Everyday Law
for Latino/as

The Everyday Law Series
Edited by Richard Delgado and Jean Stefancic
University of Pittsburgh Law School

Everyday Law for Individuals with Disabilities
Ruth Colker and Adam Milani (2005)

Everyday Law for Children
David Herring (2006)

Everyday Law for Consumers
Michael L. Rustad (2007)

Everyday Law for Gays and Lesbians and Those Who Care about Them
Anthony C. Infanti (2007)

Everyday Law for Latino/as
Steven W. Bender, Raquel Aldana,
Gilbert Paul Carrasco, and Joaquin G. Avila (2008)

Forthcoming
Everyday Law for Immigrants
Victor C. Romero (2008)

Everyday Law for Seniors
Lawrence Frolik and Linda Whitton

Everyday Law
for Latino/as

Steven W. Bender,
Raquel Aldana,
Gilbert Paul Carrasco,
and Joaquin G. Avila

Paradigm Publishers

Boulder • London

Published in the United States by Paradigm Publishers, 3360 Mitchell Lane, Suite E, Boulder, CO 80301 USA.

Paradigm Publishers is the trade name of Birkenkamp & Company, LLC, Dean Birkenkamp, President and Publisher.

Library of Congress Cataloging-in-Publication Data
Everyday law for latino/as / Steven W. Bender . . . [et al.].
    p. cm. — (The everyday law series)
  Includes bibliographical references and index.
  ISBN 978-1-59451-343-5 (hardcover : alk paper)
  ISBN 978-1-59451-344-2 (pbk. : alk. paper)
  1. Hispanic Americans—Civil rights.   2. Discrimination—Law and legislation—United States.   3. Immigrants—Civil rights—United States.   4. Emmigration and immigration laws—United States.   I. Bender, Steven.
  KF4755.5.L38E934 2009
  342.08'73—dc22
                        2008026677

Printed and bound in the United States of America on acid free paper that meets the standards of the American National Standard for Permanence of Paper for Printed Library Materials.

Designed and Typeset by Mulberry Tree Enterprises.

12   11   10   09   2   3   4   5

*To my mother and the LatCrit
community of scholars, activists, and friends.*
—Steven W. Bender

*To mom and dad, in deep gratitude for all you gave up
when you left your home to bring your children to the
United States. And to my brother and sister for reminding
me that we will always be family.*
—Raquel Aldana

*To my mother, Delia Aurora Carrasco,
with love and appreciation.*
—Gilbert Paul Carrasco

*To my family. It is only through their support that I can
continue to devote time and resources to pursue the goal of
providing Latina/os with access to the political process.*
—Joaquin G. Avila

Contents

Acknowledgments   x

1   Introduction   1

   Immigration   1
   Language   2
   Discrimination   3
   Broad Scope of Latino/a Population   4
   Sources of Law   5
   Overview of the Book   5
   Practical Guidance for Latino/as   6

2   Employment Law   7

   Discrimination in Hiring and Employment   7
   Terms and Conditions of Employment   14
   Sexual Harassment   18
   Language Requirements in the Workplace   21
   Rights of Undocumented Workers   26
   Farm Worker Wages   31
   Appendix   34

3   Discrimination in Housing   37

   Landlord Discrimination   37
   Habitability of Housing   43
   Landlord Obligations to Spanish-Speaking Tenants   44
   Discrimination in Lending   46
   Appendix   49

4   Language Discrimination   51

   Official English and English-Only Laws   52

Government Obligations to Spanish Speakers   53
Spanish Language and Family Law   56
English-Only Rules in Places of Entertainment   57
Language Fraud in the Marketplace   59
Appendix   62

5   Hate Speech   64

Hate Speech on the Job   65
Hate Speech at Home and on the Street   67
Derogatory Media Stereotypes of Latino/as   71
Walkouts, Protests, and Boycotts: Legal Limits   73
Appendix   75

6   Education   77

The No Child Left Behind Act   77
Affirmative Action and Higher Education   80
Race-Conscious Measures in K–12 Schools   87
Rights of Undocumented Children   89
Bilingual Education   92
Appendix   95

7   Voting Rights   98

Barriers to Effective Political Participation   98
Dilution of Latino/a Voting Strength   100
Section 5 Preclearance   105
Invisible Government Boards   108
Appendix   109

8   Criminal Justice System   114

Racial Profiling   114
The Right to Remain Silent   122
Pretrial Language Rights   130
Language Rights During a Criminal Trial   134
Spanish Speakers on Criminal Juries   138
Prisoners' Language Rights   140
Immigration Crimes   141
Immigration Consequences for the Commission of Crime   145
Appendix   152

9   Immigrants Choosing Lawyers and Filing Taxes   157

Choosing Legal Representation   157

Paying Taxes in the United States 164
Appendix 171

10 Documented Immigrants 173

Government Benefits 173
Citizenship 178
Family Unification 185
Removal: Reasons, Process, and Relief 194
Appendix 201

11 Undocumented Migrants 205

Government Benefits 205
Access to Higher Education 209
Ordinary Living 212
Legalization, Removal, and Relief from Removal 215
Domestic Violence: Legalization of Victims and Removal 229
Appendix 239

12 Conclusion 242

Index 247
About the Authors 253

Acknowledgments

All the authors extend their gratitude to series editors Richard Delgado and Jean Stefancic for their vision in creating the Everyday Law series as well as their scholarly efforts on behalf of subordinated communities. We also appreciate the attitude and aptitude of the Paradigm Publishers editors. And we thank our research assistant Tara Donahue for her work on the index.

Raquel Aldana thanks Sarah Nakanishi, Lianne Wakayama, Adrian Deleon, and Sang Park for their research assistance. She especially thanks Barbara McDonald for her amazing editing. Raquel is also very grateful to her colleague Steve Johnson who generously contributed to the tax chapter included in this book. She could not do her work without the support of her deans, Richard Morgan and Joan Howarth, and the financial assistance of James Rogers.

Steven Bender thanks his research assistant, Lalo Garcia; his secretary, Debby Warren, for helping to coordinate this ambitious project; and his dean, Margie Paris, for her constant support.

Gil Carrasco would like to thank Willamette law students Daniel J. Rice, Ian Jeffrey Slavin, Joseph McIntosh, and Tara M. Donahue. He would also like to thank Willamette professor Keith Cunningham-Parmeter for providing useful comments regarding the rights of farm workers. Finally, he thanks Dean Symeon Symeonides for the academic support that facilitated the writing of this book.

1
Introduction

We organized our handbook on Latino/as and the law around the three primary flashpoints that contribute to the unique legal treatment of Latino/as—immigration status, language regulation, and racial/ethnic discrimination. We examine these flashpoints in the venues of everyday life for Latino/as—from discrimination in housing to discrimination and language regulation in the workplace and the lack of protection of immigrant labor, to classrooms where the bilingual education debate rages, to the voting booth and the criminal justice system where Latino/as confront racial profiling and language barriers. Before we consider these issues, we reflect on how their histories have shaped the current treatment of Latino/as under U.S. law.

Immigration

Until enactment of the Immigration and Nationality Act of 1965, ceilings on immigration from Mexico and other Western Hemisphere countries did not exist—rather, immigration restrictions focused on excluding or limiting immigrants from Asia and Southern and Eastern Europe. Still, the absence of immigration restrictions did not prevent mass economic and racially driven deportations of Mexicans (even persons with U.S. citizenship) during the Great Depression and Operation Wetback in the 1950s. Initiated during World War II but with roots extending to World War I, the bracero (temporary worker) program facilitated the entry of Mexican workers into the U.S. fields and factories for agreed on wages and terms of employment. By 1964, however, a coalition of labor unions, religious organizations, and Mexican American groups, concerned both with the impacts of abundant bracero labor on wages and conditions for U.S. workers, and about abuses of participants in the bracero program, persuaded Congress to let the program lapse.

1

The next year, the Immigration and Nationality Act of 1965 placed the first restrictions on Western Hemisphere immigration, limiting immigration from Mexico and other Central and Latin American countries. By 1976, in addition to the overall Western Hemisphere quota, immigration from Mexico was restricted to a 20,000-person limit annually. The combination of the end of the bracero program and these new limits on Latino/a immigration created the Latino/a undocumented immigrant problem that still commands headlines. Efforts to address undocumented immigrants have taken several tacks, none of them effective. In 1986, President Reagan signed the Immigration Reform and Control Act of 1986 that offered a pathway to citizenship to undocumented workers, but aimed to curb future undocumented immigration through employer sanctions. In the 1990s, President Clinton championed restrictive legislation arming urban border entry points that resulted in immigrants' undertaking more dangerous crossings in desolate locations. For his part, President Bush favored a bracero-like guest worker program to import Mexican and other Central and South American workers without a potential for citizenship. Later, Bush supported comprehensive immigration reform that included a pathway, albeit a lengthy, expensive one, to citizenship, but Congress failed to enact reform in 2007.

Today, an estimated 12 million undocumented immigrants, many of them from Mexico, reside in the United States. As discussed herein, U.S. law in the workplace and elsewhere leaves these immigrants largely unprotected, although the Supreme Court has recognized a constitutional right to public education for undocumented immigrant children.

Language

Regulation of non-English languages under U.S. law disproportionately impacts Latino/as, most of whom speak Spanish. Some of these Latino/a Spanish speakers may also speak English, and others may speak a third indigenous language. Mexico and Guatemala alone, for example, are home to about 260 indigenous languages. Although the United States has no comprehensive official English-language law that bars the use of languages other than English in government, government operations nonetheless tend to be conducted in English. Moreover, about half the states have comprehensive English-language laws that declare English the official language, with a few going so far as to require only English for all government operations except when necessary for health or safety. This language regulation, supplemented by nongovernmental language restrictions, causes difficulty for Latino/as who wish to speak or hear the Spanish (or other non-English) language in settings as diverse as their schools, workplace, government offices, the criminal justice system, and places of entertainment.

Some language disputes, particularly those arising in the criminal justice setting over police searches and rights on arrest, involve the right to receive communications in Spanish or languages other than English. Here the sources of law that may confer the right to a Spanish-language translation include statutes as well as constitutional guarantees against unreasonable search and seizure and self-incrimination. By contrast to the right to receive Spanish translations, many language disputes seek the right to speak Spanish in settings that include school classrooms, the workplace, and even the home. Sometimes laws require English in these settings; for example, laws in California, Arizona, and Massachusetts outlaw bilingual education and mandate classroom instruction overwhelmingly in the English language. Other times the language restriction may be court-imposed, such as the possibility of a judge in a custody dispute ordering that a child hear only English from the child's Latino/a parent. Often, a private source, such as an employer, a landlord, or a neighborhood tavern imposes the restriction against speaking Spanish. Here, those who challenge private language policies rely on civil rights laws protecting against discrimination on the basis of race or ethnicity, with mixed success. Language restrictions may fall heavily on even bilingual speakers, who can understand English and thus overcome the lack of Spanish language translations, but whose desire to communicate in Spanish might be barred in workplaces and places of entertainment.

Language restrictions under U.S. law, as well as private language policies, have deep roots in history. Hostility toward Southern and Eastern European immigrants in the early 1900s prompted many states to mandate English language in schools. Schools in the Southwest have a long history of prohibiting Spanish. Texas, for example, criminalized the speaking of Spanish by teachers in the classroom for most of the twentieth century and punished or expelled students for speaking Spanish on the school grounds.

Discrimination

The history of discrimination against Latino/as includes early forms of racial profiling in California—its antiloitering Vagrancy Act, enacted in 1855 and known as the Greaser Act, targeted only persons "commonly known as 'Greasers' or the issue of Spanish and Indian blood . . . and who go armed and are not peaceable and quiet persons." In a particularly notorious example from the 1940s of abusive police practices, authorities prosecuted twenty-two Mexican gang members in Los Angeles on charges ranging from assault to murder arising out of the killing of a young Mexican near the Sleepy Lagoon swimming hole. Although a jury convicted seventeen of the Mexican boys in the sensationalized trial during which local newspapers called the defendants "zoot-suit gangsters" and "pachuco killers," a California appeals court struck down their convictions due to a "total lack of evidence" (*People v. Zammora*, 152 P.2d 180 [Cal. Dist. Ct. App. 1944]).

Discrimination historically has also taken the form of segregating or excluding Latino/as in schools, businesses, places of entertainment and recreation, and even from juries. Litigation in Texas that reached the Supreme Court in the 1950s stemmed from the finding that although 14 percent of a Texas county's residents had Latino/a surnames, for the previous twenty years not a single Latino/a surnamed resident ever served on a grand jury or criminal jury (*Hernandez v. Texas*, 347 U.S. 475 [1954]). Segregation, both by government and in the private sector was rampant in the Southwest where schools separated Mexican American from Anglo children ostensibly to protect the Anglo youth from higher rates of communicable disease among poor Mexican children, and to accommodate the alleged slower academic progress of the Mexican students. Challenges by Latino/as (*Mendez v. Westminster School District of Orange County*, 64 F. Supp. 544 [S.D. Cal. 1946]) and African Americans to segregation practices in schools culminated in the famous 1954 Supreme Court decision *Brown v. Board of Education* (347 U.S. 483 [1954]) that struck down separate but equal facilities in public education as violating the constitutional Equal Protection Clause. In addition to abolishing government-sponsored segregation in public education, the *Brown* decision enabled lawyers to eradicate longstanding segregation practices in other government facilities such as parks and buses. In the mid-1900s, for example, a Texas public park sign read: "This park was given for white people only. Mexicans and Negroes stay out. Order of Park Board." Although the *Brown* decision outlawed official segregation in public facilities, private segregation continued. For example, movie theaters and restaurants in the Southwest often excluded altogether or relegated Mexicans to certain days of use or to certain permitted areas. In the 1960s, however, Congress enacted civil rights laws that prohibited segregation and other forms of discrimination by private parties in some settings. For example, Title II of the federal Civil Rights Act of 1964 barred racial or ethnic segregation or discrimination in places of public accommodation such as hotels, restaurants, gas stations, and theaters. Further, the federal Fair Housing Act of 1968 outlawed discrimination in real estate transactions, Title VI of the Civil Rights Act of 1964 targeted discrimination in public education, and Title VII of that act prohibited employment discrimination.

Broad Scope of Latino/a Population

A broad range of groups comprise the U.S. Latino/a population. According to the 2000 U.S. Census, most (66.1 percent) are of Mexican origin, with Puerto Ricans the next largest group (9 percent), followed by those of Cuban origin (4 percent); another 14.5 percent of Latino/as identify as Central or South American in origin, and 6.4 percent as "other Hispanic origin." Although possessing unique cultural and historical backgrounds, these groups share common issues of immigration (aside from Puerto Rico), language barriers, and anti-Latino/a discrimination. Therefore, our book encompasses all these groups. But, in some instances, particularly in the context of immigration, our book will address rules applicable to Latino/as of a specified origin.

Sources of Law

The materials in this book encompass federal and state statutes, as well as constitutional provisions and judicial decisions. All of these sources of law have the potential to endanger the interests of Latino/as as well as to liberate them from unfair treatment. Federal law establishes various civil rights of Latino/as, particularly in the areas of employment, schools, voting, and housing. At the same time, restrictive federal immigration law creates a gauntlet for undocumented immigrants as well as documented immigrants seeking citizenship. State law duplicates many of the civil rights protections of federal law, in some cases providing enhanced rights and remedies. Still, some state laws target Latino/as through English-language laws, laws eradicating bilingual education and affirmative action programs, and laws denying government services to undocumented immigrants.

Latino/as rely on federal and state constitutional guarantees to ensure language rights in the criminal justice system. Constitutional guarantees may also help establish immigrant rights. For example, the Supreme Court relied on the federal Constitution's Equal Protection Clause to strike down Texas law withholding state funds to educate undocumented children. The First Amendment guarantee of free speech, however, impedes legal attack on media productions that invoke derogatory stereotypes. Still, lawyers invoked the First Amendment to strike down Arizona's former English-Only law that unconstitutionally burdened communication in Spanish and other non-English languages between politicians and their constituents and between government service providers and residents.

Courts have aided Latino/as, among other ways, by creating and applying judicial grounds to scrutinize the fairness of contracts between merchants and Latino/as with a language barrier. At the same time, some courts are reluctant to function as lawmakers to offer relief to Latino/as beyond what the legislature has provided; for example, the California Supreme Court refused to require an aspirin manufacturer to provide a Spanish-language translation of product dangers, instead suggesting translation was best mandated by the legislature, if at all (*Ramirez v. Plough, Inc.*, 863 P.2d 167 [Cal. 1993]).

Overview of the Book

Our book addresses discrimination against Latino/as in the workplace (Chapter 1), housing (Chapter 2), and the criminal justice system (see the discussion of racial profiling in Chapter 8). Language-based discrimination is the subject of Chapter 4, but language rights and language oppression are also discussed in Chapters 2 (employment), 3 (housing), 6 (education), and

8 (the criminal justice system). Protection against hate speech is addressed in Chapter 5. Recognizing the limits of legal remedies, Chapter 5 also outlines proactive nonlegal strategies such as protests and walkouts.

Affirmative rights of Latino/as are also the subject of discussion in Chapters 2 (farm worker wages), 3 (housing), 6 (education), and 8 (the right to remain silent).

Our book contains extensive treatment of the rights of Latino/a documented and undocumented immigrants in all facets of their everyday lives, including the right to education of the undocumented (Chapters 6 and 11), rights in the employment setting (Chapter 2), rights to government benefits (Chapter 11), and the needs of everyday living (Chapter 11). Rights of legalization, and of citizenship, including family reunification procedures and asylum, are addressed in Chapters 10 and 11. The criminalization of immigration and the consequences for immigrants who commit crimes are the subject of Chapter 8.

Practical Guidance for Latino/as

Our goal is to convey sometimes complex legal issues in readable, accessible text. To implement our goal of a reader-friendly text, we have kept legal citations to a minimum. In addition to summarizing applicable laws, we have included practical, nonlegal strategies for Latino/as and Latino/a community groups such as tactics in the face of workplace immigration raids (Chapter 2), advice to college applicants (Chapter 6), and advice when choosing an immigration lawyer (Chapter 9). Recognizing that the best long-term solution for unfair treatment of Latino/as under the law comes from political power, we have also included discussion of how Latino/as can protect their right to vote (Chapter 7).

2
Employment Law

Discrimination in Hiring and Employment

When the civil rights movement gained momentum in the late 1950s and early 1960s, Congress finally took comprehensive action against discrimination in employment in passing the Civil Rights Act of 1964. Regarding employment, the critical provision is Title VII (42 U.S.C. § 2000e-2[a]), which makes it an unlawful employment practice "to fail or refuse to hire or to discharge any individual, or otherwise discriminate against any individual with respect to his compensation, terms, conditions, or privileges of employment, because of such individual's race, color, religion, sex, or national origin." Among those covered by Title VII are private employers with fifteen or more employees, public employers, labor unions, and employment agencies. All hiring practices are covered by this federal law, including recruitment, job advertising, pre-employment inquiries, written application requirements, and job interviews. The law also governs the recruitment and referral actions of unions and employment agencies.

What You Can Do as a Victim of Employment Discrimination. There are two places you may initiate a claim of discrimination under Title VII. One is to complain to ("file the charge with") one of the many regional offices of the Equal Employment Opportunity Commission (EEOC). To locate the office in your area, call 800-669-4000 or go to http://www.eeoc.gov/facts/howtofile.html. This must be done within 180 days of when the discriminatory episode occurs (e.g., when the aggrieved person is informed of the decision not to hire or promote, regardless of when that decision is made).

The other place to file a charge is with a state or local agency that investigates and prosecutes violations of state or local discrimination law (which exist in almost all states). If such an agency has not resolved the matter within

60 days, the claimant must file the charge with the EEOC within 300 days of the discriminatory episode or within 30 days after receiving notice that the state or local agency has terminated its proceedings, whichever comes first.

Ironically, it wasn't until after the 1964 law was enacted that the Supreme Court in *Runyon v. McCrary*, 427 U.S. 160 (1976), gave new life to the Civil Rights Act of 1866 (42 U.S.C. § 1981, i.e.,"Section 1981"), another equal employment law enacted during Reconstruction, which followed the Civil War. The 1866 law made guarantees of equality to newly freed slaves. It confirmed a federal cause of action for racial discrimination in the formation and enforcement of employment contracts. The advantage of a Section 1981 claim for racial discrimination is that it does not require the various procedural steps and time limitations that accompany a Title VII action.

The argument has been made that the at-will employee (one without a written contract) is not covered by Section 1981. Courts generally include at-will employees within the meaning of the statute (a law enacted by a legislature), however, under the theory that an employer's promise to pay in exchange for the employee's promise to work is an employment contract. A cause of action under Section 1981 generally follows the same standards of liability that govern Title VII disparate treatment claims (discussed below).

In both Title VII disparate treatment cases and under Section 1981, compensatory and punitive damages and, hence, jury trials, are available for individual plaintiffs or for a class of plaintiffs that can show actual injury from discriminatory hiring practices, but they are not available in disparate impact cases. Courts may also grant declaratory and injunctive relief (declare the rights of the parties, and order the employer to do something to remedy the wrong or stop doing something found to be illegal), attorneys' fees, and court costs to the prevailing party.

Although Section 1981 covers discrimination based on race, the Supreme Court in *Saint Francis College v. Al-Khazraji, aka Allan*, 481 U.S. 604, 613 (1987), made it clear that Congress intended to protect from discrimination identifiable classes of persons subjected to intentional discrimination solely because of their ancestry or ethnic characteristics. Title VII explicitly protects against all discrimination that can be tied to one's "national origin," which the EEOC defines as being based on "an individual's or his or her ancestor's place of origin; or because an individual has the physical, cultural or linguistic characteristics of a national origin group."[1]

State law often provides additional protection against discrimination based on race and national origin in employment. Most states have a Fair Employment Practices (FEP) law, which covers most of the state's private employers, labor organizations, and employment agencies. States also have public employment laws prohibiting discrimination by state governments and political subdivisions. State antidiscrimination laws are typically modeled after Title VII, but some go beyond Title VII in their coverage and some address situations where federal law is silent. For example, some states expressly prohibit discrimination based on arrests or conviction records, educational background, personal appearance, height and weight, receipt of public assistance, language, and polygraph testing. Some state laws, such as California's Fair Employment and Housing Act, also contain affirmative action hiring requirements for government contractors.

Disparate Treatment and Disparate Impact

Under Title VII, the Supreme Court has defined "discrimination" in two ways. The Court has consistently recognized a distinction between claims of discrimination based on disparate treatment and those based on disparate impact.

Disparate treatment is the most easily understood type of discrimination. The employer simply treats some people less favorably than others because of their race, color, religion, sex, or national origin. Liability in a disparate treatment case depends on whether the protected trait actually motivated the employer's decision. Proof of discriminatory motive is critical, although it can in some cases be inferred from the mere fact of differences in treatment. Direct evidence of disparate treatment would include, for example, an employer's statement that he "does not hire Latinos" in rejecting a Latino/a applicant. However, discrimination by employers is usually more subtle, and most cases must be established circumstantially.

Under the Supreme Court's holding in *McDonnell Douglas Corp. v. Green*, 411 U.S. 792 (1973), an inference of disparate treatment is established by showing that the plaintiff (the person complaining) (1) is a member of a protected group, for example, is Latino/a; (2) was qualified and applied for the job for which the employer was seeking applicants; (3) was rejected; and (4) the position remained open and the employer continued to seek applicants from persons of complainant's qualifications. Proof that the position was eventually filled by a non-Latino/a strengthens a plaintiff's case, but is not required to create an inference of discrimination. Circumstantial evidence of an employer's motive can be used to establish discrimination. An example is where an employer demands more qualifications for Latino/as than for others, or where an employer discourages a Latino/a applicant from filing an application even though the employer doesn't know the applicant's qualifications. An inference of discrimination might also arise if an employer questions an applicant as to his ancestry or native language, and then does not hire the applicant. If the employer fabricates a reason for the action, for example that the position had already been filled, the applicant then has the opportunity to show that the employer's reason was a "pretext," that is, it wasn't the real reason for failing to consider the Latino/a applicant.

The second way discrimination is defined and proven under Title VII, in contrast to disparate treatment, is disparate impact. In addition to prohibiting intentional discrimination by employers in hiring, Title VII prohibits neutral hiring practices that have a disparate impact on the hiring of minority groups. When it enacted Title VII, Congress intended to stop intentional discrimination as well as other employment barriers that favored whites over other races and colors. The Supreme Court in *Griggs v. Duke Power Co.*, 401 U.S. 424 (1971), made the disparate impact claim available for plaintiffs by providing a framework for pleading a case. Congress clarified the disparate impact claim with the Civil Rights Act of 1991.

Disparate impact claims are used to challenge neutral selection criteria that fall more harshly on one group than another. Disparate impact discrimination is, therefore, systemic because it necessarily involves several members of a protected class (e.g., Latino/as). Under the statute's guidelines, selection procedures can include tests, training programs, informal or casual interviews, unscored application forms, and physical, educational, and work experience requirements. All of these methods for selecting employees from a pool of applicants can disparately impact the hiring of protected groups.

For example, the *Griggs* case involved a challenge to an employer's policy requiring that all employees in some positions have a high school diploma or pass a standardized general intelligence test. The policy, even though neutral and uniformly applied, had the effect of disparately impacting the hiring of African Americans. The Court found no significant connection between the diploma/intelligence test requirements and capability to perform the various duties required of the jobs in question. It therefore violated Title VII because it is the type of institutional barrier to hiring people of color that Congress sought to address with the Civil Rights Act of 1964, and the employer could not "demonstrate that the challenged practice is job-related for the position in question and consistent with business necessity" (42 U.S.C. § 703[k][1][A][i]).

Under the *Griggs* standard, an employer's motive in a disparate impact case is generally irrelevant. The strength of a disparate impact claim instead depends on the statistical disparity between the hiring of minorities and whites. If statistical hiring data are compared to the percentage of minorities in the workforce, the statistics must generally follow the standards explained by the Supreme Court in *Wards Cove Packing Co., Inc. v. Atonio*, 490 U.S. 642 (1989). Thus, baseline comparisons must account for the relevant labor market. There, the Court was critical of raw statistics showing that a disproportionately low number of the company's minority employees were represented in the skilled higher-paying jobs. The Court said that the disparity failed to implicate the employer's hiring decisions because the comparison assumed that the company's workforce was generally qualified for the skilled higher-paying jobs. The general rule following *Wards Cove* is that "baseline" comparisons of hiring data are not enough to establish an inference of discrimination. This is even true in some cases where the job in question requires no minimum qualifications, because other factors such as the age, health, and geographic proximity of workers to the workplace might be affecting the data. Thus, in *Llamas v. Butte Community Coll. Dist.*, 238 F.3d 1123 (9th Cir. 2001), raw statistical data that only 8.7 percent of a custodial staff was Hispanic, compared to Hispanics' 16.3 percent representation in the local labor market, were not enough to establish a case because other factors were not considered.

An example of an employment practice challenged as disparately impacting the hiring of Latino/as is height requirements. In a number of cases, successful disparate impact claims have been established based on evidence that height requirements (ranging from 5'6" to 5'9") have eliminated Spanish-surnamed applicants at a much higher rate than other applicants. A showing that 80.6 percent of Spanish-surnamed males between the ages of 17 to 26 were automatically excluded from work, compared to 48.5 percent of U.S. males who don't have Spanish surnames, was enough to establish a pattern or practice of discrimination in *United States v. City of Buffalo*, 457 F. Supp. 612 (W.D.N.Y. 1978), *aff'd as modified*, 633 F.2d 643 (2d Cir. 1980). Other types of job requirements challenged by Latino/as are language and accent requirements, which are discussed later in this chapter.

Employers may be able to show a business necessity for hiring criteria that have a disparate impact on the hiring of minorities, assuming the hiring criteria are facially neutral and uniformly applied. A valid business necessity defense requires that employers demonstrate that the hiring criteria are reasonably related to job function. For example, in *EEOC v. Steamship Clerks Union, Local 1066*, 48 F.3d 594 (1st Cir. 1995), the court rejected the union's argument that its policy of requiring that applicants be sponsored by existing members provided a way for family members to continue traditions of working in the union. The court held that the union needed to connect family traditions to the business of being a union worker to show business necessity.

Even if the employer advances a business necessity that does correlate to job function, the plaintiff can nevertheless rebut the employer's defense by "demonstrating an alternative employment practice and [that] the [employer] refuses to adopt such alternative employment practice" (42 U.S.C. § 703[k][1][A][ii]). This means that the employee's alternative must be comparable to the employer's more discriminatory practice both in terms of cost to the employer and effectiveness in achieving the employer's legitimate employment goals.

A hiring decision preferring a person based on national origin (but not race or color) could, in exceptional cases, serve a legitimate business objective. Accordingly, Title VII has an exemption for employers who can demonstrate that an applicant's national origin is a "bona fide occupational qualification (BFOQ) reasonably necessary to the normal operation of that particular business or enterprise" (42 U.S.C.A. § 2000e-2[e]). The EEOC guidelines provide that a national origin BFOQ is to be strictly construed, and will fail upon a showing that "the essence of the (employer's) business would not be undermined by employing persons of other national origins" (EEOC Compliance Manual § 625.2). To date, neither the EEOC nor courts has issued a decision squarely reaching the application of the national origin BFOQ exception to a specific fact pattern. Commentators have suggested that a BFOQ for national origin discrimination might exist where the business must maintain some degree of cultural authenticity, such as hiring a Latino/a maitre d' at a Mexican restaurant.

Discrimination Based on Citizenship

It is important to distinguish between discrimination that occurs on the basis of a person's *citizenship*, and discrimination that occurs against someone who is not a U.S. citizen but is *based on a protected trait, such as race or color*. This distinction is particularly important when the claim is based on the protected trait of national origin, which is among those specifically referenced in Title VII. *Espinoza v. Farah Mfg. Co.*, 414 U.S. 86 (1973), is a case involving a Title VII challenge to an employer's policy of hiring only U.S. citizens. It was brought by Cecilia Espinoza, a lawfully admitted resident alien born in and a citizen of Mexico. Espinoza claimed the company's policy discriminated against her based on her national origin. The Supreme Court dismissed the claim, holding that Title VII did not cover discrimination based on citizenship (or her alienage). It noted that persons of Mexican ancestry made up more than 96 percent of the employees at Farah's San Antonio division, where Espinoza applied for a seamstress job. The Court concluded that Espinoza was, therefore, not discriminated against based on her "national origin" (or ethnicity or ancestry).

Significantly, however, the Court said that under Title VII it certainly would be unlawful for an employer to discriminate against aliens because of race, color, religion, sex, or national origin—for example, by hiring aliens of Anglo-Saxon background but refusing to hire those of Mexican or Spanish ancestry. Aliens are protected from illegal discrimination under this law, but it is not illegal to discriminate on the basis of citizenship or alienage. Undocumented aliens are also protected against such illegal discrimination (*Rivera v. NIBCO, Inc.*, 364 F.3d 1057 [9th Cir. 2004]).

Federal law with regard to citizenship discrimination changed in 1986 when Congress enacted the Immigration Reform and Control Act (IRCA). This law prohibits the employment of "unauthorized" (undocumented) workers and makes employers responsible for verifying employees' identity and authorization to work (on Form I-9, the Employment Eligibility Form). Under this law, hiring the undocumented can result in sanctions against the employer (orders to cease and desist, fines, and, for repeated violations, even criminal punishment). Concerned that employers would categorically pass over Latino/a applicants to avoid the risk of hiring undocumented workers, Congress included in the IRCA an "unfair immigration-related practices" provision that prohibits discrimination by employers on the basis of national origin and citizenship (8 U.S.C. § 1324b).

Congress sought to protect U.S. citizens of Latino descent and, in some cases, Latino/a noncitizens who have obtained work eligibility. Under IRCA, the protection against discrimination based on national origin is the same as under Title VII with the exception that IRCA applies to employers with four to fourteen employees, while Title VII applies only to employers with at least fifteen employees.

The prohibition against discrimination based on citizenship status under IRCA is quite limited. It applies to those with authorization to work in all immigration categories ("protected individuals," which include, for example, refugees). Those with lawful permanent resident status (LPRs, green card holders), however, only have the protection against discrimination based on their noncitizen status until the date six months after they become eligible for naturalization (U.S. citizenship). This means that those who acquired lawful residence through marriage to a U.S. citizen lose their protection against discrimination based on citizenship status three years and six months after acquiring legal residence, and all other lawful permanent residents lose their protection five years and six months after such acquisition. In addition to the consequence of removal for conviction of one of the many crimes discussed in Chapter 8, such loss of protection against discrimination is yet another important reason for acquiring U.S. citizenship upon becoming eligible.

Those who do have protection based on citizenship status have no right to complain, however, when employers in good faith hire a citizen over a noncitizen after comparing the two and determining that both are equally qualified. This preference can only be applied to hiring, recruitment, or referral, and does not apply to discriminatory discharge (firing).

In verifying work authorization under IRCA, excessive requests by an employer for documentation are prohibited if done with a discriminatory motive under either IRCA (citizenship or national origin) or Title VII (race or national origin). One example of a Title VII claim is the case of *Zamora v. Elite Logistics Inc.*, 478 F.3d 1160 (10th Cir. 2007) (*en banc*). The employer of Ramon Zamora, a Mexican-born naturalized citizen, discovered that someone else had used Zamora's social security number. Zamora offered his naturalization certificate to confirm his work authorization, but the employer told Zamora he couldn't return to work until he proved the validity of his social security number, or provided the company with a new one. Zamora eventually provided sufficient documentation, but was fired when he demanded an apology on his first day back. The court said the employer had a legitimate, nondiscriminatory reason for suspending Zamora from work and that Zamora didn't show that the reason was a pretext (an excuse) for discrimination against him based on his Mexican heritage. The court also said that Zamora's termination was not discrimination because the employer had no legal duty to apologize.

Although the Supreme Court has not yet decided the issue, protection from discrimination based on alienage may also be available under Section 1981 (*Anderson v. Conboy*, 156 F.3d 167 [2d Cir.1998]; *Duane v. Government Employees Ins. Co.*, 37 F.3d 1036 [4th Cir. 1994]). Section 1981 prohibits government entities from discriminating based on alienage (*Takahashi v. Fish and Game Commission*, 334 U.S. 410, 419 [1942]). There are also at least two states—Colorado and Minnesota—that prohibit employment discrimination based on citizenship by state law.

Governmental entities in all states are prohibited from discriminating against lawful permanent residents based on their alienage by the Fourteenth Amendment to the U.S. Constitution. The only exception to this prohibition is if the employment involves a state elective or important nonelective executive, legislative, or judicial position and the officers in such positions participate directly in the formulation, execution, or review of broad public policy and perform functions that go to the heart of representative government. A resident alien who was a native of Mexico could not be prohibited by a Texas law from serving as a notary public for Texas Rural Legal Aid. The Supreme Court said the law was unconstitutional (*Bernal v. Fainter*, 467 U.S. 216 [1984]). As the U.S. Constitution has been interpreted however, the federal government can require that its employees have U.S. citizenship.

Terms and Conditions of Employment

Title VII prohibits discrimination based on race, color, sex, religion, or national origin by employers in the "terms, conditions, or privileges of employment." The statute covers all employers with fifteen or more employees. Section 1981 also covers the making, performance, modification, and termination of contracts, and the enjoyment of all benefits, privileges, terms, and conditions of the contractual relationship.

Terms and conditions include just about every aspect of the employment relationship, including compensation, hours, assignments, transfers, leave, training, apprenticeship programs, discipline, the working environment, and termination. All forms of compensation are covered, such as salary, overtime pay, bonuses, stock options, expense accounts, commissions, life insurance, vacation and holiday pay, and benefits. Incidental or fringe benefits provided to employees outside the employment contract are covered if given in connection with the employment relationship. For example, voluntary medical and pension programs may become benefits if they are made available to certain employees.

With respect to job assignments, for example, employers may not assign applicants or employees to certain positions based on race or national origin, even if the wages or hours are equal to those of other positions (although they may be able to assign applicants or employees based on language, if based on business necessity). The EEOC provides the following example of an unlawful job assignment based on national origin:

> XYZ Pizza Palace decides to open a restaurant at a suburban shopping mall. It runs an advertisement in local newspapers recruiting for positions in food preparation, serving, and cleaning. Carlos, a Hispanic man with a few years of experience as a server at other restaurants, applies for a position with XYZ and states a preference for a server position. Believing that Hispanic employees would be better suited for positions with limited public contact at this location, XYZ offers Carlos a position in cleaning or food preparation even though he is as well qualified for a server position as many non-Hispanic servers employed by XYZ.

Like cases involving discrimination in hiring, individual actions for discrimination in terms and conditions of employment can be brought under theories of disparate treatment or disparate impact. In disparate treatment cases, the plaintiff must generally connect an employer's discriminatory motive with an adverse employment action. Plaintiffs can do this circumstantially with proof that similarly situated white employees were treated differently. With respect to wages, employees are similarly situated if they have jobs that require the same skill, effort, responsibility, and that are performed under similar working conditions. In a Title VII case, a Latino employee terminated for falsifying a time sheet entry was not found similarly situated to other employees who falsified time sheet entries because his violations were objectively more severe in nature (*Espitia v. Procter & Gamble Co.*, 93 Fed. Appx. 707 [6th Cir. 2004]). In a separate case with respect to discipline and termination, a Latino was not found similarly situated because, unlike a non-Latino employee, he had a record of disciplinary problems and had been previously warned against the mistake or violation (*Nieto v. L&H Packing Co.*, 108 F.3d 621 [5th Cir. 1997]).

Plaintiffs may use statistics to compare the terms and conditions of minority employees and white employees in establishing a circumstantial case of discrimination. The Supreme Court gave some guidance in *International Broth. of Teamsters v. U.S.*, 431 U.S. 324 (1977), where it found a "pattern or practice" of disparate treatment supported by statistics showing a substantial disparity between a union's assignment of black and Spanish-surnamed drivers to lower-paying driving jobs, and white drivers to higher-paying jobs. Statistics are also used to make disparate impact challenges to an employer's neutral criteria that affect terms and conditions of employment of Latino/as. Using standardized criteria in evaluating the performance of employees can have a disparate impact on the terms and conditions of Latino/a employees where, for example, it prevents a disproportionate number of Latino/a employees from receiving wage raises or promotions.

Hostile Work Environment

The work environment is a term and condition of employment covered by Title VII. Title VII and Section 1981 prohibit discriminatory harassment in the workplace motivated by an employee's race or national origin. To establish a cause of action for a hostile workplace, a plaintiff must generally show that the harassment stemmed from discriminatory animus (racism) and that it was severe enough to alter the conditions of one's employment. The existence of a hostile working environment turns on the facts and circumstances of each case. Harassment can include, but is not limited to, offensive jokes, slurs, name-calling, assaults, threats, intimidation, mockery, insults, offensive objects or pictures, and interference with work performance. The standard articulated by courts and the EEOC is that harassment must be sufficiently severe or pervasive to create a hostile working environment. Under this standard, isolated or offhand racial comments are usually not enough to make a case. Instead, courts look for ongoing harassment or instances so severe that the work environment becomes a miserable place for the average person.

Racial slurs and jokes that occur on a regular basis that are both subjectively and objectively offensive will usually be enough to create a hostile work environment. Some courts describe the standard as requiring a "steady barrage" of racial comments. For example, a supervisor's ongoing comments to Jenice Torres, of Puerto Rican background, that she was a "dumb spic" and that she should stay home, go on welfare, and collect food stamps like the rest of the "spics" would have been sufficient had the victim not asked the person to whom she reported the harassment to keep the matter confidential and to refrain from taking action (*Torres v. Pisano*, 116 F.3d 625 [2d Cir. 1997]). However, in a claim under Section 1981, isolated jokes about the work ethic of Puerto Ricans and an e-mail making fun of a Spanish-speaking patient's pronunciation were insufficient to state a case. Similarly, the court ruled against Jonas Cruz even though he provided evidence that he was referred to as a "wetback" and was subjected to other racial slurs by the defendant's employees. The court said that Cruz failed to establish that such ethnic epithets were routine, regularly repeated, or constituted any pattern or practice. The court suggested they were merely the result of individual attitudes and relationships that didn't amount to violations of Title VII (*Cruz v. Standard Motor Products, Inc.*, 1990 WL 94364 [D. Kan. 1990]).

A single incident of harassment, if serious enough, or a handful of incidents, may be sufficient to create a hostile work environment. Courts usually consider as sufficient in themselves incidents of harassment that involve over-the-top humiliation or physical threats. The plaintiff must generally connect the harassment with discriminatory motive (or animus). For example, a claim was allowed where Robert Lopez, a Latino draftsman, went to a department meeting of group leaders and another group leader announced "no spics allowed" and regularly referred to Lopez as a "wetback." One of his former supervisors witnessed the harassment, including slurs such as "cockroach," "f***ing Mexican," and "f***ing spic." The court refused to dismiss Lopez's claims under Title VII and Section 1981 for racial and national origin harassment, and discriminatory and retaliatory discharge (*Lopez v. Union Tank Car Co.*, 8 F. Supp. 2d 832 [N.D. Ind. 1998]).

Even if only coworkers and not managers do the harassing conduct, an employer is still *liable* (the term used in civil cases, as opposed to the term *guilty* in criminal cases) to the extent a manager knew or should have known about the harassment. Courts will look to whether the employer took steps reasonably likely to prevent the harassment from recurring, which usually requires some affirmative response.

Employers who are indifferent to an employee's complaints of harassment are generally liable for the hostile working environment as, for instance, where an employer responded to racial harassment complaints by Federico Erebia, a Latino supervisor, by telling him to ignore the harassment, and that it was just "shop talk" (*Erebia v. Chrysler Plastic Products Corp.*, 772 F.2d 1250 [6th Cir. 1985]). There the employer had a duty to warn and thereafter to take adverse action against the workers responsible for the harassment. The court upheld an award of $30,000 in punitive damages to Erebia under Section 1981. There are no caps on the amount of punitive damages under Section 1981, but Title VII limits compensatory and punitive damages to $50,000 for employers with 15 to 100 employees and $300,000 for employers with more than 500 employees.

If the source of the harassment is unknown, the employer might have a duty to conduct an investigation into who was responsible. In a case involving a workplace bathroom anonymously spray-painted with the phrases "Tony Cerros is a Spic" and "Go Back to Mexico," the court rejected the employer's argument that it was enough to remove the graffiti immediately. The court said the employer's legal duty was to take reasonable steps to discover and rectify acts of harassment of its employees, even if that meant conducting a thorough investigation into who was responsible (*Cerros v. Steel Techs., Inc.*, 398 F.3d 944 [7th Cir. 2005]).

Employers may also be responsible for harassment by third parties, such as customers or clients, under the theory that employers have the ability to control the work environment. A court in a case involving a postmaster who alleged discriminatory harassment by community members held that the Postal Service could be liable if it failed to take reasonable steps within its power to address the problem (*Galdamez v. Potter*, 415 F.3d 1015 [9th Cir. 2005]). The EEOC guidelines also reflect that employers may be liable for harassment based on race or national origin by third parties. The EEOC provides the following example:

> Charles is a frequent visitor on XYZ Senior Community's "neighborhood days," when XYZ allows senior citizens in the neighborhood to visit its residents. During his visits, Charles often yells derogatory comments about

blacks and Latinos at Cheryl, a black employee of Puerto Rican national origin, and has even pushed and tripped her on a few occasions. Cheryl complains about the conduct to a manager, and is told that XYZ cannot take any action against Charles because he is not a resident. On subsequent visits, Charles continues to yell racial and ethnic slurs at Cheryl, and she files an EEOC charge. XYZ is liable for the actions of Charles, a nonemployee, because it had the power to control Charles's access to the premises, was aware of Charles's offensive conduct, and did not take corrective action.

Employer Retaliation

Employers are prohibited from retaliating against employees for exercising their rights to equality in employment. Title VII makes it unlawful for an employer to discriminate against a person because that person opposed any of the employer's practices that were found to be unlawful, or made a charge, testified, assisted, or participated in an investigation, proceeding, or hearing of discrimination. To establish a claim for retaliation, a plaintiff needs to connect an adverse employment action with the protected activity (e.g., filing a complaint with the EEOC). The EEOC provides an example:

> Pedro files a charge alleging discrimination because of his race, [which is black], and his national origin, Dominican. In the months following his charge, Pedro begins receiving less and less overtime work. He files another charge alleging that the denial of overtime is retaliatory. The employer states that Pedro was not assigned overtime because there is less work. The investigation reveals no significant change in the amount of overtime available before and after Pedro's charge. Other employees with similar qualifications as Pedro have continued to be assigned overtime at approximately the same rate. These facts establish that Pedro has been subjected to retaliation for filing a charge, in violation of Title VII.

If a plaintiff makes out a case of retaliation, the employer has an opportunity to demonstrate a legitimate reason for the adverse action, and the plaintiff then has a chance to show pretext. The plaintiff can show pretext (1) indirectly, by showing that the employer's proffered explanation is unworthy of credence because it is internally inconsistent or otherwise not believable, or (2) directly, by showing that unlawful discrimination more likely motivated the employer (*Reeves v. Sanderson Plumbing Products, Inc.*, 530 U.S. 133, 147 [2000]).

Sexual Harassment

In addition to experiencing a hostile work environment on account of race, ethnicity, or national origin, many Latinas experience a hostile work environment based on gender. Although Latinas face this problem much more than men, either gender may be able to bring a claim for sexual harassment under Title VII. Generally, the requirements for stating a hostile work environment claim, either on account of race or gender, are substantially the same. There are, however, some issues unique to sexual harassment that should be kept in mind.

As discussed in the previous section, words alone may be sufficient to demonstrate a hostile work environment. Therefore, for sexual harassment, the victim does not need to show that she suffered physical harm or that she was physically touched. Instead, showing that the working environment is laced with obscene or derogatory sexual language may be enough to show that the environment is hostile.

For example, in *EEOC v. Hacienda Hotels*, 881 F.2d 1504 (9th Cir. 1989), the EEOC sued a hotel general manager, the executive housekeeper, and the chief of engineering for sexually harassing several Latina housekeepers. When the housekeepers became pregnant, their supervisors made several derogatory comments such as "that's what you get for sleeping without your underwear," "[you are] stupid women who have kids," and "women get pregnant because they like to suck men's dicks." Additionally, the chief of engineering threatened to fire the housekeepers if they did not submit to his sexual advances. He even told Mercedes Flores, one of the housekeepers, that he would obtain an apartment for her to live in if she would "give him [her] body." Eventually, several of the women were fired after being informed they were too fat to work.

The Ninth Circuit Court of Appeals found that the supervisors' sexual advances and use of obscene language was sufficient to establish a hostile work environment. Additionally, the hotel violated the Pregnancy Discrimination Act, an amendment to Title VII, which makes it unlawful for an employer to discharge or otherwise discriminate against a woman because she is pregnant. Therefore, even if an aggressor asks for no sexual favors, Title VII may still be violated if a pregnant woman is forced to work under conditions different from nonpregnant women.

According to *Hacienda* and cases like it, the key to stating a claim for sexual harassment under Title VII is showing the conduct was *unwelcome*. When considering whether the conduct was in fact welcome, courts are allowed to consider evidence of the victim's past conduct. Thus, a court can consider evidence such as the victim's flirtatious nature, whether her clothes were provocative, whether she had a past relationship with the harasser, or whether she regularly used sexual, obscene, or lewd language. Although evidence of this kind will not defeat a plaintiff's case, courts will consider this evidence when there is a question of fact regarding whether she welcomed the conduct.

Title VII provides a second form of actionable sexual harassment, in addition to a hostile work environment, referred to as "quid pro quo" sexual harassment, that occurs when submission to or rejection of sexual harassment is used as the basis for employment decisions affecting the employee. This means that an employee's success or failure at work cannot be dependent on her willingness to tolerate harassment. The following are a few examples of quid pro quo sexual harassment:

- Requiring the employee to perform sexual favors to keep her job.
- Denying the employee a promotion because he or she refused to tolerate sexual advances or inappropriate sexual humor.
- Demoting or firing the employee because she complained to the employer regarding the sexually harassing behavior of coworkers or supervisors.

A supervisor or employer cannot even *threaten* to fire or demote an employee for her unwillingness to accept sexual advances. Therefore, even if an employer does not actually take retaliatory action, the threat of such action is unlawful under Title VII.

In addition to federal Title VII, many states have their own laws that may offer further protection to victims of sexual harassment. These state laws, usually called fair employment statutes or antidiscrimination statutes, may offer more protection, or may offer more monetary damages, than Title VII. Therefore, it may be advantageous to file a claim under both state and federal law.

What You Can Do as a Victim of Sexual Harassment. To receive the protections of Title VII against sexual harassment and other forms of discrimination, Latino/as and other workers must file a complaint with the EEOC. Complaints can be filed at the nearest EEOC regional office. The EEOC's main website, www.eeoc.gov, provides information about finding the nearest regional office as well as information about how to file a complaint. Generally, the worker must provide the following basic facts to make a complaint:

- The worker's name, address, and telephone number;
- The employer's name, address, and telephone number;
- The number of people who work for the employer;
- A description of the event or events that indicate that the employer discriminated against the worker;
- The date of the event or events.

Complaints can be made by mail or in person. If possible, making the complaint in person is probably the best approach. Workers can make appointments to meet with a representative in the nearest EEOC regional office to discuss their complaint, to determine whether Title VII covers their complaint, and whether the complaint is timely. The EEOC representatives can advise whether the EEOC can assist the worker or whether other avenues of relief are available. The EEOC may ultimately determine to sue the employer for the Title VII violations.

Generally, most states have local offices, similar to the EEOC, which investigate claims of sexual harassment. The easiest way to find a state agency near you is to contact the federal EEOC, which often works in conjunction with the state agencies to investigate sexual harassment. They can direct you to a local or state office.

Language Requirements in the Workplace

The federal law that prohibits race and national origin discrimination in the workplace (Title VII of the Civil Rights Act of 1964) also may protect against English-language requirements on the job. Although many states regulate workplace national origin discrimination, the discussion below focuses on federal law. The discussion confronts employer rules requiring English on the job, as well as employer discrimination against Latino/as who cannot speak English. It also addresses employers who discriminate against Latino/as because of their accents.

Bilingual Workers

Many employers have reacted to increasing numbers of Spanish-speaking workers by adopting restrictive English-language rules in the workplace. These policies may require employees to speak only English on the job. The legality of such restrictions under Title VII often turns on the existence of a legitimate business reason for the English-language rule. Under guidelines issued by the EEOC, employer language rules may potentially constitute national origin discrimination. The EEOC presumes these rules to have a disparate impact on Spanish-speaking employees and other employees whose primary language is not English. The employer must therefore demonstrate that the rule is justified by business necessity.

Despite this federal potential to protect against restrictive English-only rules in the workplace, many employer language rules have survived judicial scrutiny. Some courts believe that bilingual workers can voluntarily switch between languages and therefore suffer no adverse consequences from an English-only requirement in the workplace. For example, a federal appeals court rejected a Latino hardware store employee's Title VII claim arising from his discharge for speaking Spanish to another store employee in violation of the employer's English-only rule. The rule did not apply to work breaks, nor to employees who worked outside in the lumberyard who did not speak English. As to the bilingual discharged employee, the court felt the rule had no discriminatory impact because he could readily observe the rule as a matter of choice by speaking English as he was able. Therefore, as applied to a bilingual person, the court felt the rule could not constitute national origin discrimination (*Garcia v. Gloor*, 618 F.2d 264 [5th Cir. 1980]).

Following this decision, the EEOC issued its guidelines adopting the view that workplace English-only rules have an adverse discriminatory impact and are legitimate only where the employer shows a sufficient business justification. A federal appeals court, however, refused to follow the EEOC guidelines, finding them at odds with the court's own sense of congressional intent. Instead, it embraced the reasoning of the *Garcia* case that bilingual employees have a choice to speak their non-English language and therefore can readily comply with an English-only rule. Thus, the employer, a meat packing company, did not have to demonstrate any business justification and its English rule was valid (*Garcia v. Spun Steak Company*, 998 F.2d 1480 [9th Cir. 1993]).

Recent "code switching" research—which finds that compliance with English-only rules is not merely a matter of "choice" for bilingual speakers—suggests these court decisions are flawed. This is particularly the case where the employer hires a bilingual employee expecting that employee to respond in Spanish to Spanish-speaking customer inquiries, but then to switch to English for other conversations. Here, sociolinguists have determined that speaking in Spanish will act as an unconscious stimulus to continue speaking in Spanish in subsequent conversations. Further, English-language rules are particularly burdensome in workplaces with significant numbers of Latino/a employees, as bilingual Spanish-speakers may have learned automatically to switch to Spanish with persons they assume to be Latino/a. At least one federal court was persuaded by this linguistic evidence to reject the view that employer English-only rules have no adverse impact on bilingual workers.[2] Further, legislation enacted in California in 2001 demands that employers justify any language restriction as a business necessity, thus allowing the challenge of employer English-only rules under state law without need for proof by the employee of adverse impact on Latino/as. Latino/a organizations should pursue similar legislation in other states and resist persistent efforts in Congress to enact legislation that denies the EEOC enforcement authority over workplace English-only rules.

Business Justifications

Assuming a court is willing to find that a workplace English-only rule causes a discriminatory adverse impact, the employer may nonetheless prevail by demonstrating a sufficient business justification for the rule. The employer will have an easier time when the English rule has limited application (for example, it does not apply to employee break times); by contrast, the EEOC views blanket language rules applied at all times as constituting a burdensome condition of employment that must be carefully scrutinized. Safety considerations present the strongest justification for workplace English rules. For example, the EEOC supported an oil refinery that required employees to speak English during emergencies and when handling volatile materials. This safety rationale may extend to dangerous jobs where team communication is essential, such as in the construction and mining industries.

Employers have also tried to justify English-language rules because they need to effectively supervise employees and defuse workplace tensions among coworkers.[3] Because the Title VII legal standard allows for the employee to rebut a business justification by demonstrating a less discriminatory alternative, it is possible that an employee could prevail despite an otherwise valid supervisory rationale by, for example, demonstrating that hiring a bilingual supervisor would effectively address the employer's supervision concerns. Sometimes the supervision rationale is clearly specious. For example, a Virginia convenience store once contended it needed an English-only rule to ensure its employees weren't plotting on the job to steal from their employer. This rationale makes no sense as employees could wait to plot until their supervisor was out of earshot or could do their illicit planning off the job. Workplace tension justifications sometimes intersect with safety, such as when the employer contends that its employees may be distracted in a dangerous job by suspicions that coworkers are talking about them negatively in a language they cannot understand. Even here, the English-language rule might be countered by establishing viable alternatives to resolve these worker tensions.

What You Should Do as a Spanish Speaker at Work. Spanish-speaking workers nonetheless should be sensitive to the often unfounded insecurities of coworkers who do not speak Spanish that they are being made fun of; for example, language manners suggest that when in conversations that include a monolingual English-speaker, the bilingual worker should avoid switching to Spanish. And when English-speaking coworkers are nearby, the Spanish-speakers should avoid looking at them and laughing while speaking Spanish. A federal court permitted an employer to require a bilingual university program official to speak English based on complaints the employee was excluding English-speaking coworkers from conversations by switching to Spanish (*Roman v. Cornell University*, 53 F. Supp. 2d 223 [N.D.N.Y. 1999]). Employees of an employer where workplace language and cultural tensions exist alternatively might propose that the employer offer basic foreign language courses, as well as English courses, to help relieve workplace tensions.

Customer preference is a questionable business justification for English-only rules. Although racist persons may object to sitting near black riders on the bus or Latino/a diners at a restaurant, their prejudice does not overcome civil rights laws that outlaw segregation of the races. Similarly, although some of an employer's retail customers may object to overhearing Spanish, this does not justify English-language rules. Still, courts give the employer the right to regulate an employee's language when speaking directly to a customer. Illustrating the ability to regulate direct communications is a federal case rejecting a terminated radio disc jockey's Title VII case that challenged the employer's English rule targeting his radio broadcasts peppered with Spanish. The employer's rule was limited to on-air time and the court viewed it as reasonably related to the station's right to control its broadcast programming (*Jurado v. Eleven-Fifty Corporation*, 813 F.2d 1406 [9th Cir. 1987]). Sometimes the customer preference rationale intersects with a safety purpose that heightens the potential for judicial deference to the employer—for example, a nursing home might argue that its English-only policy applying to conversations between nursing attendants is intended to ease the fear its patients have that the attendants are speaking about their medical condition, which increases stress and imperils patient health.

Employers might also assert the business justification of improving employees' English-language skills. This justification may be invalid unless the employer can demonstrate that such skills are important for the particular job, and further that alternate means of gaining English competency, such as facilitating on- or off-the-job English-language instruction, are not feasible.

Non-English-Speaking Workers

Requiring English fluency of one's employees is constrained by similar legal standards. These requirements must have a valid business justification—EEOC commentary states that a workplace English fluency requirement is only valid when necessary for effective performance of the particular job. The EEOC commentary gives the following illustrations of permissible English fluency requirements:

> As with a foreign accent, an individual's lack of proficiency in English may interfere with job performance in some circumstances, but not in others. For example, an individual who is sufficiently proficient in spoken English to qualify as a cashier at a fast food restaurant may lack the written language skills to perform a managerial position at the same restaurant requiring the completion of copious paperwork in English. . . . [T]he employer should not require a greater degree of fluency than is necessary for the relevant position. . . .
>
> Jorge, a Dominican national, applies for a sales position with XYZ Appliances, a small retailer of home appliances in a non-bilingual, English-speaking community. Jorge has very limited skill with spoken English. XYZ notifies him that he is not qualified for a sales position because his ability to effectively assist customers is limited. However, XYZ offers to consider him for a position in the stock room. Under these circumstances, XYZ's decision to exclude Jorge from the sales position does not violate Title VII.[4]

In validating English fluency requirements as necessary for job performance, court decisions give considerable leeway to employers. For example, an employer validly denied a monolingual Spanish-speaking hotel chambermaid a promotion to a front office cashier's position because of her inadequate

English skills (*Mejia v. New York Sheraton Hotel*, 459 F. Supp. 375 [S.D.N.Y. 1978]). Another federal court upheld an English-fluency requirement imposed by a medical care facility as a necessary job-related requirement (*Garcia v. Rush-Presbyterian-St. Luke's Medical Center*, 660 F.2d 1217 [7th Cir. 1981]). Also, a trucking firm's English-ability requirement for its truck drivers passed scrutiny due to the employer's business justifications of increased communication with English-speaking customers and the ability to understand the owner's English-language instructions (*Vasquez v. McAllen Bag & Supply Co.*, 660 F.2d 686 [5th Cir. 1981]).

Accent Discrimination

Accent discrimination by employers is also a potential Title VII civil rights violation that turns on whether the accent interferes materially with the worker's job performance. EEOC commentary elaborates on this legal standard:

> An employment decision based on foreign accent does not violate Title VII if an individual's accent materially interferes with the ability to perform job duties. This assessment depends upon the specific duties of the position in question and the extent to which the individual's accent affects his or her ability to perform job duties. Employers should distinguish between a merely discernible foreign accent and one that interferes with communication skills necessary to perform job duties. Generally, an employer may only base an employment decision on accent if effective oral communication in English is required to perform job duties and the individual's foreign accent materially interferes with his or her ability to communicate orally in English. Positions for which effective oral communication in English may be required include teaching, customer service, and telemarketing. Even for these positions, an employer must still determine whether the particular individual's accent interferes with the ability to perform job duties.

Although customer preference against hearing an accented voice presumably will not justify accent discrimination, customers may play a role in gauging the understandability of the worker, as illustrated by the following example from the EEOC:

> A major aspect of Bill's position as a concierge for XYZ Hotel is assisting guests with directions and travel arrangements. Numerous people have complained that they cannot understand Bill because of his heavy Ghanaian accent. Therefore, XYZ notifies Bill that he is being transferred to a clerical position that does not involve extensive spoken communication. The transfer does not violate Title VII because Bill's accent materially interferes with his ability to perform the functions of the concierge position.

Consistent with this analysis, a federal appeals court upheld the denial of a Title VII claim following the government's refusal to hire an applicant with a heavy Filipino accent for a clerk position that involved delivering services to the general public. The court viewed the ability to communicate effectively as a legitimate occupational qualification for this clerk job (*Fragante v. City and County of Honolulu*, 888 F.2d 591 [9th Cir. 1989]). By contrast, a federal appeals court found an employer was not justified in demoting a Filipino with a noticeable accent from his position as a university dental laboratory supervisor. Here, the court concluded the worker's accent did not interfere with his job performance and thus the demotion constituted national origin discrimination (*Carino v. University of Oklahoma Board of Regents*, 750 F.2d 815 [10th Cir. 1984]).

What You Can Do When Targeted for Your Accent. An employee targeted for his Spanish accent should counter by asking coworkers and customers to vouch for his or her ability to be understood. This effort will be most persuasive if those asked to do so are themselves English-speakers with understandable diction. Further, the employee should remind the employer of the benefits of his or her bilingual ability on the job.

Rights of Undocumented Workers

Concerns about immigration and the loss of jobs for U.S. workers in the early 1980s led to various measures to curb illegal immigration, but with little success. Congress concluded that it was necessary to enlist employers to enforce immigration policy. Through the Immigration Reform and Control Act of 1986 (IRCA), Congress made the hiring of undocumented workers illegal and made employers responsible for enforcing the law by verifying the identity and work authorization of employees. Under this law, to work legally in the United States all employees must complete Form I-9 and show documents (such as a driver's license or state-issued identification card) to their employers to prove who they are and whether they are authorized to work (if they have a "green card" evidencing lawful permanent resident status or a social security card). A U.S. passport is sufficient to prove both identity and authorization to work.

Of course, by definition, the undocumented don't have valid documents of this kind. Some run the risk of using counterfeit documents or those of others, both of which can lead to charges of document fraud and identity theft. These are felonies (serious crimes) that can lead to arrest and, upon conviction, removal (deportation). These issues are discussed in great depth in Chapter 11 on undocumented immigrants.

National Labor Relations Act (NLRA)
This federal law guarantees nonagricultural workers the right to organize into unions and to bargain collectively to secure decent wages and working conditions. Workers can actively participate in enforcing the law by filing

claims against employers who interfere with their rights. The remedy for unfair termination by an employer is usually job reinstatement and back pay for time missed. The Supreme Court had to decide whether the rights under the NLRA apply equally to both documented and undocumented workers.

In *Hoffman Plastic Compounds, Inc. v. National Labor Relations Board*, 535 U.S. 137 (2002), an unauthorized worker named Juan Castro used a friend's birth certificate fraudulently to obtain a California driver's license and a social security card, which he provided to Hoffman as documentation of his work status. Six months after being hired, Castro was discharged for supporting a union organizing campaign. Castro complained this was an unfair labor practice, and Hoffman was ordered by the National Labor Relations Board to pay $67,000 to Castro in back pay for earnings lost after his unlawful discharge. The Supreme Court reversed the board's decision, finding an award of back pay for Castro inconsistent with IRCA because Castro's employment was illegal and was obtained through fraud. The Court noted that compliance with immigration law was more important than Castro's interest in holding the employer responsible for interfering with unionization. The *Hoffman* decision has, in some cases, had an impact on remedies available to undocumented workers under other federal and state laws.

Title VII of the Civil Rights Act of 1964

Title VII protects workers from discrimination by employers based on race, color, religion, sex, and national origin. Wrongfully terminated workers are entitled to the remedies of reinstatement, back pay, and other forms of wage loss compensation. In cases involving undocumented workers, courts have often analogized Title VII's coverage to that of the NLRA. The EEOC has also looked to NLRA cases in issuing its guidelines. Accordingly, after the *Hoffman* decision the EEOC removed its guideline saying undocumented workers are entitled to federal remedies.

Nevertheless, questions remain as to *Hoffman*'s bearing on Title VII, as reflected in the case of *Rivera v. NIBCO, Inc.* There, twenty-three Latina and Southeast Asian female immigrant workers at NIBCO's factory were tested on their basic job skills with an English-only examination. The workers had limited English proficiency and performed poorly on the tests. The company demoted and eventually terminated the workers, which led to their Title VII suit for discrimination. During the pretrial discovery (evidence-gathering) period, NIBCO tried to question the workers about their immigration status. The court said that such questions were not relevant to the issue of discrimination and would have an unacceptably chilling effect on Title VII claims. Recall the discussion of national origin in the section on discrimination based on citizenship earlier in this chapter.

Other circumstances may also allow undocumented workers to receive back pay. A federal district court awarded back pay to undocumented workers from India who had been misled into thinking they were authorized to work by their employer. The employer recruited the workers from India, gave them visas for living in the United States, and told them they were authorized for employment. The district court awarded back pay for the work actually performed, which it distinguished from NLRA's back pay for time missed. The court also distinguished the fraud in the case from that in *Hoffman*, which involved fraud in obtaining employment on the part of the worker.

Fair Labor Standards Act (FLSA)

The Fair Labor Standards Act mandates minimum wage and overtime standards for employers. Courts are authorized to award back pay for minimum wage and overtime violations concerning work performed by an employee. Undocumented workers generally have been afforded full protection under FLSA, even after IRCA was passed. For example, in *Patel v. Quality Inn South*, 846 F.2d 700 (11th Cir. 1988), the court found that extending FLSA's protection to undocumented workers removes any incentive employers might have in hiring persons unlawfully in this country. The court reasoned that no conflict existed between the objectives of FLSA and IRCA. Courts have also held that undocumented workers are protected from retaliation by an employer for filing a wage claim with the Labor Board. One form of unlawful retaliation against an undocumented worker for filing a FLSA claim is an employer threat to report the employee to U.S. Immigration and Customs Enforcement (ICE).

State Laws

Worker compensation laws provide injured workers with medical and wage loss benefits. Even after IRCA, most state courts treat undocumented workers as statutory "employees" under state compensation laws, with some variation. California courts generally extend worker's compensation coverage to undocumented workers but withhold vocational rehabilitation benefits from undocumented workers. Undocumented workers in Texas are covered as long as the worker's employment contract or arrangement did not aid him in his illegal entry into the country. Florida claimants usually must demonstrate a good faith job search to establish wage loss, but courts will excuse the work search and award benefits to undocumented workers with serious enough injuries. Undocumented workers have also been generally included in the worker's compensation statutes of Oregon, Georgia, Maryland, Louisiana, Oklahoma, Minnesota, Connecticut, North Carolina, and Virginia, among others. Jurisdictions that exclude coverage for undocumented workers include Nevada, Wyoming, and the District of Columbia.

Undocumented employees who suffer injuries in the course of employment may also pursue claims outside the worker's compensation framework. For example, New York's highest court allowed recovery in a personal injury action by an undocumented worker who sued his employer for violating workplace safety requirements. The court held that damages awarded to the undocumented worker under state tort laws for lost wages were not pre-empted (superseded) by IRCA (*Balbuena v. IDR Realty LLC*, 6 N.Y.3d 338 [2006]).

Immigration Raids at the Workplace

"Factory surveys," as they have euphemistically been called, continue to be a problem for both employers and, particularly, Latino/a employees. Although ICE wants to apprehend those without legal immigration status, it is often the case that all Latino/a employees, including lawful permanent residents and U.S. citizens, bear the brunt of these immigration raids. As explained in Chapter 8, and particularly in its section on racial profiling in immigration enforcement cases, decisions that virtually exempt such raids from Fourth Amendment protections necessitate the identification and utilization of the remaining available means of protecting the rights of all Latino/as, regardless of immigration status.

It is not uncommon for the undocumented to use someone else's social security number or counterfeit documents to satisfy the employer of the employee's authorization to work for purposes of completing Form I-9 (discussed earlier in the section on discrimination based on citizenship). The employer must honor documents tendered that on their face reasonably appear to be genuine, that is, are not obviously fake. A cautious employer will photocopy the documents submitted and put them in the employee's personnel file.

Employers who satisfy these requirements and who don't want their workplaces to become a scene of pandemonium when ICE arrives can use strategies together with their workforce to safeguard the rights of all. First, they can take steps to protect their own legal rights. If ICE arrives at the workplace, the employer has the right to request a copy of the warrant and read it carefully before permitting government agents to enter. If possible, the employer should ask the ICE agents to wait until the employer has an opportunity to call a lawyer and read the warrant to the lawyer and ask for advice on how to proceed. In any event, the employer need only permit a search of the particular places named in the warrant. The ICE agents, upon entry, only have a right to arrest particular persons named in an arrest warrant, unless other facts give them "probable cause" for an arrest (e.g., employees who are running away).

What Employers, Community Groups, and You Can Do to Protect Your Rights in Workplace Immigration Raids. Employers can also assist their workers in protecting their rights. The Supreme Court has said that employees in immigration raids have no reason to believe they will be detained if they "simply refused to answer" (*Immigration and Naturalization Service v. Delgado*, 466 U.S. 210, 218 [1984]). This is because, under the Fifth Amendment of the U.S. Constitution, "no person shall be compelled in any criminal case to be a witness against himself, nor be deprived of life, liberty, or property, without due process of law" (see Chapter 8). Employers can, therefore, simply inform their employees that, if ICE ever enters the workplace, everyone should simply continue their work and remain silent. To facilitate this process, a worker could carry and silently show a card (that could be provided by the employer or by a civil rights organization) when approached by a government agent. The card could say, "I do not wish to speak with you and shall not do so unless first advised by a lawyer."

Absent some reasonable suspicion of misconduct, detaining someone, even if for the purpose of determining identity, violates the Fourth Amendment "right of the people to be secure in their persons, houses, papers, and effects, against unreasonable searches and seizures" (*Brown v. Texas*, 443 U.S. 47, 52 [1979]). If the employee says nothing, does not flee, and simply continues to work, the ICE agent has two choices: to make an illegal arrest, without probable cause, or to leave. Although ICE has the right to ask questions, they do not have the right to have those questions answered before an arrest. And they only have the right to arrest a person if they have a warrant with the person's name on it (and the employer should so advise that employee, if that is the case) or "if there is reason to believe that the alien so arrested in the United States is in violation of the immigration laws" (see Chapter 8). Mere Latino/a appearance does not give an ICE agent such "reason to believe" that the person has any particular immigration status. If the employees don't speak, there is no basis upon which the ICE can acquire such reason.

This strategy, of course, requires some solidarity among workers. The privilege against self-incrimination (right to remain silent) would be most effective in this context if *everyone* in the workplace exercised their right, U.S. citizen, lawful resident, and undocumented alike. It also requires some courage, because the show of force of armed, uniformed ICE agents can be very intimidating. Nevertheless, in a unanimous decision, the Supreme Court made it clear that "a person is seized by the police and thus entitled to challenge the government's action under the Fourth Amendment when the officer, 'by means of physical force or show of authority,' 'terminates or restrains his freedom of movement'" (*Brendlin v. California*, 127 S.Ct. 2400 [2007]). Because of the Supreme Court's retrenchment in protecting individual rights and liberties in the context of immigration law enforcement, increased resort to the privilege against self-incrimination until counsel can be consulted appears to be one of the few avenues left to ensure self-protection.

Where such raids occur with some frequency, other strategies have been used. Latino/a, church, and immigrants' rights activists can establish coalitions ready for action when raids occur. People with video cameras can go to the workplace and obtain permission from the employer to film the workplace during a raid to monitor potential abuses and violations of the

Constitution. If arrests are made, a telephone tree can be used to share information and make arrangements for children with detained parents. Some churches provide sanctuary to affected families or those in fear of removal (deportation). Some communities, such as Portland, Oregon, have established "raid watch teams" that mobilize when rumors of raids surface. They go to the Federal Building and monitor outbound immigration agents. It is, of course, always helpful to have lawyers who can be called to advise on all of these matters.

Farm Worker Wages

Two significant laws address wages for agricultural workers: the Migrant and Seasonal Agricultural Worker Protection Act (MSAWPA) and the Fair Labor Standards Act. MSAWPA has some important provisions that relate to wages, as well as many other provisions primarily concerned with the conditions of agricultural work. Most protections related to agricultural wages are addressed under FLSA. Both laws are quite technical in the definitions they use and how their protections actually function.

The Farm Labor Contractor Registration Act of 1963 (FLCRA) is an earlier law enacted to protect agricultural workers whose employment had been historically characterized by low wages, long hours, and poor working conditions. Congress found this law was largely ignored and not adequately enforced, which led to the enactment of MSAWPA.

While we generally understand the term "migrant worker" to mean low-wage workers performing manual agricultural labor, MSAWPA actually protects two different categories of such workers. A "migrant agricultural worker" is defined as "an individual who is employed in agricultural employment of a seasonal or other temporary nature, and who is required to be absent overnight from his permanent place of residence." A "seasonal agricultural worker" is defined as "an individual who is employed in agricultural employment of a seasonal or other temporary nature and is *not* required to be absent overnight from his permanent place of residence" (emphasis supplied).

MSAWPA does have some exemptions. It does not apply to family businesses, if the business is owned or operated exclusively by an immediate family member, and the work is performed only for that business operation and by an immediate family member (small family farms). It does not apply to anyone (other than a farm labor contractor) for whom the employer did not use more than five hundred person-days of agricultural labor in any calendar quarter of the preceding year. There are also other miscellaneous exemptions, such as for labor organizations, nonprofit charitable organizations, and several others where the principal activity is typically not agricultural employment. But undocumented workers *are* protected by this law (*In re Reyes*, 814 F.2d 168 [5th Cir.1987]).

MSAWPA requires employers (whether an agricultural employer, agricultural association, or farm labor contractor) to disclose to each migrant agricultural worker, in writing, the wage rates to be paid, and the disclosure must be in the worker's language if not fluent or literate in English. (This requirement also applies to seasonal workers who request it.) The wages are to be paid when due, and this "failure to pay wages" provision is quite effective. An employer who willfully and knowingly (deliberately) violates these provisions can be fined or imprisoned, or both. The U.S. Department of Labor (USDOL) can also request a court to order that an employer cease the violation. Of course, complaints don't go to court right away. A complaint to USDOL would be addressed first by an administrative officer. Employers who are assessed a fine can appeal—first, to an administrative law judge specializing in labor law, and then to the federal district court. However, a worker with a complaint under MSAWPA has the choice of suing the employer in a United States District Court, and does not need to wait for the administrative process to finish (or even to go through the administrative process at all). This is unlike the process under the discrimination law, Title VII, which requires the complaint to be filed initially with an administrative agency before going to court.

One of the important differences between MSAWPA and FLSA is that, under MSAWPA, the worker may have more time after the violation to sue. MSAWPA adopts the same statute of limitations as analogous state claims. So, for example, if the state requires a worker to sue for a violation of a state minimum wage law within six years of the violation, the worker can also sue under MSAWPA within six years. This contrasts with cases under FLSA, which usually have to be filed within two years of the FLSA violation (or within three years for "willful" violations).

Under MSAWPA, upon request the court may even provide the complaining worker with an attorney. The worker can obtain damages—an award of money the employer must pay—in the amount the employee actually lost, or, in the court's discretion, up to $500 per violation (or, in some cases, even both). (Multiple violations of a single provision are lumped together, however, when applying the $500 per violation provision.) For claims of small amounts, therefore, MSAWPA is preferred over FLSA. The court can also make other awards it finds fair. However, while the complaining worker need not go through the administrative process, the court can consider whether an attempt was made to resolve the dispute in determining how much money to award. Unfortunately, attorney's fees are not available under MSAWPA (although they are under FLSA).

Furthermore, an employer is utterly prohibited—by intimidation, threat, coercion, blacklisting, firing, or any manner of discrimination—from retaliating against a worker who files or testifies in a lawsuit, or because another worker has done so, to assert rights under MSAWPA.

What You Can Do If Your Employer Retaliates Against You. If a worker believes retaliation has occurred, the worker may, within 180 days of the violation, file a complaint with USDOL, which will investigate. If the agency finds just cause for complaint, it will bring legal action against the employer in the U.S. District Court, which can order any appropriate remedy, including rehiring or reinstatement, back pay, or other money awards.

The other important law that relates to the wages of farm workers is FLSA, which Congress passed in 1938. FLSA applies to employees of businesses engaged in interstate commerce and established a national minimum wage. It also guaranteed an increased wage for working "overtime," or more than forty hours in a week (but this FLSA provision, importantly, does not apply to agricultural workers. The law *does* protect the undocumented *(Patel v. Quality Inn South)*.

FLSA has been amended several times to raise the minimum wage, including the Fair Minimum Wage Act of 2007 that established a minimum wage of $5.85 per hour on July 24, 2007; increasing to $6.55 per hour on July 24, 2008; and increasing again to $7.25 on July 24, 2009. However, an employer may pay a new employee under age 20 a lower wage, but it must be at least $4.25 per hour for the first 90 days of employment. Employers are prohibited from displacing (whether by dismissal, or reduction in hours or benefits) any regularly paid employee to hire a lower-paid employee under age 20.

Under FLSA, an employer must pay nonagricultural employees at least one and one-half times their regular rate ("time-and-a-half"), if the employees work more than forty hours in one work week. The employer may not count certain things as part of an employee's regular rate, including gifts, holiday or sick-time pay, reimbursement for reasonable travel expenses, amounts paid for life or health insurance, contributions for pension or retirement funds for the employee's benefit, extra compensation at a premium rate for working extra hours in a day or on other unusual days or holidays, any value derived from exercising stock options, or other exceptional payments not measured by or dependent upon hours worked, production, or efficiency as compensation for hours of employment.

There are some kinds of employment exempt from the minimum wage and overtime requirements. As it relates to migrant or seasonal agricultural workers, the minimum wage requirements do not apply to agricultural employees if the employer did not use more than 500 person-days of agricultural labor in any calendar quarter in the preceding year. They also do not apply to an employee who is a member of the employer's immediate family. Also exempt are seasonal (but *not* migrant) agricultural workers employed as hand harvest laborers customarily paid at a piece rate, if they were employed in agriculture less than thirteen weeks in the preceding calendar year.

And while employees who work at a piece rate need not earn the minimum wage for each hour worked, the total earned in the work week must bring the average hourly rate up to the minimum wage (*United States v. Rosenwasser*, 323 U.S. 360, 363 [1945]).

These exemptions only apply to employers who can prove they are engaged in an agricultural operation. Under FLSA (also adopted by MSAWPA), the definition of "agriculture" includes farming (including the cultivation and tillage of the soil); dairying; the production, cultivation, growing, and harvesting of any agricultural or horticultural commodities; the raising of livestock, bees, fur-bearing animals, or poultry; and any practices (including any forestry or lumbering operations) performed by a farmer or on a farm incident to or in conjunction with such farming operations, including preparation for market, delivery to storage or to market, or to carriers for transportation to market.

As is the case with violations of MSAWPA, an employer can be subject to criminal penalties for FLSA violations. Additionally, an employee has the right to sue in federal or state court for unpaid minimum wages and overtime (but agricultural workers are not entitled to overtime under FLSA). Workers entitled to recover compensation unlawfully withheld under FLSA can also request the court to order the employer to pay an equal, additional amount in "liquidated damages." Employees can also sue for other court orders, such as for re-employment, reinstatement, or promotion, and can recover from the employer reasonable costs and attorney's fees incurred in bringing the lawsuit.

Additionally, USDOL may sue (or remedy the matter administratively, without taking the case to court) on behalf of one or more employees. If USDOL does so and the employee agrees to the collection activity of USDOL in getting the employer to pay the unpaid compensation, the employee waives the right to sue. Similar to MSAWPA, the employer is forbidden to retaliate against employees who assert their rights to proper compensation.

Appendix

Resources on Employment Discrimination

- *U.S. Equal Employment Opportunity Commission.* Investigates complaints of employment discrimination based on national origin, color, and race, and sexual harassment by employers having fifteen or more employees. Instructions in English and Spanish on how and where to file a complaint are available at www.eeoc.gov/index.html. The nearest EEOC field office may be contacted by calling toll-free 800-669-4000.
- *Office of Special Counsel for Immigration-Related Unfair Employment Practices, U.S. Department of Justice.* Investigates complaints of

employment discrimination based on national origin and citizenship status by employers with four to fourteen employees. Instructions in English and Spanish on how and where to file a complaint are available at www.usdoj.gov/crt/osc. The toll-free worker hotline at the central office in Washington, D.C., is 800-255-7688.

- *Employment Litigation Section, Civil Rights Division, U.S. Department of Justice.* Investigates complaints of systemic employment discrimination and those referred by the EEOC. Answers to frequently asked questions about Title VII of the Civil Rights Act of 1964 are available in English and Spanish at www.usdoj.gov/crt/emp/faq.html.

Resources for Farm Workers

- *U.S. Department of Labor.* Information regarding the laws and regulations that protect migrant and seasonal farm workers is available at www.dol.gov/topic/training/migrantfarmworkers.htm. The central office in Washington, D.C., can be reached toll-free at 866-4-USA-DOL.
- *United Farm Workers.* Information regarding organizing and protecting the rights of farm workers is available at www.ufw.org.

Resources on Language Discrimination in the Workplace

- Equal Employment Opportunity Commission Workplace Language Compliance Manual: http://www.eeoc.gov/policy/docs/national-origin.html#V.
- Equal Employment Opportunity Commission materials in Spanish: http://www.eeoc.gov/es/origin/index.html.
- Workplace Fairness (nonprofit organization) materials on language discrimination: http://www.workplacefairness.org/language.

Notes

1. For a discussion of national origin discrimination, see EEOC Compliance Manual, "Section 13: National Origin Discrimination" (December 2, 2002), available at http://www.eeoc.gov/policy/docs/national-origin.html; Guidelines on Discrimination Because of National Origin, at 29 C.F.R. § 1606.1; and see discussion of discrimination based on citizenship, later in this chapter.

2. *Equal Employment Opportunity Commission v. Premier Operator Services, Inc.,* 113 F.Supp.2d 1066 (N.D. Tex. 2000); see also *Maldonado v. City of Altus,* 433 F.3d 1294 (10th Cir. 2006) finding sufficient evidence to present jury question on whether municipal English-only policy for all employees created a hostile work environment that adversely affected Spanish-speakers; among proof of adverse impact was testimony of ethnic taunting because of the language policy, as well as contentions the policy made them feel like second-class citizens.

3. See *Barber v. Lovelace Sandia Health Systems,* 409 F. Supp. 2d 1313 (D. N.M. 2005), in which a medical clinic's justifications for its English-only rule—employee complaints about their discomfort when employees around them spoke Spanish, and a complaint that derogatory remarks were made about a patient in Spanish—were legitimate and nondiscriminatory.

4. EEOC Compliance Manual, "National Origin Discrimination," available at www.eeoc.gov.

3
Discrimination in Housing

Landlord Discrimination

Although the purchase of housing will also be discussed to some extent in this chapter, the focus will be primarily on the rental of housing. Latino/as are more likely than others to have the following characteristics associated with lower home-ownership rates:

- householder is not a citizen;
- householder is foreign-born;
- foreign-born householder recently arrived in the United States;
- young householder;
- low income;
- low educational attainment level;
- residence located in central city;
- residence in multifamily housing unit;
- residence in high-cost housing market.[1]

Many of the cases discussed in this chapter relate to African Americans, but a study conducted by the U.S. Department of Housing and Urban Development (HUD) reveals that discrimination against Hispanic renters has become more common than discrimination against African Americans.[2]

The Civil Rights Act of 1964, although fairly comprehensive, did not prohibit private discrimination in housing. The need for such a provision became clear to Congress, however, in subsequent years, especially as young African Americans and Latino/as returned from fighting in Vietnam only to be denied housing because of their race. The assassination of Dr. Martin Luther King Jr. on April 4, 1968, helped spur Congress into action, and the Civil Rights Act of 1968 was enacted a week later. As amended, Title VIII

(8) of the 1968 law, also known as the Fair Housing Act (FHA), prohibits discrimination in housing based on race, color, national origin, and familial status, among other categories.

At about the same time Congress enacted Title VIII, the Supreme Court revived a federal remedy for violations of the housing discrimination provision of the post–Civil War Civil Rights Act of 1866, 42 U.S.C. § 1982 (*Jones v. Alfred H. Mayer Co.*, 392 U.S. 409 [1968]). The statute provides that "all citizens of the United States shall have the same right, in every state and territory, as is enjoyed by white citizens thereof to inherit, purchase, lease, sell, hold, and convey real and personal property."

Section 1982 covers landlords who might be statutorily exempt from Title VIII, but discrimination under Section 1982 must include a racial component. Interpretation of race in this context (*Shaare Tefila Congregation v. Cobb*, 481 U.S. 615 [1987]) is the same as under Section 1981 (another provision of the Civil Rights Act of 1866, discussed in Chapter 2). Both provisions, therefore, include within their scope discrimination based on ethnic origin. Section 1981 is also applied to discrimination by landlords because it provides that "all persons . . . shall have the same right . . . to make and enforce contracts . . . as is enjoyed by white citizens." Finally, a number of states and municipalities have enacted their own fair housing laws, some of which prohibit discrimination based on citizenship.

The central provision of Title VIII is 42 U.S.C. § 3601(a), which makes it an unlawful housing practice "to refuse to sell or rent after the making of a bona fide offer, or refuse to negotiate for the sale or rental of, or otherwise make unavailable or deny, a dwelling" based on race, color, or national origin. Making a case for housing discrimination is similar to employment discrimination under Title VII. Similarly, the two methods available to prove discrimination under Title VIII are disparate treatment and disparate impact (see discussion in Chapter 2). The disparate treatment methodology is the only one available when proceeding under Sections 1981 and 1982.

What You Can Do to Help Prove Discrimination. To prove discrimination in housing under the disparate treatment model, typically the plaintiff must

- show membership in a protected class (e.g., be Latino/a);
- apply for and be qualified to rent or purchase the unit involved;
- be rejected by the defendant;
- and demonstrate that the housing opportunity remained available thereafter.

Plaintiffs can use such evidence to show that a denial of housing was based on a landlord's discriminatory motive (i.e., was intentionally based on the applicant's ethnicity). For example, a Latino applicant named Raymond Pina called about a vacancy after seeing the landlord's advertisement. After

Pina told the landlord his name, she informed him there were no vacancies and ended the conversation. Later that day, a non-Latino coworker friend of Pina's inquired in person about the apartment and was told it was available. The landlord then told other Latino friends of Pina who expressed interest in the unit that it was not available, and the unit was ultimately rented to a non-Latino. Using that evidence, Pina established an inference of discrimination in court. To defend her decision, the landlord said she told Pina there were no vacancies because Pina had been "mean" over the phone. The court found the landlord's justification inadequate ("pretextual") and indicated that, at the least, some evidence supporting the landlord's explanation beyond her word was needed to establish a legitimate defense (*Ventura v. State Equal Opportunity Commission*, 517 N.W.2d 368 [Neb. 1994]). Although this is a decision of the Nebraska Supreme Court under the state's fair housing act, it applied Title VIII because the state law was patterned after Title VIII. Even more direct evidence of disparate treatment and discriminatory intent is where a landlord tells a Latino/a housing applicant that he does not rent to Latino/as because he believes they are less likely to make timely payments, or more likely to be involved in criminal activity.

Landlords are allowed to defend housing selections on nondiscriminatory grounds. Courts will generally defer to landlords who can show objective financial reasons for their decision. For example, in a case under Title VIII and Section 1981, a landlord's selection of a white person over an African American couple was justified where the white person's salary was $90,000 compared to the couple's collective salary of approximately $50,000, and the applicant-wife had previously filed for bankruptcy (*Sullivan v. Hernandez*, 215 F. Supp. 2d 635 [D. Md. 2002]).

Plaintiffs, nevertheless, have successfully challenged decisions as discriminatory by showing that financial criteria are applied differently to whites and people of color. For example, a landlord's use of credit histories to explain why minority applicants were rejected was found pretextual because almost half of the landlord's white tenants were never asked about their credit histories, and some had been unemployed or bankrupt on or about the time they were accepted as tenants (*Marable v. H. Walker & Associates*, 644 F.2d 390 [5th Cir. 1981]).

Occasionally, landlords use income formulas or minimum income requirements for selecting tenants. These are generally accepted unless applied selectively to people of color or otherwise implemented with a discriminatory motive. Under Title VIII and Sections 1981 and 1982, therefore, race need not be the sole reason for refusal to rent to establish a violation of the law.

A handful of other reasons for denying housing are generally accepted as measures of an applicant's ability to be a successful tenant. Most relate to an applicant's character, which landlords are allowed to inquire about through references, letters of recommendation, and criminal histories. But these decisions are usually more subjective and easier to challenge as discriminatory than those involving an applicant's finances (*e.g.*, *Allen v. Muriello*, 217 F.3d 517 [7th Cir. 2000]).

Sometimes landlords give nonracial priorities to certain groups. These are generally allowed, but can be challenged as a pretext for discrimination, especially where there is evidence that whites and people of color are treated differently under a priority system. One such case was successfully made against the manager of New York's Cooperative Village, a group of housing cooperatives on the Lower East Side of Manhattan. The cooperatives offered 4,432 low-cost units, and thousands of applicants wanted to live there. The manager's stated policy gave priority to newlyweds, young people, and children of tenants. Julio Huertas and other Latino/a and black plaintiffs were able to demonstrate that nonminorities were almost always accepted before people of color, even where the priority system favored the minority applicant. They prevailed under Title VIII and Sections 1981 and 1982 (*Huertas v. East River Housing Corp.*, 674 F. Supp. 440 [S.D.N.Y. 1987]).

In some circumstances, a fair housing violation might take place even before an application for housing is made. Title VIII makes it unlawful to indicate racial preferences for housing (42 U.S.C. § 3601[c]) and to steer applicants away from housing based on their race or national origin (42 U.S.C. 3601[d]). Both of these provisions targeted practices that discourage people of color from applying for housing in the first place. They are sometimes used against advertisers and real estate agents, but landlords can just as easily be held liable for indicating racial preferences in conversations with potential applicants.

For example, a landlord's questioning of a prospective tenant's race in a telephone interview was found to violate Title VIII even though the landlord did not indicate to the prospective tenant his preferences (*Jancik v. Department of Housing and Urban Development*, 44 F.3d 553 [7th Cir. 1995]). In contrast, in *Campbell v. Robb*, 162 Fed. Appx. 460 (6th Cir. 2006), a landlord's offhand racial joke referring to a black cat in the neighborhood as a "nigger in the haystack" to a white prospective tenant who had a black fiancée was not unlawful because the landlord did not yet know about the black fiancée, so he could not have intended to discourage African Americans from applying. The court concluded the remark was, therefore, not "with respect to the sale or rental of a dwelling." After he did know, the landlord also stated, "I don't have any problems with black people, but I do not want a lot of them hanging out in my parking lot," which, the court said, would have violated Title VIII if the couple had been financially qualified to rent the apartment.

In terms of printed advertisements, courts have found that the routine use of human models of only one race can constitute an indication of preference in violation of Title VIII. For example, a claim was allowed under 42 U.S.C § 3604(c), which prohibits discrimination in the advertisement of the sale or rental of dwellings, where the landlord ran a series of about thirty rental advertisements, all of which featured white models, over the course of twenty years (*Ragin v. New York Times Co.*, 923 F.2d 995 [2d Cir. 1991]). A single advertisement that featured only white models was not enough to constitute a Title VIII advertising violation (*Housing Opportunities Made Equal v. Cincinnati Enquirer, Inc.*, 943 F.2d 644 [6th Cir. 1991]).

Even though a preference is benign, it still may violate Title VIII. A management company sought to maintain a racial balance of 64 percent Anglo, 22 percent African American, and 8 percent Latino/a in its housing complex to avoid setting off a wave of "white flight." To do so, it considered the applicants' race as a factor in its rental decisions. The court found this inconsistent with the Fair Housing Act even though the law aimed to promote integrated housing. Because the percentages were viewed as rigid quotas of indefinite duration that operated to restrict the access of people of color to scarce and desirable housing, the court said it was a preference that violates Title VIII (*United States v. Starrett City Associates*, 840 F.2d 1096 [2d Cir. 1988]).

Under Title VIII, discrimination in transactions relating to "dwellings" is prohibited. The law defines a dwelling as any building or structure occupied as a residence and any vacant land offered for sale or lease for the construction of such a building. Temporary housing provided for migrant farm workers qualifies as a "residence" under Title VIII. Even if the migrant laborer owns a permanent residence elsewhere, the seasonal lodging provided farm workers by the farm owner is covered by Title VIII, at least in the circumstance of the migrants staying in the housing for four or five months (*Villegas v. Sandy Farms, Inc.*, 929 F. Supp. 1324, 1328 [D. Or. 1996]; *Hernandez v. Ever Fresh Co.*, 923 F. Supp. 1305 [D. Or. 1996]).

In addition to proving discrimination under the disparate treatment model, a showing of *discriminatory effect* suffices to demonstrate a violation of the Fair Housing Act. Title VIII prohibits not only direct discrimination but also practices with racially discriminatory effects. Therefore, it is not necessary to prove racial or ethnic animus using this methodology, as it is under the disparate treatment model. Instead, statistics are usually used to prove that a particular housing practice has a discriminatory impact.

For example, the exclusion by officials of Okaloosa County, Florida, of public housing from an unincorporated five-mile area of the county had a harsher impact on African Americans than whites because 86 percent of the persons on the waiting list were African American, and the neighborhood where the public housing probably would have been built was racially impacted. Okaloosa County was 8 percent African American at that time, and excluding the five-mile area would have resulted in the housing being built in Fort Walton Beach, which was 38 percent African American already. Such action would have worsened existing segregation (would have had a discriminatory effect) in the county (*Jackson v. Okaloosa County*, 21 F.3d 1531 [11th Cir. 1994]). Housing practices or policies that have discriminatory effects are only lawful if the defendant can present bona fide (good faith) and legitimate justifications for its action and can show there are no less discriminatory alternatives available.

Terms and Conditions

Federal law not only guarantees that tenants must be able to obtain housing on a nondiscriminatory basis, but also guarantees their right to equal treatment once they become tenants. Title VIII makes it unlawful "to discriminate against any person in the terms, conditions, or privileges of sale or rental of a dwelling, or in the provision of services in connection therewith" based on race, color, or national origin (42 U.S.C. 3604[b]).

The most obvious cases of discrimination involve landlords who provide Latino/a tenants with worse rental terms than Anglo tenants. Examples would include landlords who ask higher rents of Latino/a tenants, do not provide them with equal maintenance or repair services, ask for a higher damage deposit, or refuse to return the deposit after the tenancy ends in situations where deposits are returned to other tenants. A landlord also discriminates in terms and conditions of housing when tenants are placed in units according to their race or ethnicity, that is, when an apartment building or complex is segregated.

Discrimination can also occur with regard to terms and conditions not expressly referenced in the lease agreement. As a general rule, any right or privilege incidental to housing must be provided to tenants on equal terms. One landlord was held liable for a pattern or practice of discrimination under Title VIII where his manager refused to allow African American guests to attend a tenant's party (*United States v. L & H Land Corp.*, 407 F. Supp. 576 [S.D. Fla.1976]). An Asian American landlord was found to have discriminated against white tenants in violation of Title VIII where only children of the Asian and Middle Eastern tenants were allowed to play in the building's common areas and only they were provided repairs and maintenance (*Jordan v. Khan*, 969 F. Supp. 29 [N.D. Ill. 1997]). Courts have also found landlords liable for failing to respond to complaints of racial harassment by other tenants. Although landlords are not under a duty to provide a harassment-free living environment, they must take reasonable efforts to stop harassment once reported. In a case under Section 1982, a court indicated that, in cases of ongoing and extreme racial harassment, the only reasonable response of landlords is to move or evict the harassing tenant (*Bradley v. Carydale Enterprises*, 730 F. Supp. 709 [E.D. Va. 1989]).

A landlord's decision to terminate or not to renew a tenant's lease is also a term and condition of housing. Violations of fair housing laws are sometimes established by showing that Anglo tenants were not terminated for the same reason that resulted in a Latino/a tenant's termination, as, for example, where a Latino/a tenant is terminated for missing a rent payment, but Anglo tenants are given second chances. If no immediate comparison can be made, courts may consider other evidence suggesting that a termination was out of custom for the landlord.

One such case under Title VIII and Sections 1981 and 1982 involved a landlord who terminated the lease of an African American couple after their initial rent check failed to clear with the bank. The landlord's justification was that past experience had taught him that problems with the first check usually meant the tenant would be unreliable. The court rejected the landlord's explanation because the landlord had many years of experience dealing with white tenants and failed checks, yet he had never been so quick to conclude that one of those tenants would have problems making timely payments. The plaintiffs were awarded $10,000 in compensatory and $5,000 in punitive damages (*Shaw v. Cassar*, 558 F. Supp. 303 [E.D. Mich. 1983]).

Habitability of Housing

Most states imply, either through statute or common law, a warranty of habitability in lease contracts. The warranty requires that rental property be delivered and maintained in good living condition for the duration of the lease. Many states have enacted versions of the Uniform Residential Landlord and Tenant Act (URLTA) or similar statutes to guide courts as to the standard for habitability. Courts will also look to housing codes and sanitary regulations where available.

At the least, habitability means the property is free of known hazards. Known hazards are problems within the dwelling that might make it unsafe for tenants, such as asbestos, lead paint, structural defects, faulty electrical wiring, infestations, and other health and safety problems. In most jurisdictions, landlords are also required to make the property reasonably fit for living. URLTA requires that landlords "maintain in good and safe working order and condition all electrical, plumbing, sanitary, heating, ventilating, air-conditioning, and other facilities and appliances, including elevators, supplied or required to be supplied" (URLTA § 2.104). However, landlords are not required to provide living amenities or make the property aesthetically pleasing. So wall cracks, bad painting, malfunctioning blinds, and even water leaks will not make a property uninhabitable, assuming they do not create a significant health or safety problem.

What You Can Do If the Rental Is Not Habitable. A landlord who fails to make the property habitable is legally in breach of the lease. Tenants may withhold rent and, in some cases, may be entitled to damages if rent was paid when the property was uninhabitable. Courts, however, will not hold landlords liable for defective conditions of which they were unaware, or about which they were not reasonably required to know.

Landlord Obligations to Spanish-Speaking Tenants

Translation Requirements

A few states by statute require residential landlords to provide the Spanish-speaking tenant with a Spanish-language translation of the lease agreement. For example, California requires translations before the contract is signed from persons in the business of renting apartments and other dwellings who negotiate a lease primarily in the Spanish language (or other specified Asian languages) that exceeds one month (Cal. Civ. Code § 1632). Translation rights normally must be based on a state statute, as many courts are reluctant to impose translation requirements as a matter of judge-made law. For example, although a judge in New Jersey believed the landlord adopting new rules for pets should have translated them for Spanish-speaking tenants (*5000 Park Associates v. Collado*, 602 A.2d 803 [N.J. Super. Ct. 1991]), another New Jersey judge criticized this decision for undertaking a legislative function (*New York East Coast Management v. Gonzalez*, 870 A.2d 314 [N.J. Super. Ct. 2004]). That judge also decried the burden on landlords of determining a tenant's proficiency in English and obtaining translation of leases, rules, and eviction notices. Still, even in the absence of legislative mandate there is some chance a court will require translation of lease-related documents, particularly demand letters and eviction notices,[3] where the tenant is known to speak only Spanish. For example, a New York court concluded that a landlord could not provide an English-language rent demand, in connection with an eviction, to a tenant the landlord knew spoke only Spanish (*Metz v. Duenas*, 702 N.Y.S.2d 745 [Dist. Ct. 1999]).

Tenant Language Ability

Consistent with the burgeoning anti-Spanish sentiment in the United States, some landlords have resorted to imposing English-ability requirements on their tenants. These requirements may violate federal and state civil rights laws that protect against national origin discrimination in housing, particularly the federal Fair Housing Act (42 U.S.C. § 3601 *et seq.*). Pursuing a housing discrimination claim for a landlord's English-language policies, however, presents challenges similar to lawsuits targeting employer English-only and English-ability restrictions. The claimant must demonstrate discriminatory intent, or alternatively that the English-ability rule has a disparate impact on Latino/as. A California lawsuit illustrates the claimant's difficulty (*Veles v. Lindow*, 243 F.3d 552 [9th Cir. 2000], unpublished opinion). This litigation targeted a San Jose landlord who allegedly would rent only to tenants where at least one adult in the household spoke fluent English. The landlord allegedly told a Latino/a applicant: "If you can't understand English, don't even bother turning in an application. . . . We're not going to rent the house to Spanish-speaking people." The applicants framed their lawsuit as whether civil rights laws allowed a landlord to exclude the huge class of monolingual

Spanish-speaking tenants by adopting an English-ability requirement. By contrast, the landlord argued that civil rights laws did not intend to force a contract between two people who could neither communicate nor understand each other. The jury rejected the claim for discriminatory intent (treatment) under the federal Fair Housing Act, embracing the landlord's argument that the English-ability rule was meant to ensure effective communication with the tenants in an emergency. Although proof of disparate (discriminatory) impact can also establish a discriminatory housing claim, the Spanish-speaking applicant failed to prove disparate impact. Presumably disparate impact can be shown by statistical proof of the number of monolingual Spanish-speakers in the area, and by equating Spanish-speaking with Latino/a ethnicity. A federal court in New York failed to find disparate impact in a claim by a public housing tenant who contended she was entitled to notice in Spanish of the termination of her public housing rights (*Vialez v. New York City Housing Authority*, 783 F. Supp. 109 [S.D.N.Y. 1991]). The court rejected her Fair Housing Act national origin claim despite her showing that substantial numbers of tenants in the area did not speak English well or at all. Instead, the court assumed that if these non-English-speaking Latino/a residents received documents from the public housing authority they would obtain a translation. Thus, there was no sufficient showing that persons of the plaintiff's national origin would lose their apartments as a result of their inability to speak English. In the case of a landlord's English-fluency requirement, however, monolingual Spanish speakers or poor English speakers would indeed lose their right to rent based on their language inability and thus should be able to demonstrate the requisite disparate impact on Latino/as of the landlord's policy.

Still, landlords can defeat a disparate impact claim by demonstrating a valid business justification for their English-fluency rule. Here, the landlord's excuse of effective communication in an emergency might also insulate it from a disparate impact claim. Nevertheless, the tenant might demonstrate a less discriminatory alternative—such as requiring the tenant to obtain a translation and submit all housing complaints in English—that overcomes this business justification.

In Florida, a cooperative apartment building voted to restrict residency to English speakers as a means of enhancing tenant protection with the residents stating, "We don't want undesirables living here." This specious business justification masks racial stereotypes and should be invalid; under housing discrimination laws, renters and purchasers are entitled to be evaluated on their individual merits without the trappings of derogatory group stereotypes.

In the case of home loans, a rule of the federal Office of Thrift Supervision warns banks that "requiring fluency in the English language as a prerequisite for obtaining a loan may be a discriminatory practice based on national origin" under federal housing antidiscrimination law (12 C.F.R. §

528.9[c][2]). Still, the landlord setting is somewhat different because a home lender could be hard-pressed to identify a sufficient business justification, whereas landlords will point to a safety justification.

What You Can Do as a Tenant to Protect Your Rights as a Spanish Speaker. Because of the challenges in pursuing litigation against landlords who require English fluency, Spanish-speaking tenants should consider proposing a reasonable alternative if they want to convince the landlord to rent to them despite this restriction. For example, the tenant could propose to submit any requests for repairs in a written English translation. Landlord English-fluency requirements might also be changed following community-organized protest (see Chapter 5). Because of the spotty requirements in law requiring the landlord to translate certain crucial documents for its tenants, such as apartment rules and eviction notices, tenants must be prepared to protect themselves by obtaining translations of communications from the landlord. First, however, the tenant may want to ask the landlord for its willingness to supply a translated version of important information given the tenant's lack of fluency in English. This is best accomplished at the inception of the lease and can be memorialized by writing into the lease that "all notices to tenant will be provided in Spanish."

Discrimination in Lending

Federal law prohibits discrimination by home mortgage lenders. The two most important federal statutes are the Fair Housing Act (Title VIII) and the Equal Credit Opportunity Act (ECOA) (15 U.S.C. § 1691). Title VIII specifically covers housing-related financing, while ECOA is broader and covers all applications for credit. ECOA was enacted in 1974 with the original purpose of protecting women applying for credit, but subsequent amendments expanded its scope to protect race, color, national origin, and other factors. ECOA requires that lenders disclose their reason for denying a loan (15 U.S.C. § 1691[d]). Typically, applicants denied a home loan are given a fairly standard list of financial reasons for the decision. These usually relate to the applicant's income, assets, and credit history. Sometimes lenders base their decisions on uniformly applied scores, which carry a strong presumption of validity. Where some subjectivity is involved in the decision, however, there is the potential for race becoming a factor.

Plaintiffs can generally make a case for discrimination under the same framework used in employment and housing discrimination cases. Plaintiffs can show a lender's discriminatory motive through statements or conduct. For example, a plaintiff could show that the lender required more documentation than is usually asked of similar Anglo applicants. Evidence that a lender was unusually difficult to work with or provided less assistance or information to Latino/as than to others could also be used to make a case. Most courts will also allow plaintiffs to make a disparate treatment case by showing that the plaintiff was qualified, was denied the loan, and the lender continued to approve loans for white applicants with similar qualifications.

ECOA has specifically been interpreted to incorporate the disparate impact standard of Title VII (Regulation B § 202.6). So, when a lender determines an applicant's creditworthiness, its policies can be scrutinized to ascertain whether they have harsher effects on Latino/as than others. Immigrants and other Latino/as are more likely to be lacking credit histories and conventional forms of identification, for example. As a result, many banks have changed their policies, practices, and cultures to serve nontraditional customers more effectively.

Although a denial of credit is the most obvious violation of fair lending laws, Title VIII, ECOA, and Sections 1981 and 1982 also prohibit discrimination in terms and conditions. One area where fair lending law has become more visible is predatory lending. Predatory lenders are those who offer loans with unfair and abusive terms to vulnerable borrowers. When borrowers are targeted for predatory loans because of their race or national origin, there is a fair lending violation.

An example of this type of discrimination is *Hargraves v. Capital City Mortgage Corp.*, 140 F. Supp. 2d 7 (D. D.C. 2000). The plaintiffs were an African American pastor whose church was having financial problems and others who also lived in predominantly African American neighborhoods. A mortgage broker made an unsolicited call to the pastor and convinced him to enter a loan agreement with the church as collateral. The pastor soon discovered that hidden in the terms were a huge origination fee and a 25 percent interest rate for the first four years, making repayment impossible. The broker foreclosed on the property and sold it for a huge profit. The predatory broker directed his marketing almost exclusively toward borrowers in African American neighborhoods, engaging in the practice known as "reverse redlining." This is contrasted with "redlining," which is the practice of *denying* credit to those in specific geographic areas because of race, color, or ethnicity, which is illegal under Title VIII.

A claim was also possible under the Home Ownership and Equity Protection Act (15 U.S.C. § 1639). This law provides protection against "equity-stripping," a predatory lending practice based on the value of the asset, rather than on the borrower's ability to pay. The lender makes the loan and knows that the borrower won't be able to afford the payments. When the borrower gets behind on payments, the lender, as planned, forecloses on the property (strips the owner of the equity in the property).

This is similar to what happened to several Spanish-speaking Latino/a homebuyers in California targeted for a predatory lending scheme by a group of real estate agents and loan brokers. The brokers had negotiated in Spanish with the homebuyers for the purchase and financing of new homes. During those negotiations, the plaintiffs were told that, based on their income, they could afford to repay the loans and that the mortgage payments would not exceed a certain amount. On the closing date, however, the plaintiffs were "baited and switched" into signing loans they did not understand, and that contained higher principals and interest rates than they originally wanted or were able to repay. Six of the seven plaintiffs were then unable to make the loan payments, and the defendants foreclosed on the houses. The court found there was enough evidence to find that the plaintiffs had been targeted because of their race or national origin. The court, therefore, allowed federal and state claims for discrimination to proceed against all the defendants, including claims under Title VIII, ECOA, and the Real Estate Settlement Procedures Act (RESPA) (12 U.S.C. § 2601–2617). RESPA prohibits paying kickbacks and giving or receiving a portion, split, or percentage of charges made or received for the rendering of a real estate settlement service (*Muñoz v. International Home Capital Corp.*, 2004 WL 3086907 [N.D. Cal. 2004]).

Of course, one of the vulnerabilities of first-time home buyers, especially immigrants and those who speak Spanish at home, is their general lack of experience with borrowing and their relative lack of knowledge about the process of shopping for homes and mortgages. Unscrupulous professionals in the real estate industry, therefore, try to take advantage of them, as illustrated by Table 3.1.

Another issue is subprime lending in minority neighborhoods. Subprime lending means charging higher interest rates from borrowers with bad

Table 3.1   Borrowing Fallacies and Home Buyers Who Know the Statement Is False (in percentage)

	All	English-Speaking Hispanic	Spanish-Speaking Hispanic
You need to have stayed in the same job for at least five years to qualify for a mortgage.	65	55	39
Information on home buying is only available in English.	89	93	60
Housing lenders are required by law to give you the best possible rates on loans.	59	42	25
If you want a mortgage, you have to accept a 30-year commitment.	74	65	27
You need a perfect credit rating to qualify for a mortgage.	73	64	22

Source: Fannie Mae, 2004.

credit, which is generally not considered predatory because the interest rate compensates for increased risk. The problem is that people of color, especially Latino/as, appear to be overrepresented in the subprime lending market. Data gathered from the Home Mortgage Disclosure Act reveal that 20 percent of first mortgages to Hispanics were subprime loans, compared to only 10 percent for non-Hispanics. Such loans are even more common for junior liens (second mortgages); 57 percent of Hispanics' junior liens are categorized as subprime loans, compared to 34 percent for all others.

Part of the problem is that big banks offering prime rates have historically avoided lending in minority neighborhoods. Even though significant efforts have been made to reverse these lender "redlining" practices, the loan market in many minority neighborhoods still appears to be dominated by subprime lenders. Courts have recognized claims for discrimination against subprime lenders under the disparate impact theory, but so far there have not been many successful challenges.

Appendix

Resources on Housing Discrimination

- *Office for Civil Rights, U.S. Department of Housing and Urban Development.* Investigates complaints of housing discrimination in violation of the Fair Housing Act. Instructions in English and Spanish on how and where to file a complaint are available at www.hud.gov .complaints/housediscrim.cfm. The central office in Washington, D.C., can be reached toll-free at 800-669-9777.
- *Housing and Civil Enforcement Section, Civil Rights Division, U.S. Department of Justice.* Investigates complaints of systemic housing discrimination and those referred by the U.S. Department of Housing and Urban Development. Answers to frequently asked questions about the Fair Housing Act, the Equal Credit Opportunity Act, and the Civil Rights Act of 1964 are available in English and Spanish at www.usdoj.gov/crt/housing/faq.htm.
- *Housing and Community Development Project, Lawyers' Committee for Civil Rights Under Law.* Litigates fair housing lawsuits under the Fair Housing Act to challenge discrimination in rental and private markets as well as in public and assisted housing. The central office in Washington, D.C., can be reached at 202-662-8331, and Joe Rich, the director, can be reached at jrich@lawyerscommittee.org.

Resources on Lending Discrimination

- *Federal Deposit Insurance Corporation.* A Guide to Fair Lending is available at www.gov.fdic/regulations/resources/side/index.html.

- *Federal Reserve Board.* Home Mortgages: Understanding Your Rights to Fair Lending is available at www.federalreserve.gov/pubs/mortgage/morbro_3.htm. This site also has a directory of federal agencies having responsibility for monitoring the lending practices of particular types of lenders (banks, credit unions, and savings and loan associations).

Selected Publications

Brooks, Roy L., Gilbert Paul Carrasco, and Michael Selmi. *Civil Rights Litigation: Cases and Perspectives.* Durham: Carolina Academic Press, 2005; 2007.

Fannie Mae. *Understanding America's Homeownership Gaps: 2003* Washington, D.C.: Fannie Mae National Housing Survey, 2004; available at www .fanniemae.com/global/pdf/media/survey/survey2003.pdf.

Paulson, Anna, Audrey Singer, Robyn Newberger, and Jeremy Smith. *Financial Access for Immigrants: Lessons from Diverse Perspectives.* Chicago: Federal Reserve Bank of Chicago and the Brookings Institution, 2006; available at www .chicagofed.org/community_development/files/fai-lessons_from_diverse _perspectives.pdf.

Ready, Timothy. *Hispanic Housing in the United States.* South Bend, Ind.: Institute for Latino Studies, University of Notre Dame, 2006.

Rustad, Michael L. *Everyday Law for Consumers.* Boulder: Paradigm Publishers, 2007.

Notes

1. Timothy Ready, *Hispanic Housing in the United States 2006* (South Bend, Ind.: Institute for Latino Studies, University of Notre Dame, 2006), 12.

2. Margery Austin Turner, Stephen L. Ross, George C. Galster, and John Yinger, *Discrimination in Metropolitan Housing Markets: National Results from Phase I HDS 2000* (Washington, D.C.: HUD, 2002).

3. District of Columbia legislation, for example, requires notice to vacate under a month-to-month lease to be given in English and Spanish to all tenants. D.C. Code § 45-1406.

4

Language Discrimination

Language "vigilantes"—who might be teachers, employers, landlords, business owners, or even judges—guard against the Spanish language in virtually all reaches of everyday life for Latino/as. Imagine the English gauntlet in a typical day in the life of María Sanchez, a bilingual Latina. As María walks her son to school, she reminds him not to speak Spanish or his teachers will punish him in the all-English classroom mandated by state law. Later, while talking with a coworker at her bus stop, a passerby scolds María for speaking Spanish because, "You're in America now." Once at work, her supervisor at the supermarket tells María and her coworkers they may no longer speak Spanish to Spanish-speaking customers or between themselves as some customers are irritated when they overhear Spanish. On break, María studies for her driver's license exam, which she must take in English. In the afternoon, María leaves work to attend a child custody hearing in her divorce; the judge tells María she is abusing her son by speaking Spanish and that he will remove the child if she will not speak English at home. After work, María meets a friend for dinner at a neighborhood tavern. Hanging over the bar is the sign, "It's English, or Adiós, Amigo." After dinner María picks up her son from her mother's apartment. While there, María translates for her mother, who cannot speak English, some new rules on pets and visitors from the apartment manager written in English. María obeys the judge's order by speaking English to her son as they walk home. Many of these language issues are addressed below—those language issues discussed in other chapters include workplace language rules (Chapter 2), Spanish-language discrimination by landlords (Chapter 3), bilingual education (Chapter 6), and language rights in the criminal justice system (Chapter 8).

Official English and English-Only Laws

Most states have laws that require use of the English language in specific circumstances, such as in testing for occupational licenses (see below). But about half the states have more comprehensive laws that declare English the state's official language.[1] Some also require the protection and preservation of English, while others go further still to outlaw using other languages in government business. These laws have roots in xenophobic hostility toward Southern and Eastern European immigrants in the early 1900s that prompted many states to require English language in schools. Nebraska, for example, reacted to anti-German sentiment and amended its constitution in 1920 to declare English the official state language. Modern English-language laws, however, target Spanish-speaking Latino/as, as well as Asian immigrants.

The Colorado Constitution, for example, provides that "the English language is the official language of the state of Colorado" (Colo. Const. Art. II, § 30a). Such official English-language laws probably have little legal effect. In concluding that the Illinois official English law did not prohibit local elections officials from assisting voters in Spanish, a federal appeals court noted the Illinois law appears with those naming the state bird and the state song and has "never been used to prevent publication of official materials in other languages" (*Puerto Rican Org. for Political Action v. Kusper*, 490 F.2d 575, 577 [7th Cir. 1973]).

California's English-language initiative illustrates an intermediate variety of these language laws by declaring English the state's official language and instructing the legislature and California officials to "take all steps necessary to insure the role of English as the common language of the state of California is preserved and enhanced." Further, "the Legislature shall make no law which diminishes or ignores the role of English as the common language of the state of California" (Cal. Const. Art. III, § 6). As with official English laws, these intermediate language laws apparently have little substantive effect on government operations. California's attorney general interpreted the law to permit other language translations to accompany English in official publications, and a California appeals court rejected a lawsuit to prevent the California State Bar from printing and distributing a legal pamphlet in Spanish intended for persons under arrest (*Levy v. Davis*, 2003 WL 157555 [Cal. Ct. App. 2003] unpublished opinion).

The most far-reaching English-language laws (known as English-only laws) are found in a few states, such as Utah that require English for all government business except in specified circumstances, such as when necessary for public health or safety reasons (Utah Code § 63-13-1.5). Arizona's language law provides similarly that the state must act in English and in no other language except in specified circumstances (Ariz. Const. Art. XXVIII). As construed by the Arizona Supreme Court, Arizona's former English-only law struck down by that court in 1998 could prohibit a public school teacher from speaking in Spanish to Latino/a parents about their child's education and prevent a town hall discussion in Spanish between Arizona voters and their elected officials. That law unconstitutionally infringed on the First Amendment free speech rights of the public, public employees, and elected officials (*Ruiz v. Hull*, 957 P.2d 984 [Ariz. 1998]). But Arizona voters revived the English-only law in 2006, passing a similar initiative that questionably aims to cure the constitutional defect by allowing government representatives, such as legislators, to communicate "unofficially" in languages other than English.

Although state and local English-language laws vary in format from official English to English-only requirements, generally they are restricted to government speech and do not purport to regulate language used in homes, businesses, or churches.[2] Still, these language laws prompted a private backlash against Spanish-speakers in many states that reached nongovernment speech. For example, after the passage in 1986 of California's English-language initiative, civil rights organizations received complaints that employers adopted English-only rules to govern their employees in private businesses such as hospitals, hotels, manufacturing firms, insurance companies, banks, and charitable organizations. Following voter approval in 1998 of the Colorado English-language initiative, a Colorado school bus driver told students that speaking Spanish on the bus was illegal. After the Florida English-language initiative passed, a bank rejected checks written in Spanish; residents told Latino/as, "Speak English. It's the law now"; and a Florida supermarket manager suspended a cashier for speaking Spanish. State law mandated none of these reactions, and they illustrate the tendency of the public to wildly misconstrue the meaning of these English-language laws. Despite the narrow interpretation of these laws by courts and other legal authorities such as state attorneys general, the experience of these harmful impacts on private use of languages other than English suggests that Latino/as and others who respect language rights ought to oppose the adoption of these laws and oppose the strengthening of existing English-language laws.

Government Obligations to Spanish Speakers

Several federal and state statutes and regulations mandate accommodation of language barriers by requiring government to supply translations of government documents for the benefit of Spanish and other non-English-speaking groups. These laws differ widely from state to state and may extend to a variety of situations—from mortgage loan disclosures and summaries of employee rights in the workplace to door-to-door contracts, home repair contracts, rent-to-own contracts, public school notices, and rights of nursing home patients. Federal law also supplies a smattering of translation requirements. For example, the federal Voting Rights Act mandates voting materials (such as ballots) be translated to another language if at least 10,000 (or 5 percent) of a state or political district's voting age citizens are members of a single-language minority group, are unable to speak or understand English adequately, and have a rate of failure to complete the fifth grade that exceeds the national failure rate (42 U.S.C. § 1973aa-1a). In the absence of such legislative or administrative requirements of translations, however, courts typically refuse to recognize a constitutional or other judicial obligation of the government to translate or otherwise accommodate non-English speakers. For example, although the right to a court-appointed interpreter in criminal trials is constitutionally grounded (see Chapter 8), courts refuse to recognize a constitutional right to an interpreter at public expense when a non-English-speaking Latino/a is sued in a noncriminal case (*Jara v. Municipal Court for San Antonio Judicial Dist. of Los Angeles County*, 145 Cal. Rptr. 847 [1978]).

These court decisions often address the receipt of benefits by non-English speakers under government programs. The typical scenario involves an adverse government decision to deny benefits, such as those for unemployment or under welfare programs. The monolingual Spanish-speaker receives notice in English that specifies the recipient has a narrow window of time within which to request a hearing, or the recipient will forfeit the right to contest the rejection. Almost uniformly, courts refuse to compel an unwilling government to supply a Spanish-language translation in these circumstances. For example, the California Supreme Court rejected a challenge by Spanish speakers to the state's refusal to send notice of reduction or termination of welfare payments in Spanish to recipients the state knows or has reason to know cannot read English. The lawsuit was based on the due process clause of the federal Constitution that guarantees an evidentiary hearing before termination of welfare benefits, as well as adequate notice of the right to a hearing. Based on its assumption that Spanish-speakers "experience strong and repeated incentives either to learn the English language or to develop a reliance on bilingual persons who can translate for them when necessary," the court deemed the English-only notice adequate (*Guerrero v. Carleson*, 109 Cal. Rptr. 201, 204 [1973]).

The court's assumption that the recipients should have obtained a translation from their children or someone else is flawed. Because the welfare office had appointed Spanish-speaking caseworkers and printed some forms in Spanish, the Spanish-speaking recipients arguably were led to believe that any notice they received in English was not important enough to warrant immediate translation. Further, the period to request a hearing (fifteen days) was not much time to obtain a translation, which might result in problems of cost and transportation.

Courts that assume adult Spanish speakers can rely on their English-speaking children to translate government documents ignore the possibility that the documents may expose potentially embarrassing personal information (such as revealing the receipt of welfare or allegations of failing to comply with conditions for receipt of unemployment benefits) and also contain technical or legal terms their bilingual children may be unfamiliar with.

Still, the California Supreme Court approach reflects how courts disregard translation claims for other government forms, such as those that detail the denial of unemployment benefits, the termination of a public housing lease, and the provision of social security benefits. The parties often challenge these English-only policies under the constitutional equal protection guarantee as well as due process, but the courts easily find reasonable grounds to uphold the government policy. In addition to the assumption that recipients will obtain a translation, these court decisions often point to the burden on government of having to pay for translations, as well as the slippery slope of whether obligating the government to accommodate Spanish would require the government to translate into every language spoken by service recipients, no matter how many languages or how obscure.

Spanish speakers seeking language accommodation for government occupational testing, or license tests and applications, are similarly left unprotected by the courts. Pointing out limited government resources, a federal appeals court concluded the City of Cleveland was not constitutionally required to administer a carpentry exam in Spanish to a Puerto Rican applicant who could read English with great difficulty (*Frontera v. Sindell*, 522 F.2d 1215 [6th Cir. 1975]). Claimants trying to establish an equal protection violation must prove intentional discrimination, which is unlikely in this setting because the courts tend to view a government decision to provide English-only services as reflecting a nondiscriminatory government preference for English. Federal regulations promulgated under Title VI of the federal Civil Rights Act of 1964 allow for challenges to certain government programs that have a discriminatory effect on protected groups. But when a Latina invoked these regulations to challenge the practice in Arkansas of administering English-only driver's license exams, even to the exclusion of translation dictionaries or other interpretive aids, the U.S. Supreme Court concluded that Congress did not intend a private legal action under these regulations, rejecting her challenge (*Alexander v. Sandoval*, 532 U.S. 275 [2001]).

Although Latino/as not fluent in English at least can obtain their own accommodation when they receive a government notice in English, government testing requirements in English cannot be overcome by translators and imperil the economic progress of Latino/as. These court decisions also run counter to the overwhelming sentiment of Latino/as favoring accommodation—one opinion poll measured 90 percent of Mexican Americans and 94 percent of Puerto Ricans and Cuban Americans who agreed that government services should be provided in Spanish. The Latino community can soften the absence of the government's legal obligation to translate government documents by arranging for convenient and free translation services at local Latino social service centers, community centers, and churches.[3]

The imperative of the right to vote garners special treatment in the courts. Here, California's Supreme Court applied the federal Equal Protection Clause to strike down a state constitutional provision that conditioned the right to vote in state elections on the ability to read English (*Castro v. State*, 466 P.2d 244 [Cal. 1970]).

Spanish Language and Family Law

The English-only language movement advocates using English for all government communications, but tends to disavow the regulation of non-government speech. For example, a publication of the pro-English organization U.S. English contends that "official English has nothing to do with the language of the home, church, community center, private enterprise or with the conversation between two neighbors over the back fence." Still, the anti-Spanish climate has sparked efforts to regulate language even within the sanctity of the home. In 1995, for example, a Texas judge presiding in a child custody dispute instructed a bilingual Latina mother of a five-year-old daughter: "Now get this straight. . . . The child will hear only English." The judge was concerned the mother was speaking Spanish to her child at home, and likened her insistence on Spanish to child abuse: "If your daughter starts first grade with the other children and cannot even speak the language that the teachers and other children speak and she's a full-blooded American citizen, you're abusing that child, and you're relegating her to the position of a housemaid." The judge later apologized to housemaids and then vacated his order in response to criticism his ruling sparked. The judge's ruling and his characterization of Spanish as child abuse, though, spread alarm across Texas among Latino/a families who feared losing their children if they spoke Spanish in the household. Later, in 2003, a Nebraska judge issued a similar order requiring English as the principal form of communication during visitation periods between a Latino father and his five-year-old daughter.

What You Can Do If a Judge Is Prejudiced Against Spanish Speakers. Protests against the close-minded Texas judge proved effective and signaled the potential susceptibility of judges to local pressure, particularly in districts where judges are elected.

Generally, the law respects the autonomy of parents in raising their children—the autonomy even has constitutional foundations in due process, equal protection, the right to privacy, and the free speech guarantee in the First Amendment. In striking down a state statute that guaranteed visitation rights based solely on the child's best interest as contrary to a parent's due process rights, the Supreme Court articulated the constitutional standard that "so long as a parent adequately cares for his or her children (i.e., is fit), there will normally be no reason for the state to inject itself into the private realm of the family to further question the ability of that parent to make the best decisions concerning the rearing of that parent's children" (*Troxel v. Granville*, 530 U.S. 57 (2000]). Ordinarily the government must have a compelling interest to interfere with the fundamental right of autonomy in the parent-child relationship—such as preventing intellectual or physical harm to the child that may compel parents to educate and provide medical care for their children. The Texas ruling involved a bilingual mother who presumably could have communicated with her daughter in English as the judge demanded, although no doubt the judge's ruling constrained her constitutional liberty and privacy rights to choose the language spoken at home.

When a parent is fluent only in Spanish, an anti-Spanish ruling by a domestic relations judge will be even more devastating. A Tennessee judge confronting this situation took a different approach: in 2005 he instructed an eighteen-year-old mother from Oaxaca, Mexico, who spoke only the indigenous language Mixtec, to learn English (and use birth control in the future) or risk termination of her parental rights. She was before the judge on a hearing to monitor custody after she allegedly failed to immunize her child. The judge explained the mother had "turned her back" on U.S. culture and that he had "to look out for the best interests of the child" who might lose out "on all the opportunities [of a U.S. citizen] if she's not assimilated into the culture." He explained further, "I'm not against someone retaining a sense of their culture. . . . But at the same time, I have to do what I can to see that child develop in as normal of a manner as possible." The same Tennessee judge in 2004 warned a Latina mother accused of neglect that she risked permanent parental termination over her eleven-year-old daughter if the mother did not learn English to a fourth-grade level in six months. The Southern Poverty Law Center, a national civil rights organization representing the mother in challenging the ruling, put the litigation in historical perspective: "If the millions of immigrants who built this great nation over the generations had been required to learn English or lose their children, we'd have a country full of motherless children."

English-Only Rules in Places of Entertainment

Older Mexican Americans may still remember hateful signs in some Southwest taverns that read, "No Mexicans or dogs allowed." Now that civil rights laws have reined in more blatant discrimination, the sign is more likely to mirror that in a Washington state tavern in the 1990s reading, "No English, Shirts, Shoes, [No] Service." The courts have not adequately confronted whether this Spanish-language discrimination is lawful, as few if any lawsuits have reached the appellate courts.

The federal Civil Rights Acts give all persons (including noncitizens) the same right to make contracts (42 U.S.C. § 1981), and all citizens (which would not encompass Latino/a noncitizens) the equal right to purchase and sell real and personal property (42 U.S.C. § 1982). These lofty statutes extend to contracts and purchases as simple as a meal at a restaurant or a beer at a tavern. Many states have complementary state civil rights laws, as do certain cities. The discussion below focuses on federal law, but state law requirements are similar.

Two significant obstacles potentially impede the use of these federal civil rights laws to prevent or redress English-only policies in such arenas as restaurants and taverns. First, the claimant under these statutes must prove racial discrimination. Although it is clear that Latino/as constitute a (nonwhite) race (or races) for purposes of these laws, it is unclear whether discriminating on the basis of language constitutes racial discrimination. But a 1973 federal court decision held that an Oregon tavern's English-only policy targeting Spanish-speaking customers constituted "patent racial discrimination" that violated these federal civil rights laws (*Hernandez v. Erlenbusch*, 368 F. Supp. 752, 755 [D. Or. 1973]).

The second and more significant obstacle is that the Supreme Court requires claimants to demonstrate purposeful (intentional) discrimination, as opposed to the potential under fair employment and fair housing laws of establishing violations through proof of disparate (discriminatory) impact of the policy or practice on a protected group without sufficient business justification. Indeed, the 1973 Oregon tavern decision preceded the Supreme Court's insistence on proof of intent and relied on the language rule's impact on Mexican American customers, not the tavern owner's intent, in finding a civil rights violation.

A 1990s lawsuit against a Washington state tavern illustrates the challenge of overcoming the purposeful discrimination requirement. In 1996, Latino Spanish-speaking customers relied on similar state civil rights laws to redress their removal from a tavern with a sign above the bar reading, "In the U.S.A. it's English, or adios amigo." The claimants failed to establish the tavern owner had discriminatory intent. Rather, the tavern owner contended she meant the English-only policy to help keep the peace by enabling the bartenders to understand whether "fighting words" were being exchanged. The trial judge believed the owner, finding her rule was intended to ensure safety of others and her property and thus was not discriminatory. The legal standard under the applicable civil rights laws is whether the business intended to discriminate. In contrast to employment and housing litigation, identifying a less discriminatory alternative, such as the bartender looking for hostile customer behavior and inflammatory tone of voice instead of speech, will not be helpful. Still, the Washington tavern owner made statements to the press, such as, "We don't want Spanish gibberish here, and we mean it," that suggested purposeful discrimination, although at trial she claimed these remarks were quoted out of context. Her condescending bar sign seemed to signal a prejudicial attitude, but the court concluded that while "insensitive," it did not constitute actionable discrimination.

The earlier Oregon court decision signaled that some judges (and juries) might scrutinize a tavern or restaurant safety justification more carefully. In that case, the tavern's policy was meant to ensure the peace and reduce friction that developed in the town between Anglos and Mexican Americans, prompting Anglo customers to contend the Mexican customers were using Spanish to talk about them. The court called this justification "lame" and one that catered to prejudice.

As of this writing, city officials in Philadelphia were investigating potential official action against the owner of a restaurant whose sign demands "This Is America. When Ordering, Speak English." A city agency plans to take the position the sign's unwelcome message violates the law prohibiting discrimination in places of public accommodation.

What Community Groups and You Can Do When Businesses Target Spanish Speakers. Given the potential difficulty of establishing the purposeful intent needed for a civil rights violation, as well as the modest damages likely even for proof of intentional discrimination in these circumstances, options other than civil rights litigation should be used against anti-Spanish business policies. Community leaders might defuse the concern over fighting words and vulgar language by offering tavern employees a crash course in Spanish vulgarities. The Washington "adiós amigo" tavern case suggests another avenue—the state liquor board with wide discretion to regulate taverns required the tavern remove its condescending bar sign. A business English-only policy might galvanize local community members of all backgrounds to protest the anti-Spanish and anti-Latino/a sentiments often embodied in these policies. In a related context, uproar from Latino/as and others led America Online to reverse its English-only policy for its international sports chatroom that aimed to protect against vulgar language. Outcry also followed a Little League baseball game in Massachusetts in 2005 where baseball officials prohibited coaches from instructing players in Spanish, prompting a league spokesperson to confirm there is no rule against players speaking Spanish on the field.

Language Fraud in the Marketplace

Unscrupulous merchants in the United States often target Latino/as unable to understand English. For example, in California, a satellite dish vendor who was selling door-to-door allegedly targeted Spanish-speaking homeowners to exploit their language barrier. A separate home equity loan scam in East Los Angeles preyed on non-English-speaking Latino/a homeowners who unknowingly signed deeds to their homes conveying full title rather than just a lender's mortgage interest. A car dealer in Oregon allegedly used Spanish-speaking employees to entice Latino/a immigrants to sign contracts written in English that sold them unwanted extras such as extended warranties and credit insurance, all financed at 39 percent interest. Another Oregon car dealer allegedly misrepresented to a Spanish-speaking Latina that an "as is" warranty meant the customer had fifty days to rescind the purchase. Another car dealer leased a car to a Spanish-speaking Latino customer pursuant to an English-language contract despite assurances in Spanish he was purchasing the car outright by making the agreed upon monthly payment.

U.S. law has reacted slowly to these rampant language abuses in the consumer marketplace.[4] Still, Latino/a Spanish-speakers have a few potential sources of protection—primarily statutes and regulations that require merchants to translate their consumer contacts, and the safety net of courts that occasionally protects against egregious advantage taken of a language barrier.

Statutory or administrative translation requirements are spotty and no comprehensive protection exists. Federal law singles out door-to-door and used car sales. Door-to-door sellers must provide buyers with a contract in the same language used principally in the oral sales presentation (16 C.F.R. § 429.1[a]). Used car sellers who conduct a sale in Spanish must deliver certain warranty information in Spanish (16 C.F.R. § 455.5). But the federal Truth in Lending Act, which requires disclosures of interest rates and fees in loan transactions, does not mandate Spanish-language disclosures.[5] Nor do other federal consumer protection statutes that require English-language disclosures, such as the Truth in Savings Act, the Real Estate Settlement Procedures Act, or the Magnuson-Moss Warranty Act. But a few states have translation laws with broad coverage. For example, California requires written translations of certain loan contracts (but not home loans), residential property leases, and other consumer contracts, when these transactions are negotiated primarily in Spanish (Cal. Civ. Code § 1632). An Illinois statute addresses retail transactions negotiated in a language other than English and requires an acknowledgment by the customer signed in the non-English language that the merchant orally explained the English-language contract to the customer (Ill. Ann. Stat. ch. 815, para. 505/2N).

U.S. law typically does not require translations of dangerous product warnings. Courts tend to refuse to impose liability on manufacturers who forego warnings in Spanish of product dangers and medicine side effects, even where the product is marketed extensively in Spanish-speaking communities. For example, the California Supreme Court rejected a lawsuit against the manufacturer of St. Joseph children's aspirin for failing to warn in Spanish of serious product dangers that permanently damaged a Latina's child. The court felt that although the manufacturer advertised in Spanish-language media, it was the legislature's job, not the court's, to require a duty to warn in languages other than English (*Ramirez v. Plough, Inc.*, 863 P.2d 167 [Cal. 1993]).

Businesses that misrepresent the terms of the written English contract to the Spanish-speaking consumer face the prospect of judicial intervention and invalidation of the contract or affirmative damages for fraud. Bolstering these judicial actions is the codification of consumer fraud in federal law that prohibits "unfair or deceptive acts or practices" in interstate commerce (15 U.S.C. § 45) and laws of all fifty states and the District of Columbia prohibit unfair or deceptive consumer practices such as fraud. Consent agreements in the 1970s between several merchants and the federal government enforcing this federal law went beyond fraud to require the merchants to translate certain consumer contracts for Spanish-speaking consumers, effectively treating the failure to translate in certain circumstances as "unfair or deceptive."

Apart from fraud, courts might also refuse to enforce consumer contracts that contain unfair terms procured by exploiting a language barrier. For example, a New York court used the judicial fairness doctrine of unconscionability to strike down a non-English-speaking Latino buyer's remaining payment obligation under an English-language contract that waived warranties in the purchase of a defective automobile (*Jefferson Credit Corp. v. Marcano*, 302 N.Y.S.2d 390 [Civ. Ct. 1969]). Similarly, a New York court nullified the purchase obligation of a non-English-speaking Latino who bowed to high pressure sales tactics and signed an untranslated English-language contract for the purchase of a gas furnace that later broke (*Brooklyn Union Gas Company v. Jimeniz*, 371 N.Y.S.2d 289 [Civ. Ct. 1975]).

What Community Groups and You Can Do to Protect Spanish-Speaking Consumers. Because U.S. law does not broadly compel merchant translations, and legal remedies for Spanish-speaking consumers may demand a showing of a false representation by the merchant or an egregiously unfair bargain, as well as the trouble of pursuing a lawsuit, Latino/a community leaders and other concerned parties might address these growing marketplace abuses by nonlegal strategies. Consumer education programs at the community level for Latino/as should address concepts and staples of the American marketplace that include the "as is" sale of used cars, credit insurance, extended product warranties, variable interest rates, arbitration clauses, rent-to-own transactions, car title pawn loans, and alternatives to payday loans and check cashing services. Because language barriers present additional opportunities for abuse in consumer transactions, adult English-language instruction plays a role in this consumer education model. Spanish-speaking consumers should request a merchant to supply a written translation of the English-language contract. Failing to acquire a written translation, the consumer should obtain an oral translation from a trustworthy person other than the merchant before signing any contract. The burden of merchants translating contracts should ease markedly as technology advances are seen in computer translation software programs. Still, unscrupulous merchants in the many states without statutorily mandated translation laws will be waiting to prey on language barriers of consumers who fail to protect themselves by demanding a written translation.

Appendix

Websites on Language Issues

James Crawford's Language Policy Website, http://ourworld.compuserve.com/homepages/JWCRAWFORD/.

English Only Policy, a university database of language policy resources, http://www.indiana.edu/~reading/ieo/bibs/englishonly.html.

Mexican American Legal Defense and Educational Fund, extensive testimony in 2006 against federal English-only/Official English legislation, http://www.maldef.org/pdf/Trasvina_Testimony.7.26.06.pdf.

"The National Language Policy," position statement (against English-only legislation) of the Conference on College Composition and Communication, National Council of Teachers of English, http://www.ncte.org/cccc/resources/positions/123796.htm.

TESOL (Teaching English to Speakers of Other Languages), Advocacy Resource Documents, a list of documents with testimony against restrictive language legislation, http://www.tesol.org/s_tesol/seccss.asp?CID=80&DID=1550.

TESOL Sociopolitical Concerns Committee Recommendations for Countering the Official English Movement in the United States, http://www.ncela.gwu.edu/pubs/tesol/official.

TESOL U.S. Action Advocacy Center, resources on key language and anti-immigrant legislation in Congress, http://capwiz.com/tesol/home/.

Books and Articles

Bender, Steven W. "Consumer Protection for Latinos: Overcoming Language Fraud and English-Only in the Marketplace." *Am. U.L. Rev.* 45 (1996): 1027.

Crawford, James. *At War with Diversity: U.S. Language Policy in an Age of Anxiety.* Clevedon, UK: Multilingual Matters, 2000.

Crawford, James. *Hold Your Tongue: Bilingualism and the Politics of English Only.* Reading, MA: Addison-Wesley, 1992.

Simon, Paul. *The Tongue-Tied American: Confronting the Foreign Language Crisis.* New York: Continuum, 1980, 1992.

Notes

1. Half the states have adopted these comprehensive English-language laws—Alabama, Alaska (in November 2007 the Alaska Supreme Court struck down part of this law as violating constitutional free speech rights, but left intact its requirement that English be used for all official documents and records), Arizona, Arkansas, California, Colorado, Florida, Georgia, Hawaii (English and Hawaiian), Idaho, Illinois, Indiana, Iowa, Kentucky, Mississippi, Missouri, Montana, Nebraska, New Hampshire, North Carolina, North Dakota, South Carolina, South Dakota, Tennessee, Utah, Virginia, and Wyoming. As part of a package of comprehensive immigration reform never adopted, the U.S. Senate in 2006 approved official English legislation

by voting 63-34 to designate English as the "national language," and 58-39 to declare English the "common and unifying language."

2. But see *Asian American Business Group v. City of Pomona*, 716 F. Supp. 1328 (C.D. Cal. 1989) invoking the First Amendment and equal protection to invalidate a local ordinance requiring English-language business signs.

3. There are Internet translation services available for a fee and also for free, such as those at http://www.freetranslation.com/.

4. See generally Steven W. Bender, "Consumer Protection for Latinos: Overcoming Language Fraud and English-Only in the Marketplace," *Am. U.L. Rev.* 45 (1996): 1027.

5. Arizona state law does require the consumer lender to provide a Spanish-language truth in lending disclosure on request; see Ariz. Rev. Stat. § 6-651.

5

Hate Speech

"Congress shall make no law . . . abridging the freedom of speech."
—U.S. Constitution, Amendment 1

Edgardo Valdez, a U.S. citizen of Mexican descent, served seven years in the U.S. Army before accepting a sales position at Big O Tires. In just a few months' time Valdez became a leading salesperson, generating over 30 percent of all sales for the company. Yet his rise to the top was quickly stunted when he met his new supervisor, Craig Secia. A self-proclaimed racist, Secia had a favorite phrase: "A good Mexican's a dead Mexican." Throughout the course of Edgardo's employment, Secia insulted him daily, calling him "a sand nigger," "a wetback," "a dumb Mexican," or "a stupid-ass beaner." When a Mexican or Hispanic customer would enter the store, Secia told Valdez to "handle" them. "These are your stupid, motherf***ing people," he said. "F***ing wetbacks."

Secia's abuse even followed Valdez at home. He frequently called Valdez and left offensive messages on the answering machine. One night, Valdez picked up the phone only to hear Secia on the other line. He claimed to be from the INS and told Valdez that the agency was going to pick him up because "his green card has expired."

After enduring months of abuse, Valdez informed Secia he did not appreciate being called a "wetback" and asked him to stop using the term. Secia was unsympathetic. "I don't care if you like it or not," he replied. "You are a wetback. Your parents are from Mexico." Valdez then went to both of Secia's supervisors and reported the abusive conduct. Equally unhelpful, they replied that Secia was "just that way" and that Valdez should get over it. After tolerating racial harassment and verbal abuse for nearly seven months, Valdez was finally forced to resign his position.

Like many Latino/as in America, Valdez was the victim of "hate speech." Hate speech refers to any speech that incites hatred toward a group of persons because of their race, ethnicity, national origin, gender, religion, or sexual orientation. The general rule in the United States is that hate speech is protected by the First Amendment and cannot be punished; individuals are free to say what they want when they want to say it—regardless of how offensive their message may be to someone else. There are some circumstances, however, where the legal system recognizes exceptions to this general rule. For example, in the employment context, Title VII of the Civil Rights Act (discussed in Chapter 2) prohibits any employer from creating a "hostile work environment," which can include allowing the repeated use of racial epithets or insults. Valdez sued his employer under Title VII, and the court held he met his burden of proving a hostile work environment existed (*Valdez v. Big O Tires, Inc.,* 2006 WL 1794756 [D. Ariz]).

Outside the context of employment, hate speech enjoys much more protection. In the absence of a federal statute, like Title VII, "free speech is the rule, not the exception" (*Dennis v. United States,* 341 U.S. 494, 585 [1951] [Douglas, J., dissenting]). Yet there are still some situations where hateful words alone may be enough to invoke civil and possibly criminal penalties.

Hate Speech on the Job

As discussed in Chapter 2, Title VII forbids private employers from discriminating against any individual with respect to his or her compensation, terms, conditions, or privileges of employment on the basis of race, color, religion, sex, or national origin (42 U.S.C.A. §2000[e]). In an important case, *Meritor Savings Bank, FSB v. Vinson,* 477 U.S. 57 (1986), the Supreme Court held that this law includes the right to be free from a "hostile or abusive work environment." According to *Meritor,* Title VII is violated when "the workplace is permeated with discriminatory intimidation, ridicule, and insult sufficiently severe or pervasive to alter the conditions of the [victim's] employment." Therefore, if a plaintiff can show that he was the victim of hate speech while on the job, and that the speech was so repetitive and severe that it made the conditions of his employment different from all of the other employees of a different race, he can sue his employer for permitting the hate speech to continue. Thus Title VII has become a powerful tool for Latino/a employees in situations similar to Edgardo's.

Before a plaintiff can recover under Title VII, typically he must satisfy four basic judicially created requirements needed to state a claim for hostile work environment (*Harris v. Forklift Systems, Inc.,* 510 U.S. 17, 20 [1993]). First, the harassment must have been based on race. This requirement is clearly met in Edgardo's case because of the repeated derogatory comments Secia made regarding Latino/as. In other cases the intent was not so clear. For example, in *Alvarado v. Health Net, Inc.,* 21 F.3d 1111 (9th Cir. 1994), the court denied the plaintiff's Title VII claim, in part because it was unclear that the supervisor's insulting comments were based on the plaintiff's Latino heritage. A supervisor made comments to a Latino employee such as, "I don't understand you people," "you people have too many babies," and "you people drive up the cost of health insurance." The court said that these comments were not necessarily based on the plaintiff's race; the supervisor could have been referring to all employees under her supervision or even to women without a college education. Since there was no proof that the comments were made because the plaintiff was Latino, the court denied the claim.

Significantly, this first requirement does not mean that the harassment needs to be based on the race of the victim. For example, if Secia had only made derogatory comments about African Americans or Asians, and had never spoken unkindly of Mexicans, Valdez may still have a claim. When "racial hostility pervades a workplace, a plaintiff may establish a violation of Title VII, even if such hostility was not directly targeted at the plaintiff" (*McGinest v. GTE Service Corp.*, 360 F.3d 1103, 1117 [9th Cir. 2004]).

Second, the harassment must have been "unwelcome." This is a subjective test, in which the victim must actually perceive the environment to be abusive. This requirement is necessary because, if the victim is not subjectively offended, the conduct has not actually put the plaintiff in a situation different from that of his coworkers and there has been no alteration of the conditions of employment on the basis of race. Therefore, if Valdez had never taken offense to the racial epithets slung in his direction—if he had laughed along and never felt insulted—his claim under Title VII would fail, even if objectively his environment *was* in fact hostile. Notably, Valdez does not have to show he suffered actual psychological harm. He only needs to show that the conduct was unwelcome and that he personally perceived the environment to be hostile and abusive.

Third, the harassment needs to be "sufficiently severe or pervasive to alter the conditions of employment and create an abusive atmosphere." This is an objective test, which looks to whether an actual hostile or abusive work environment exists. As *Meritor* and later Supreme Court cases make clear, a few offensive remarks are not enough to make an environment objectively hostile. Often, courts frame this test by asking the question, "Would a reasonable person of the same race in the same position as the plaintiff consider the environment to be hostile?" To answer this question, judges look at all of the surrounding circumstances, such as the frequency of the hate speech, to whom the hate speech is directed, and the degree to which the hate speech interferes with the employee's ability to work. In Edgardo's case, the court stated it could "hardly envision a situation where the acts alleged could be more severe or pervasive" (*Big O Tires*, 2006 WL 1794756 at 7).

It is important to note, however, that this third "objective" test is still somewhat subjective because it turns on what the judge or jury personally consider to be "hostile." Thus the outcomes of cases are not always easy to predict. For example, a New York court found no hostile environment when supervisors of a Latino employee mocked the Spanish language, told him to "act more white" and to "lose his cocky Spanish attitude," and frequently called him "spic" (*Citroner v. Progressive Casualty Insurance Co.,* 208 F. Supp.2d 328 [E.D. N.Y. 2002]). Much of a plaintiff's success seems to depend on how sympathetic a judge is to the case.

The fourth requirement is based on what is called the theory of *respondeat superior,* which means there must be some reason to hold the employer responsible for the actions of his or her subordinates. In Title VII cases, this requirement is automatically met if a supervisor at the place of employment created the hostile work environment (*Burlington Industries, Inc. v. Ellerth,* 524 U.S. 742 [1998]; *Faragher v. City of Boca Raton,* 524 U.S. 775 [1998]). However, even if a supervisor causes the problem, the employer is not liable if he can prove two things: first, that the employer exercised reasonable care to prevent and correct any harassing behavior; and, second, that the employee unreasonably failed to take advantage of the preventive or remedial opportunities so provided.

What You Can Do as a Victim of Hate Speech on the Job. Despite the threat of Title VII liability, many employers still permit or even engage in derogatory and insulting hate speech. If you believe that you have been the victim of hate speech at your place of employment, contact the nearest U.S. Equal Employment Opportunity Commission. To find an office near you, call 800-669-4000 or access the site: http://www.eeoc.gov/offices.html.

Hate Speech at Home and on the Street

If the words spoken to Valdez had been spoken on the street, they probably would have been legally protected under the First Amendment. This is because hate speech enjoys much more protection outside of the context of employment. The rationale behind this broad protection is best stated by former Supreme Court Justice Black, who suggested that the protections "guaranteed by the First Amendment must be accorded to the ideas we hate or sooner or later they will be denied to the ideas we cherish" (*Communist Party of the United States v. Subversive Activities Control Board,* 367 U.S. 1, 137 [1961] [Black, J., dissenting]). The Supreme Court has, however, held that freedom of speech "must on occasion be subordinated to other values and considerations" (*Dennis,* 341 U.S. at 503). Five of these exceptions are "incitement," "fighting words," true threats, "captive audience," and "hostile audience."

Incitement of an Immediate Crime
The "incitement" exception means that an individual is not allowed to "incite" or provoke another person to commit a crime. Under the "clear and

present danger test," the government cannot prohibit the mere advocacy of ideas unless (1) the speaker is advocating the use of violence or the commission of a crime; (2) the nature of the speech is in fact likely to incite violence or commission of a crime; and (3) the unlawful action is likely to happen immediately (*Brandenburg v. State of Ohio*, 395 U.S. 444 [1969]). Thus, the mere advocacy of unlawful ideas is not punishable in and of itself. Instead, there must be the likelihood that people will listen to the ideas and immediately act on them. Therefore, laws that simply prohibit the advocacy of lawlessness are unconstitutional. In *Brandenburg*, a leader of the Ku Klux Klan spoke at a white supremacist rally and stated, "If our [government] continues to suppress the white, Caucasian race, it's possible that there might be some revengeance [*sic*] taken." The Court unanimously overturned the leader's conviction, because the law under which he was convicted had no requirement that the speech actually incite listeners to commit the crime. Instead, the law only prohibited "advocating . . . the duty, necessity, or propriety of crime, . . . violence, or unlawful methods of terrorism as a means of accomplishing . . . political reform." Because the law did not require that lawlessness was likely actually to occur, it was an attempt to prohibit the expression of ideas and thus violated the First Amendment.

The incitement exception could permit the punishment of hate speech if an individual incited others to inflict bodily harm on a group of Latino/as because of their race. But if an individual were to advocate for the total eradication of all Latino/as in America, and either no one heard his speech or no one was likely to listen, his speech would be constitutionally protected. If, however, the same individual said the same words to a mob of white supremacists, armed with deadly weapons, standing in the middle of a Latino/a neighborhood, this speech may be punishable under an appropriately written incitement law.

Fighting Words

The "fighting words" exception allows states to prohibit hate speech that is likely to cause violence. The Supreme Court recognized this exception in *Cantwell v. State of Connecticut*, 310 U.S. 296 (1940). In that case, Cantwell, a Jehovah's Witness, was walking through a predominately Catholic neighborhood, and asked two passersby, who happened to be Catholic, if they would listen to a recording. The recording contained a hostile attack on Roman Catholicism, and the two men became angry and demanded that Cantwell get off the street before something happened to him. Cantwell took his record player and went home, but was later charged with breaching the peace. The Court upheld the conviction, and stated that words likely to "provoke violence or disturbance of good order" could be punished. Although this language would appear to prohibit hate speech, this exception has proved to be ineffective.

True Threats

When a speaker utters a true threat, he threatens to commit criminal harm against someone else. True threats are different from incitement, because the speaker himself is threatening to commit the harm, rather than encouraging someone else to do it. True threats are similar to fighting words, except that the fighting words exception focuses on the reaction of the listener to the speaker—is the listener likely to retaliate in reaction to what the speaker just said? A true threat focuses more on the content of the speaker's words—is the speaker threatening unlawfully to inflict bodily harm on another person?

The Supreme Court has defined a true threat as speech that communicates a serious expression of intent to commit an unlawful act of violence against an individual or a group of individuals (*Virginia v. Black*, 538 U.S. 343 [2003]). The speaker need not intend to carry out the threat, but instead only must intend to place the victim in fear of bodily harm or death.

The Supreme Court has held that intimidation is a type of true threat; therefore, burning a cross in someone's yard with the intent to intimidate is a form of expression not protected under the First Amendment. This means, for example, that actions such as burning a Mexican flag in the yard of a Mexican family with the intent to intimidate them may fall within the true threat exception and be punishable as a crime.

Captive Audience

The "captive audience" exception comes into play when the speaker uses offensive speech to an audience incapable of declining to receive it so that it amounts to an intolerable invasion of privacy. This exception applies in situations where the audience lacks the choice not to hear the message of the speaker. An example of this exception is *FCC v. Pacifica Foundation*, 438 U.S. 726 (1978). In that case, the Supreme Court determined that the First Amendment permitted the Federal Communications Commission (FCC) to punish a broadcaster who played a twelve-minute monologue called "Filthy Words" by George Carlin every weekday at 2 o'clock in the afternoon. The broadcast was laced with four-letter words and other indecent language, and the FCC wanted to restrict radio shows with explicit content to times when children would most likely not be listening.

A five-to-four majority of the Court decided that the government may regulate the time, place, and manner of vulgar, offensive, and shocking speech broadcast over the airwaves. Notably, the Court did not say that the FCC could prohibit the speech altogether. Instead, the Court stated that the government in this context could decide when, where, and how indecent speech is communicated. The Court based its holding on the medium of the speech—the radio. Crucial to the Court's holding was that radio listeners are in a unique situation. They are constantly tuning in and out, which means that any prior warnings about the indecent content on a radio show would be insufficient. Also, the program occurred during the middle of the day, during a time where the show was accessible to children. Therefore, because radio listeners are a "captive audience," the government has the authority to regulate when they will be exposed to indecent language.

Hostile Audience

The "hostile audience" exception refers to speech so extremely inflammatory to a hostile audience that all good faith efforts to control the audience are futile. This exception allows the government to prevent riots and other public unrest from occurring. Under this exception, it is not enough to allege that an audience became angry upon hearing the speaker's words; speech, after all, can be expected to be provocative and controversial (*Terminiello v. City of Chicago*, 337 U.S. 1 [1949]). However, when there is a clear threat of a riot, disorder, interference with traffic on the streets, or any other immediate threat to public order, the state has the power to punish or prevent such disorder (*Feiner v. People of State of New York*, 340 U.S. 315 [1951]).

Hate Crimes

Of course, when the expression goes beyond speech and is actually criminal conduct such as assault, it may be punished. Importantly, if the crime is committed against a person *because* he is Latino (i.e., on account of ethnicity, race, or some other protected characteristic), the law can punish the criminal more severely. Such laws are called "penalty enhancement statutes." One such law was challenged, but the Supreme Court said the law did not prohibit free expression. Like the law in many states, the Wisconsin statute increases the criminal sentence of anyone who "intentionally selects the person against whom the crime . . . is committed . . . because of the race, religion, color, disability, sexual orientation, national origin, or ancestry of that person." The Court noted that such crimes are likely "to inflict greater individual and societal harm" (*Wisconsin v. Mitchell*, 508 U.S. 476, 486–487 [1993]).

When officials of state or local governments, including the police, "willfully" deprive any person of rights protected by the Constitution or other federal law, "on account of such person being an alien, or by reason of his color, or race," it is a federal crime (18 U.S.C. § 242). If death results from the police or other government action or if the acts include aggravated sexual abuse or an attempt to kill, the penalty can be life imprisonment or the death penalty. The Criminal Section of the Civil Rights Division of the U.S. Department of Justice prosecutes such willful deprivations by state or local governmental authorities of any federal "rights, privileges, or immunities." Complaints may also be filed with one of the ninety-five Offices of the United States Attorneys, located in most major cities (listed in the telephone book in the "Federal Government" pages).

Derogatory Media Stereotypes of Latino/as

Degrading portrayals of Latino/as in such media as motion pictures and television are a form of hate speech the Latino/a community should not tolerate. In the motion picture industry at least, a voluntary industry watchdog (the Production Code Administration) in the 1930s, 1940s, and 1950s protected against the most virulent derogatory depictions of Latino/as and other races and national origins, but media portrayals of Latino/as in recent times regularly depict Latino/as in unflattering terms: Latinos are heartless, hot tempered criminals and drug dealers quick with a switchblade; Latinas are sexually available and immoral. Both are portrayed as lazy, dumb, and poor, occupying the lowest stations of the workplace, if they are working lawfully.

The constitutional guarantee of free speech and limitations under state defamation law, however, derail legal remedies targeting derogatory media depictions of Latino/as. The upshot of these restrictions is that media have little legal constraint on the content of their programming that propagates hateful stereotypes. In the mid-1900s, most states had laws criminalizing media defamation on the basis of race. Racial and religious tensions surrounding African Americans and immigrant groups such as Jews prompted these laws. But since the 1950s, states have repealed or narrowed their criminal defamation laws to eliminate explicit references to race or religion, and the Supreme Court has chipped away at defamation actions by using the constitutional guarantee of free speech. Among other burdens in establishing defamation, challenging a media stereotype may require proof of the statement's falsity. For example, consider how one would legally prove the falsity of a ludicrous but hurtful media comparison of Mexicans to dogs or cockroaches. Further, many negative depictions impugn Latino/as through indirect negative connotations instead of direct false statements. For example, in the 1960s and early 1970s, Latino/a groups railed against the depiction of Mexicans in the "Frito Bandito" corn chips advertising campaign. Although the Frito Bandito was a gunslinging, sneaky thief of corn chips, the commercials and advertisements did not state explicitly that Mexicans are all lawless, gun-toting bandits. Moreover, parodies receive protection under the First Amendment, preventing a defamation lawsuit against a parody that cannot reasonably be seen as stating actual facts. For example, in 2002 tourism officials in Rio de Janeiro threatened to sue the makers of the animated sitcom *The Simpsons* for falsely depicting the Brazilian city's image in an episode filled with exaggerated perils and unsavory characters. Because no reasonable person would interpret these outrageous exaggerations as stating actual facts about Rio, they are constitutionally protected as parody.

In addition to federal constitutional free speech constraints, state laws render defamation unsuitable for lawsuits arising from racial or ethnic defamation of societal groups such as Latino/as. For example, the Latino/a campaign against the Frito Bandito image led to the announcement in 1971 by the National Mexican-American Anti-Defamation Committee of its intent to file a $610 million lawsuit against the corn chip company, its advertising agency, and national television networks, seeking $100 damages each for the "fictitious defamation" of the over 6 million Mexican Americans in the United States. Although never filed, this lawsuit would have faced insurmountable state law impediments. Courts deny organizations the right to bring defamation actions if the false statements do not address the organization—the National Mexican-American Anti-Defamation Committee was not itself the object of the falsehoods and would lack legal standing to bring the lawsuit. The following illustrates this limitation: in the 1980s a New York court dismissed a defamation action against a corporate executive who, in his role as chairperson of a Reagan-appointed private initiative, allegedly slandered Puerto Ricans. As part of an official presentation, he stated that the 900,000 Puerto Ricans living in New York are "all on food stamps," so that the government food stamp program was "basically a Puerto Rican program." Five Puerto Rican nonprofit community organizations sued for defamation, but the court dismissed their claims because the remarks did not target their organizations (*Puerto Rican Legal Defense Fund v. Grace*, 9 Media L. Rptr. 1514 [NY. Sup. Ct. 1983]). When the defamatory remarks target a large group, such as Mexican Americans, courts also preclude defamation actions by both individual members of the targeted class (on the theory that group statements cannot be regarded as referring personally to any one individual), and by group members suing in a class action. For example, a Massachusetts court upheld dismissal of a defamation action brought as a class action on behalf of all persons of Polish descent against the makers of a film that allegedly defamed Polish people. Because no single member of the class had a claim (as the defamatory remarks did not refer to them individually), all of them together as a class similarly had no legal claim (*Mikolinski v. Burt Reynolds Prod. Co.*, 409 N.E.2d 1324 [Mass. App. Ct. 1980]).

What Community Groups and You Can Do to Address Media Stereotypes. Given the shortcomings of legal remedies against derogatory media stereotypes, Latino/as must consider nonlegal strategies to confront stereotypical productions. Over the years, Latino/a organizations and other supporters have targeted media with mixed success. For example, a 1999 protest by students at a Los Angeles area high school, joined by the Mexican American Legal Defense and Educational Fund, prompted the Walt Disney company to remove a Mexican bandit character from its Toy Story 2 video game.[1] The Frito-Lay company ultimately terminated its Frito Bandito campaign in response to protest and threats of legal action. And in 1970, Hungarian comedian Bill Dana bowed to protest in the Mexican American community and abandoned the dimwitted Mexican persona José Jiménez that he created for television, stage, and record. More recently, NBC agreed to drop a Seinfeld episode from reruns after the National Puerto Rican Coalition and other Latino/a groups protested an episode disparaging Puerto Ricans. Protest from the Puerto Rican community also prompted the cancellation of a high school production of the musical West Side Story that depicts Puerto Ricans as knife-wielding gang members. Latino/a groups protested other media productions with less success—for example the television show *Chico and the Man,* the barrio gang films *Boulevard Nights* and *Walk Proud* that drew Mexican American protest, and the crime movies *Badge 373* and *Fort Apache, The Bronx* that sparked Puerto Rican protest and a failed lawsuit.

Supplementing protest, the National Council of La Raza has called on media to adopt a self-policing code of ethics against stereotyping on racial and ethnic grounds. Certain retailers, such as Wal-Mart, readily censor media on their conception of family values but tolerate derogatory stereotypes. Latino/a groups might urge retailers, particularly those that attract large numbers of Latino/a shoppers, to adopt retailer ethics codes against merchandise portraying derogatory stereotypes.

Walkouts, Protests, and Boycotts: Legal Limits

Latino/as have a storied history of community and labor protest that encompasses the grape strike and national grape boycott of César Chávez and the farm labor union in the 1960s, the "East LA Blowouts" when school children walked out of classes in several East Los Angeles high schools in 1968, protests and boycotts of derogatory stereotypical media productions, and pro-immigrant rallies and marches in spring 2006 that brought millions of Latino/as to the streets decrying anti-immigrant and border security at-any-cost proposals. The following materials address the legal constraints on and guidelines for such protest activities as boycotts, marches, rallies, and sit-ins in furtherance of Latino/a interests.

Boycotts
The courts distinguish between boycotts arising out of labor disputes and those that are political in nature, such as a community-organized boycott of a manufacturer that uses advertising with derogatory racial connotations. Boycotts in labor disputes are governed by federal and state laws that often limit or prohibit secondary boycotting—for example, the boycotting of a supermarket that sells a product manufactured by a company with whom the union pushing the boycott has a labor dispute. Enacted by Congress in 1935, the National Labor Relations Act (NLRA) protects the organizational rights of employees but was amended by the 1947 Taft-Hartley and 1959 Landrum-Griffin Acts to restrict secondary boycotts. Still, from its inception the NLRA has excluded agricultural employees, leaving growers the freedom to fire or discriminate against farm workers who unionize but freeing farm

workers and their unions from its limitations on union activity such as boycotts. Thus, the United Farm Worker union boycotts in the 1960s and later generally fell outside this federal restriction, but were subject to antisecondary boycotting laws in a few states, such as Arizona, Idaho, and Kansas, that passed strict laws regulating farm workers. For example, the Arizona law enacted in 1972 outlawed secondary boycotts and harvest-time strikes.

As distinct from labor disputes in which states have broad power to regulate economic and competitive business practice, politically minded boycotts receive strong protection from regulation under the First Amendment. The Supreme Court's decision in *NAACP v. Claiborne Hardware Co.*, 458 U.S. 886 (1982) established the free speech protection for boycotts by persons not engaged in economic competition with the business owners. This decision involved a lawsuit by white-owned businesses against black civil rights activists who orchestrated a boycott of these merchants as part of an antisegregation campaign in the South. Their boycott was protected under the First Amendment and the organizers were not financially responsible for the merchants' lost business profits under the tort of interference with business relations. Protection is not absolute, however, as violence or threats of violence against a business fall outside free speech protection: "The use of speeches, marches, and threats [to potential shoppers] of social ostracism cannot provide the basis for a damages award. But violent conduct is beyond the pale of constitutional protection" (458 U.S. at 933). Nevertheless, organizers or members of the protest are not liable to the merchants simply because some members of the group end up committing unprotected violent acts. In this case, the store owners unsuccessfully sought to hold the boycott leaders responsible for damages arguing that the leaders failed to prevent and reprimand those who engaged in unprotected violence against the person and property of those who ignored the boycott. Rather, for liability to be imposed based on membership in the protesting group, the business must establish that "the group itself possessed unlawful goals and that the individual held a specific intent to further those illegal aims" (458 U.S. at 920).

Rallies, Marches, and Walkouts

The city or other applicable local government body may, consistent with the First Amendment, regulate parades, marches, or gatherings in public places by requiring the organizers to obtain a marching or gathering permit in advance for a reasonable fee (*Cox v. New Hampshire*, 312 U.S. 569 [1941]), and by imposing reasonable constraints on the time and place of the event, so long as these restrictions, and the issuance of permits, are content neutral (*Thomas v. Chicago Park District*, 534 U.S. 316 [2002]). In other words, the government cannot favor one type of activity or speech over another and cannot treat an antiabortion protest more favorably than a rally for immigrant rights. Further, any restrictions imposed must be narrowly drawn to further a significant government interest. These restrictions might include limits on use of amplified sound, restrictions on the marching route, and requirements designed to ease impact on street traffic.

As with boycotts and merchant protests, violence is not permitted. Further, disorderly behavior such as disrupting traffic is unprotected. The Mexican American Legal Defense and Educational Fund advised students participating in the spring 2006 pro-immigrant student walkouts to avoid disrupting class and any students who opted to stay behind. In the East LA Blowouts in 1968, students voiced demands that included bilingual education, more Mexican teachers, and reduced class sizes. A couple of months after the protest, police arrested walkout organizers and charged them with the felony of conspiring to disturb the peace, itself only a misdemeanor, but these trumped up conspiracy charges were overturned on appeal under the First Amendment (*Castro v. Superior Court*, 88 Cal. Rptr. 500 [Ct. App. 1970]). Recently, high school student protesters in Round Rock, Texas, were arrested en masse on charges they violated a local daytime curfew law when they left school to protest a repressive immigration law passed by the U.S. House in 2006. Authorities required the students to prove they left school for the purpose of protesting immigration reform—under the local Texas law, skipping school without this proof is not protected as free speech. In order to boost their case under similarly construed curfew laws, students should document their presence at the rally, such as by photographs; in the event of a boycott, students can document their participation by spending their day writing letters to the local newspaper editor, making and carrying signs to protest the conditions leading to the boycott, or similar strategies that both can document the protest-oriented purpose of the absence and further the cause.

Sit-ins

Although the expressive nature of a sit-in is protected under the First Amendment, the Constitution does not insulate the protester against the crime of trespass or related state and federal property crimes. Therefore, blocking the entrance to a business or other private property, or refusing to leave private property when asked to do so, can be illegal.

Appendix

Websites

Anti-Defamation League report, "Immigrants Targeted: Extreme Rhetoric Moves into the Mainstream," http://www.adl.org/civil_rights/anti_immigrant/.

Fairness and Accuracy in Reporting, "Challenging Hate Radio: A Guide for Activists," http://www.fair.org/index.php?page=112.

Los Angeles County District Attorney's Office, website for hate crime victims in Los Angeles County, http://da.co.la.ca.us/hate/default.htm.

Not in Our Town, national movement of community response to hate crimes, http://www.pbs.org/niot/.

Partners Against Hate, comprehensive hate crime prevention and response resources for communities, educators, parents, and law enforcement; a joint project of Anti-Defamation League and other groups, http://www.partnersagainsthate.org/about_pah/index.html.

The Prejudice Institute, anti-prejudice resources for lawyers, activists, and social scientists, http://www.prejudiceinstitute.org/.

Teaching Tolerance, web project of the Southern Law Poverty Center with resources for teachers, parents, and children on preventing bias, http://www.tolerance.org/teach/?source=redirect&url=teachingtolerance.

Tex[t]-Mex Galleryblog, Mexican stereotypes in U.S. culture, http://textmex.blog spot.com/.

United States Department of Justice Community Relations Service, federal "peacemaker" for resolving community racial conflicts, http://www.usdoj.gov/crs/index .html.

Books

Bender, Steven W. *Greasers and Gringos: Latinos, Law, and the American Imagination.* New York: NYU Press, 2003.

Matsuda, Mari J., Charles R. Lawrence, Richard Delgado, and Kimberle Williams Crenshaw. *Words That Wound: Critical Race Theory, Assaultive Speech, and the First Amendment.* Boulder: Westview Press, 1993.

Rodríguez, Clara E., ed. *Latin Looks: Images of Latinas and Latinos in the U.S. Media.* Boulder: Westview Press, 1998.

Video

The Bronze Screen: 100 Years of the Latino Image in Hollywood. Questar, 2002.

Notes

1. Disparaging clothing has also been the subject of protest, with Guess stores responding to protest by stopping sales of t-shirts reading, "Ski Colombia—always plenty of fresh powder." In 2006, protesters targeted Urban Outfitters for selling t-shirts with the slogan, "New Mexico, Cleaner Than Regular Mexico," that tapped the racist, stereotypical image of the dirty Mexican.

6
Education

The No Child Left Behind Act

Many of today's students can no longer count on earning a high school diploma solely by passing all their classes through the twelfth grade. Instead, students' chances for a diploma often hinge on their ability to pass standardized tests that states have created. States either adopt such tests on their own or to comply with federal law, namely the No Child Left Behind Act (NCLB) (20 U.S.C. § 6301 *et seq.*). The movement emphasizing standardized tests, with NCLB as its impetus, significantly impacts the education of Latino/as. Enacted in 2001, NCLB has many provisions important to Latino/a students individually and, more broadly, to their schools. The law, which seeks to ensure that students have attained "proficiency" in basic subjects before they graduate, has reshaped K–12 education for Latino/as and all other students (20 U.S.C. § 6311[b][2][A]).

NCLB requires states to develop a method for ensuring that, by the 2013–2014 school year, 100 percent of K–12 students are proficient. Until then, schools must show through reliable assessments that they are making "adequate yearly progress" toward proficiency. For schools that receive federal Title I funds, several progressive corrective measures greet schools that fail to achieve adequate yearly progress. Although schools could conceivably turn down federal Title I funds to avoid these corrective measures, many schools currently depend on this federal funding. Therefore, for almost all school districts, compliance with the corrective measures is in reality mandatory. Some of the corrective measures include the following:

Schools that fail to achieve adequate yearly progress for *two* consecutive years must:
- develop an improvement plan.

- receive technical assistance from their school district.
- allow students to transfer to other nonfailing schools and provide transportation for students who choose this option.

Schools that fail to achieve adequate yearly progress for *three* consecutive years must:
- provide tutoring and other supplemental services to the low-performing and disadvantaged students who request the services.
- dedicate at least 5 percent of their federal funding to transporting students to other schools and another 5 percent to tutoring and other supplemental services.

Schools that fail to achieve adequate yearly progress for *four or five* consecutive years:
- may have to replace staff members.
- may have to change their curriculum.
- may be subject to a dramatic restructuring or takeover by a state educational association.
- risk losing all federal funds (20 U.S.C. § 6316[b]).

Standardized tests provide the tool for measuring schools' progress toward achieving proficiency. NCLB itself does not specify that passing the tests must be a graduation requirement. Many states, however, have made the tests a requirement for graduation. Thus, in addition to the effects NCLB has on schools, the law also has very practical repercussions for students and their chances of earning a high school diploma.

Spanish-Language Accommodations

Standardized tests stemming from NCLB present unique challenges for Latino/as whose primary language is Spanish. These students could score low on the exam because of language barriers, even though they understand the subject matter. NCLB contains a provision that addresses these language barriers. The act requires that states provide for "the inclusion of limited English proficient [LEP] students, who shall be assessed in a valid and reliable manner . . . including to the extent practicable, assessments in the language and form most likely to yield accurate data on what students know and can do in academic content areas, until such students have achieved English language proficiency" (20 U.S.C. § 6311[b][3][C][ix][III]). NCLB presumes that students will become proficient in English within three to five years. This three- to five-year presumption means that states are not required to test an LEP student differently from English-proficient students after this time period expires.

States have responded inconsistently. Many schools and students argue that, under NCLB, states should be required to provide language accommodations for standardized tests, whether through printing the test in a student's native language or through other measures, such as allowing the student to use a bilingual dictionary during the examination. However, while at least fourteen states have created language accommodations for testing LEP students, the majority of states do not make any accommodations. Providing language accommodations does pose difficulty for some schools because, among other reasons, accommodations are expensive and educational specialists argue about the best method. Despite these concerns, language accommodations may become more widespread in the future.

In some states with no language accommodations, parents, school districts, and individual schools have sued to force the states to provide accommodations. The lawsuits have produced mixed results. For example, in *Reading School District v. Pennsylvania Department of Education*, 855 A.2d 166 (Pa. 2004), the court held NCLB does not impose an unconditional obligation on states to provide language accommodation. Instead, the states have to provide accommodations only "to the extent practicable." Other plaintiffs have sued under state constitutions or other theories, although no consensus has emerged from the cases.

Nevertheless, increasingly more states are voluntarily providing accommodations. This is particularly true in states with a large population of students whose primary language is Spanish. Texas, Massachusetts, and New York, which all have large populations of Latino/a students, a significant portion of whom are considered LEP students, provide language accommodations for their standardized tests. California, where 25 percent of K–12 students are considered English learners, began offering Spanish-language standardized tests in the 2005–2006 school year. Therefore, depending on where they live, many Latino/as who are considered LEP students may find that their school offers some type of language accommodations on standardized tests. With so much riding on the test results, Latino/a students with concerns about ability to perform to full potential because of language barriers should investigate whether accommodations are available at their school and, if so, what type.

Other Legal Issues

Besides language accommodations, NCLB has raised a host of other legal issues that carry potential effects for Latino/a students and the schools they attend. These issues include potential litigation about funding choices that school districts make to comply with NCLB and the effect that provisions allowing students to transfer from underperforming schools will have on school desegregation plans. The first issue stems from the NCLB requirement that states divide students into subgroups, including racial subgroups, to evaluate performance and close achievement gaps. NCLB directs states to develop methods for improving the performance of minority students and other disadvantaged students whose performance lags behind nonminority students. This directive may prompt states to direct more of their education funding to these subgroups of students. Eventually, students who are not in these subgroups may complain that this funding focus violates their constitutional right to equal protection and other federal or state laws. Therefore, some have predicted that NCLB may lead to legal disputes over funding.

A second issue involves the extent to which NCLB's school choice provisions will affect the racial desegregation plans in place in many school districts. Since the landmark Supreme Court case of *Brown v. Board of Education*, 347 U.S. 483 (1954), which held that racial segregation in schools was unconstitutional, school districts have taken proactive measures to ensure that their schools are racially integrated. Many school districts operate under court-ordered desegregation plans or a voluntary desegregation plan. One goal of these desegregation plans is to avoid the concentration of poor, minority students in segregated schools. Research has documented that this concentration further hampers the ability of poor, minority students to close the achievement gap between them and their wealthier, nonminority peers.

Some fear that NCLB's school choice provisions for allowing students to leave an underperforming school for a performing one in the district will undermine the goal of desegregation plans. Indeed, the NCLB implementing regulations state that school districts under a court-ordered desegregation plan that conflicts with the NCLB school choice provisions should seek a modification of the court order to accommodate NCLB (34 C.F.R. § 200.44[c]). Because increasingly more schools, through underperformance, become subject to the school choice provisions every year, the provisions have the potential significantly to alter the demographics of the nation's schools and contribute to greater concentration of traditionally lower-performing students. For Latino/a students, already considered the most segregated student group, this is not a positive trend. Further, voluntary desegregation plans face a potentially larger legal hurdle following the Supreme Court decision in *Parents Involved in Community Schools v. Seattle School District No. 1*, 127 S.Ct. 2738 (2007), discussed later in this chapter.

Affirmative Action and Higher Education

Access to a college education provides individuals with one of the best opportunities available to achieve career and personal success. Much research has documented that higher education provides the key factor separating the flourishing from the struggling in the United States. Therefore, the future success of the nation's Latino/as depends in large part on access to college education. For Latino/as who wish to enter the country's most prominent and well-compensated professions—medicine, business, law, science, and academia—an undergraduate, and in most cases a graduate, degree acts as a prerequisite to achieving their goals. Yet, Latino/as and other minorities often encounter many obstacles to obtaining a college education. These obstacles include generally lower family income levels, admissions policies that give great weight to standardized tests, and language barriers. Latino/as and other minorities can, however, increase their chances of gaining admission to their college of choice through highlighting how their background will add to the student body's diversity. Many higher education programs, both public and private, use admission programs that treat the race of people of color as a positive factor in the admissions process. The following discussion covers the legal status of these programs, classified popularly as one form of affirmative action.

Although controversial since affirmative action began in the 1960s, the permissible structure for these programs has been largely defined by three key United States Supreme Court opinions: *Regents of University of California v. Bakke*, 438 U.S. 265 (1978); *Grutter v. Bollinger*, 539 U.S. 306 (2003); and *Gratz v. Bollinger*, 539 U.S. 244 (2003). Even though public colleges and universities, as governmental bodies, are subject to constitutional standards not applicable to private institutions, private institutions face similar legal scrutiny through other federal laws.[1] Therefore, while the Supreme Court cases focus on the constitutionality of affirmative action in the admissions process for public universities, the cases supply valuable insight for both public and private institutions. For the Latino/a applicant to a college or university, the cases carry importance not only for defining the limits for what type of affirmative action program will withstand a legal challenge, but they also may offer clues to minority applicants on how best to tailor their applications to improve their chances of gaining admission or securing a scholarship.

In its opinions, the Supreme Court has recognized the value of a diverse student body and has held that, to achieve diversity, universities may consider the race or ethnicity of applicants as one factor in deciding admission. An admissions program, however, cannot be based on race alone or set quotas for how many applicants of each race will be admitted. Instead, a permissible program must feature an individualized assessment of each applicant and ensure that each application is weighed against all others, as opposed to considering the applications from minorities in isolation from the other applications. Admissions officials may treat an applicant's race as a "plus" in an application, but they may not predetermine how much weight automatically to assign to applicants who indicate they are members of a certain race.

What You Should Do in Crafting an Application for Admission. For the Latino/a university applicant, the Supreme Court's holdings and the resulting commentary provide some general tips about how to craft an application. Of course, each institution will likely feature its own unique admissions criteria. Applicants are well advised to research institutions to learn the best strategies for gaining admission. Likewise, in selecting a college, the Latino/a applicant should consider whether it has an affirmative action program that might increase the applicant's chances of being admitted or of receiving an increase in scholarship money.

Latino/a applicants should highlight how their race, background, and unique experience will contribute to the diversity of the student body. In this context, it is also very important for Latino/a applicants to discuss any obstacles they have overcome to get to this point in their academic career or in their personal lives. Given the Supreme Court's holdings, the applicant should recognize that many institutions will have admissions programs that define diversity to include characteristics in addition to race. In *Bakke*, the Supreme Court said, "it is not an interest in simple ethnic diversity, in which a specified percentage of the student body is in effect guaranteed to be members of selected ethnic groups. Diversity . . . encompasses a far broader array of qualifications and characteristics of which racial or ethnic origin is but a single though important element" (438 U.S. at 315).

Thus, Latino/a applicants should highlight all their unique characteristics. Identification as a Latino/a is a good start and might be considered a plus on the application. However, an explanation of how that heritage could add to the educational experience of the student body is even better. In addition to identifying their race and ethnicity, applicants should take advantage of opportunities such as personal statements, interviews, or résumés to communicate all their positive traits to the admissions committee. A summary of the Supreme Court's cases will help place these points in context.

Achieving a Critical Mass:
The Supreme Court's Admissions Programs Decisions

The Supreme Court's cases involving affirmative action in the admissions arena originated with lawsuits from white applicants who did not get into the university they subsequently sued. The applicants claimed their right to equal protection of the laws under the Fourteenth Amendment to the United States Constitution and federal laws was violated because, as white students, they were being treated unfavorably compared to students of color. The Court first considered the issue in 1978 in *Bakke*.

The case originated when Allan Bakke, a white man, applied for admission into the medical school at the University of California at Davis. The medical school's admission program accepted only 100 applicants out of the nearly 2,500 who applied. Sixteen of these 100 spots in the medical college were reserved for blacks, Latino/as, Asians, and Native Americans. A special admissions program was designed to consider most of the minority applicants in isolation from the other applicants. Thus, white applicants could compete for only 84 of the 100 seats available for each year's entering class. This program, the Supreme Court held, violated Bakke's equal protection rights.

Still, the Court expressly recognized that diversity, in a broader sense than just racial diversity, serves as a sufficient reason to consider race and ethnicity in an admissions program. While race can serve as a plus for an application, a constitutional program cannot consider minority applicants separately from other applicants.

The Supreme Court provided further guidance fifteen years later in *Grutter v. Bollinger* and *Gratz v. Bollinger*. Both cases involved challenges to the University of Michigan's admissions policies. *Grutter* started with a lawsuit by a white Michigan resident rejected by the law school. The law school's admissions program required all applications be weighed against each other and that admission officials consider all the information included in an application, including past academic performance, a personal statement, letters of recommendation, and an essay on how the applicant would add to the diversity of the law school. The admissions policy did not define diversity in terms of ethnic diversity alone, but it did note that the law school had a special commitment to having African Americans, Latino/as, and Native Americans included in the student body.

The Court held that this type of program was constitutional. The school had not set a quota for students of color, a practice the *Bakke* case expressly disapproved. Instead, the Court found the law school's program sought to attain a "critical mass of underrepresented minority students" through ensuring individualized assessments of all applications and accounting for other factors besides race that may contribute to diversity (*Grutter*, 539 U.S. at 336–337). This program violated neither the Equal Protection Clause of the Constitution nor the applicable federal laws.

By contrast, the Court in *Gratz* found that the admissions policy employed by the University of Michigan's College of Literature, Science, and the Arts (LSA) violated the constitutional rights of two white applicants denied admission. The LSA admissions program relied in part on a point system to evaluate applications. The university generally admitted those receiving 100 or more out of a possible 150 points. Applicants from underrepresented minority groups were automatically awarded 20 points. The Court found that this policy did not feature the individualized assessment of applications that serves as a hallmark of a constitutional race-conscious admissions program. "The LSA's automatic distribution of 20 points has the effect of making 'the factor of race . . . decisive' for virtually every minimally qualified underrepresented minority applicant" (*Gratz*, 539 U.S. at 272).

These Supreme Court decisions help illuminate how admissions officials are likely to consider Latino/as' ethnicity in the application process. Latino/a applicants should investigate whether the institutions to which they apply have a race-conscious admissions policy and, if so, its details. That way, applicants can best tailor an application to highlight their diversity, not only as Latino/as, but also as individuals with unique experiences (such as overcoming economic obstacles), abilities (e.g., bilingual or trilingual), and traits.

The Future of Affirmative Action for the University and in Other Contexts

The Supreme Court has recognized the value of achieving a diverse student body, yet the debate over affirmative action continues. As potential beneficiaries of affirmative action programs, Latino/as and other minorities have an important role to play in shaping this debate.

Political Challenges: Public Opposition to Affirmative Action. At least four states, Michigan, California, Washington, and Florida, prohibit the consideration of race in not only university admissions but in other contexts. In Michigan, California, and Washington, the ban resulted from voter initiatives, while in Florida it resulted from an executive order of then-governor Jeb Bush. Additionally, opponents of affirmative action, such as Ward Connerly, who led the effort to pass Proposition 209 in California to ban affirmative action, have their sights on promoting voter initiatives in other states. Affirmative action opponents have been successful in convincing voters to approve the bans by casting the debate in terms of promoting equality, although critics say the opponents failed to explain the consequences of eliminating affirmative action. Latino/as who vote in a state where affirmative action is being challenged through voter initiative play an important role in preserving the programs, not only through their votes but also through lending their perspective to the debate. It is extremely important for those who are knowledgeable about these issues to spread the word to others in the Latino/a community. Many of those in California who voted in favor of the so-called civil rights initiative, Proposition 209, were people of color, including thousands of Latino/as, who were duped into believing that the law would confer additional protection, rather than deprive them of affirmative action programs.

An Affirmative Action Alternative: Percentage Plans. In the face of legal and political challenges to affirmative action, universities have sought other ways to achieve diversity. Three states, Texas, California, and Florida, adopted an alternative to race-conscious affirmative action in university admissions. These programs seek to achieve diversity in university student bodies by guaranteeing admission to students who graduate in the top of their high school class. The plans do not provide a way for students to pay for their undergraduate program or address admissions into graduate or professional schools.

Many commentators have concluded these programs have not proven successful at diversifying college campuses. Nevertheless, for a Latino/a high school student living in one of these states, the programs do provide one option for gaining admission to an in-state university. The information provided below is for summary purposes only. Students in these states should check with their high school guidance counselor or other knowledgeable individual for more specific details about each program and to check for any updates in the programs.

The Texas Ten-Percent Plan. In Texas, students in the top 10 percent of their high school class are automatically eligible for admission to any public university in the state, regardless of their race or other factors. For Latino/a students in Texas who rank in the top 10 percent of their class, this program provides opportunities to attend quality institutions like the flagship universities of the Texas system, the University of Texas at Austin and Texas A&M at College Station. These students should recognize, however, that the Ten-Percent Plan guarantees only admission into a university program. The admitted student must figure out how to pay tuition and other costs of attending such a university.

Many commentators have concluded that the Texas plan does not create the same level of racial diversity that can be achieved through a race-conscious admissions program. At Texas A&M University at College Station, for example, Latino/as and African Americans comprised 18.8 percent of the student body before implementation of the plan. By 2003, when the Ten-Percent Plan had been in place for five years, Latino/a and African American enrollments made up 12.6 percent of the Texas A&M freshman class. This decrease in Latino/a and African American enrollment came despite a significant increase in the proportion of Latino/a and African American high school graduates during the same time period.

At the University of Texas at Austin (UT–Austin), Latino/a and African American enrollment has been slightly higher under the Ten-Percent Plan, but disproportionality still exists between the percentage of Latino/a and African American high school graduates and the freshman enrollment at UT–Austin of students from these groups. The Texas experience illustrates that race-neutral alternatives to affirmative action should be closely scrutinized to determine if they truly achieve the same level of racial diversity available through affirmative action.

California's Four-Percent Plan. California enacted its percentage plan after voters approved Proposition 209. The plan works much like the one in Texas, with a couple of significant differences. First, the plan guarantees admission only to students who graduate in the top 4 percent of their high school class. The California university system has, however, expanded the program so that students who graduate between the top 4 percent and 12.5 percent of their high school class will be guaranteed admission to an in-state university provided they first complete an approved two-year program at a community college.

The second major difference between the Texas and California plans is that, while the Texas plan guarantees admission to any in-state university, the California plan guarantees only that a qualifying student will be admitted into one of California's ten campuses. In other words, qualified students in California are not guaranteed admission into their university of choice. This excludes students of color from the university system's most elite campuses and pushes them into the least exclusive ones.

Florida's Talented 20 Program. Florida instituted its Talented 20 Program at the same time then-governor Jeb Bush issued the executive order that eliminated affirmative action and "racial preferences" in the state. The program guarantees admission into a state university for students who graduate in the top 20 percent of their high school class. Like the California plan, Florida's Talented 20 Program guarantees only that students who qualify under the program will be admitted into a state university, not that they will be admitted to their university of choice. Also, as with the California and Texas plans, many have criticized the Florida plan as an ineffective substitute for affirmative action.

Some Specific Programs That May Benefit Latino/as

Besides affirmative action and percentage plans, several other programs and organizations described below assist Latino/as in higher education.

Financial Aid Programs. The trends for Latino/a students in higher education are mixed. In recent years, Latino/a student representation has significantly increased on college and university campuses across the nation. At the same time, however, Latino/as, who represent the largest minority group in the United States, still lag behind other groups in obtaining higher education. Latino/as' relatively low receipt of financial aid contributes heavily to their relatively low level of higher education attainment. Like many students, Latino/as' access to financial aid and the cost largely control their ability to attend college and the type of program they pursue there. Yet, Latino/a students have long trailed all other ethnic groups in accessing scholarships and other forms of financial aid. In the 2005 study, *How Latino Students Pay for College*, the Institute for Higher Education Policy and *Excelencia* in Education reported that Latino/a students received an average of $6,250 in financial aid in the 2004–2005 academic year, compared to the national average of $6,890.

Several groups seek to raise awareness and find solutions to the financial aid issue for Latino/as, including the Hispanic Scholarship Fund Institute (www.hsfi.org). In addition, several federal and state programs exist that could potentially benefit Latino/as in their pursuit of higher education. Many of the federal programs are funded through the Higher Education Act (20 U.S.C. § 1070 *et seq.*). Congress reauthorizes the program every five years, and through this process dictates how much funding the individual programs receive. Some of the programs include the following:

- *Developing Hispanic Serving Institutions (HSIs) Program.* The Developing HSIs Program provides a variety of development aid to higher education institutions that qualify as HSIs under the program. The aid goes to everything from curriculum development, improved technology, endowment support, and student services, to faculty development. More than 230 higher education institutions now qualify for aid through the program. The extent to which the Developing HSIs Program directly benefits Latino/a students, however, remains unclear.
- *Minority Science and Engineering Improvement Program.* The Minority Science and Engineering Improvement Program seeks to address the low representation of Latino/as and other people of color in the science and engineering fields. The program makes grants available to institutions for recruiting Latino/a and other minority students into science and engineering programs and for providing support services to these students. This program appears to have helped increase Latino/a representation among science and engineering graduates, although this representation still remains low.
- *College Assistance Migrant Program (CAMP).* The federal College Assistance Migrant Program (CAMP) provides grants to about 42 colleges and universities. The colleges and universities use the grant money to provide financial aid, mentoring, and tutoring services to migrant farm workers and children of migrant farm workers. Students from this background often face extra obstacles to higher education, including low family incomes, frequent relocation, and language barriers. The program places special focus on helping Latino/a students. Students must be legally in the country to be eligible for assistance through CAMP. The student's parents, however, do not have to be legally in the country for their child to be eligible. Migrant workers and their children should check whether colleges or universities in their area provide CAMP assistance or similar programs that can help educational aspirations become reality.

Race-Conscious Measures in K–12 Schools

Efforts to attain greater racial and ethnic diversity in a student body are not unique to higher education. Hundreds of grade K–12 school districts across the nation have developed plans, either voluntarily or by court order, that seek to achieve racially integrated schools. In such districts, a student's race may determine what school within a district the student attends. While school districts' plans vary, their general goal is to avoid racial isolation of the student body. Many of these plans were initially adopted to comply with

Brown v. Board of Education, where the Supreme Court held school segregation unconstitutional. Others were implemented in recognition that neighborhood trends and demographics were leading to "resegregation." Now, these districts' plans, in particular those operated voluntarily, could face newfound legal scrutiny following the Supreme Court's decision in *Parents Involved in Community Schools v. Seattle School District No. 1*, 127 S.Ct. 2738 (2007).

The Supreme Court held unconstitutional voluntary racial integration plans in the Seattle and Louisville school districts. The Court, in a narrow five-to-four holding, stated that the districts' methods for assigning some students to schools based on their race violated students' federal constitutional right to equal protection of law. Both districts provided students with some level of choice about which school in the district they attended. However, the students' race and the impact it would have on the existing racial makeup of their requested school in some cases determined whether the students received the school of their choice. The Louisville and Seattle school districts argued that the demographics and neighborhood makeup of their communities would produce racially isolated schools without these assignment plans. A majority of the members of the Supreme Court, however, still found the districts' plans unconstitutional.

While based specifically on an analysis of the Seattle and Louisville districts, *Parents Involved in Community Schools* will almost certainly affect other districts. For districts with large Latino/a populations, the case's impact could be particularly significant. Latino/a students are the most isolated of any ethnic group in the United States; Latino/a students attend schools that, on average, are 55 percent Latino/a. Districts that seek to establish exclusively race-based remedies to this isolation face new constraints following *Parents Involved in Community Schools*.

The Court's decision rested on essentially two related points. First, four of the nine Justices on the Court determined that a school district's goal of achieving diversity, defined solely in terms of racial diversity, does not provide a compelling state interest that will justify treating students differently based on race. The Court discussed how the Seattle and Louisville school districts' goals for racial diversity differed from the type of diversity the Court embraced in *Grutter*, which upheld the University of Michigan Law School's admissions program. Whereas the law school defined its interest in diversity broadly, with the student body's racial makeup representing just one element of the diversity it sought, the school districts' goals for diversity focused exclusively on racial diversity.

Secondly, a majority of the Court (five Justices) found fault with the methods by which the districts sought to achieve diversity. The Louisville district's plan rested on a classification of students as either black or white, and the Seattle district classified students as either white or "other." These binary classifications, the Court concluded, ran contrary to achieving true racial diversity. The Court noted that in Seattle, where the district suspended its program following the lawsuit, subsequent statistics showed that "enrolling students without regard to their race yields a substantially diverse student body under any definition of diversity." Therefore, a majority of the Court disapproved of the manner in which students were treated differently based on their race for the exclusive purpose of achieving racial diversity.

The exact effect that *Parents Involved in Community Schools* will have on other school districts remains to be seen. The opinion, however, should not be interpreted as striking down all race-conscious measures in K–12 school assignments. First, the opinion deals most directly with voluntary, race-based school assignment plans, not plans ordered by a court as a remedy for past discrimination in the district. If a school district was found to have operated racially segregated schools in the past, it could, and indeed may be required by court order to have a race-based student assignment program that seeks to remedy the effects caused by past segregation.

The decision appears to have left some options for districts to continue voluntarily to create or maintain diverse schools. Race, however, clearly cannot serve as the sole factor in deciding where a student attends school in the district. Rather, a permissible, voluntarily adopted plan must more closely resemble the law school's holistic admission program in *Grutter*.

Rights of Undocumented Children

Access to K–12 Education

In 1982, in a case called *Plyler v. Doe*, 457 U.S. 202, the Supreme Court struck down a 1975 Texas law that prohibited the use of state funds to educate undocumented children. In a five-to-four decision, the Court declared access to K–12 education to be a quasi-fundamental right and held that the Texas law violated equal protection under the Fourteenth Amendment of the U.S. Constitution. Since *Plyler*, undocumented children have the same right as U.S. citizen children to attend any K–12 school in the United States and to participate in special public school programs.

Plyler violations or attempts to undermine it, however, still occur throughout the nation. In 2006, for example, an Illinois school district denied enrollment to a fourteen-year-old student from Ecuador because she held a tourist visa and was not undocumented. *Plyler* did not directly address the issue of students with tourist visas; its holding, however, clearly instructed educators to stay out of determining students' immigration status. It was not until the Illinois Board of Education voted to cut off state funding that the district abandoned what had been a four-year-old practice of refusing to enroll students with tourist visas. Colorado also attempted to pass in 2006 a law that would require school districts to collect student citizenship data. While the bill's stated purpose was to assess the financial cost of educating undocumented children, its "chilling" effect on undocumented children enrolling in Colorado public high schools would also have run afoul of *Plyler.* For immigrant parents especially, then, it becomes crucial to understand the scope of *Plyler* guarantees in order to monitor and challenge violation of the rights of their children.

Minimum Plyler *Requirements*

At a minimum, *Plyler* requires K–12 schools not to adopt policies or take actions that would deny access to or dissuade the enrollment of undocumented children in public schools. School employees, therefore, cannot

- Deny admission to students on the basis of actual or alleged undocumented status.
- Ever ask students' immigration status or request related documentation. Schools may ask for an immunization form and a birth certificate or other paperwork that proves the child's age.
- Treat undocumented students differently from others when establishing residency. Schools may seek proof of residency in a given locality when by law students must attend school in a district where their parent or legal guardian lives. Residency may be established through utility, rental agreements, or affidavits from third parties. When a child lives with someone other than a parent, she may attend school in a different district. In such cases, districts or schools should avoid inflexible rules for establishing residence, such as requiring that the caretaker be a legal guardian, as it is not uncommon for immigrant children to live with extended families.
- Make inquiries of a student or parent that might expose the undocumented status of either.
- Require undocumented students or their parents to apply for or provide social security numbers (SSNs), for which they are ineligible under federal law (Social Security Act, 42 U.S.C. § 402[y]). If an identification number is needed, districts or schools should assign a school-generated number.
- Contact or disclose immigration status information or otherwise expose undocumented children and families to immigration officials,[2] absent a valid subpoena or warrant. When immigration officials furnish a subpoena, schools should check with an attorney to ascertain the validity of the subpoena. Schools should minimally determine that the warrant lists the school by its correct name and address, lists the students by correct name, is signed by a judge, is less than ten days old, and is served by an immigration officer with proper identification. To protect the privacy of other students, school employees should escort the immigration officials to a private place and have the students

named in the warrant brought to them. School officials should also immediately inform the superintendent and school attorney.

- Engage in any other practice to "chill" undocumented students' access to schools or participation in special programs. "Chilling" actions include those that create fear among undocumented students or their families, such as mandating completion of forms that ask for immigration status without explanation or assurances of strict confidentiality.

Special Programs

Plyler also entitles undocumented students to varied benefits provided by a number of special programs. These include (1) the Emergency Immigrant Education Program (No Child Left Behind Act of 2001, 115 Stat. 1425 at §§ 3241–3248); (2) programs that receive funds under Section 204 of the Immigrant Reform and Control Act (SILG Funds); (3) bilingual or English-language learning programs; (4) Chapter 1 funds, which are used to supplement the educational services provided to low-achieving students in low-income neighborhoods; (5) Head Start programs; (6) special education; and (7) free and reduced meal programs.

These programs require schools to maintain student applications that document eligibility to receive services. Many of these federal programs, for example, ask for SSNs of all household members over the age of twenty-one. To ensure that parents are not afraid to apply, schools should carefully explain that if a student or household member over the age of twenty-one does not have an SSN, "none" should be written in that space. Schools should also assure parents and students who are filling out the applications that federal law prohibits schools from disclosing any information on the forms to any other federal agency, including those charged with enforcing immigration laws.[3]

The Future of Plyler

The right of undocumented students' access to K–12 public education is settled in the legal domain, despite attempts to overturn the decision. One such attempt occurred in 1994, when California voters passed Proposition 187. At the core of Section 7 of Proposition 187 was the denial of K–12 education to undocumented children. The Central District Court of California, however, struck down Section 7 because federal law trumped California law (*League of United Latin American Citizens v. Wilson*, 908 F. Supp. 755 [C.D. Cal. 1995]).

In the Personal Responsibility and Work Opportunity Reconciliation Act of 1996, which disqualified undocumented migrants from nearly all public assistance, Congress preserved *Plyler* by prohibiting states from denying children access to elementary public schools (8 U.S.C. §§ 1643[a][2]). The continued viability of *Plyler* took center stage in 2005 with the confirmation of Supreme Court Chief Justice John Roberts, who opposes *Plyler* based on the legal doctrine of judicial restraint, which generally disfavors courts' "lawmaking" function, including defining individual rights and liberties. Overturning *Plyler*, however, will take more than just a change in the Court's composition, as long as federal legislation continues to affirm the holding. Nevertheless, with Justice Roberts on the Court, today the possibility is greater that the Court would permit Congress to adopt legislation to disallow *Plyler*, construing the holding as not constitutionally mandated.

What Community Groups and You Can Do to Protect the Rights of Undocumented Schoolchildren. Anti-immigrant groups understand the possibility that legislation could be passed to overturn *Plyler* and, in the hope of influencing Congress, are likely to continue producing studies that contend immigrants are a significant drain on public education.[4] For this reason, it is imperative that supporters of *Plyler* protect its legacy. Supporters should lobby against legislative measures that seek to undermine *Plyler*, strengthen the constitutional standing of *Plyler* in court, and produce studies that reveal the fallacy of anti-*Plyler* arguments.

At the same time, *Plyler* violations will persist and parents, especially, must remain vigilant. When these occur, parents should file a formal complaint with school leadership or with the state's board of education if school leadership is unresponsive. If the violations persist or if the climate is particularly hostile, parents should seek the intervention of local or national civil rights groups, such as the Mexican American Legal Defense and Educational Fund.

Bilingual Education

Spanish has often been unwelcome in the U.S. classroom. The Southwest, particularly, long tolerated punishing schoolchildren for speaking Spanish. For much of the past century Texas even criminalized the teaching of Spanish in its public schools. In 1970, for example, a Mexican American teacher in Texas was indicted for teaching a U.S. history class in Spanish, but the indictment was later dismissed. Texas enforced its no-Spanish rule against schoolchildren even for conversations outside the classroom—one student was corporally punished for asking a friend in Spanish to throw him a ball. Illustrating that the current renewed wave of anti-Spanish sentiment has reached the schools, in 2005 a public school suspended a Kansas City teenager for speaking Spanish in the hallway. The youth merely replied "no problema" when asked to lend a friend a dollar. The local school district ultimately rescinded his punishment and overturned its policy against Spanish on the school grounds. Earlier, in 2002, an Arizona elementary school with a predominantly Latino/a student body allegedly instructed its teachers to encourage its students to speak English in the hallways, cafeteria, and playground.

Hostility toward non-English languages in schools extends beyond Spanish. In the early 1900s, more than half the states passed laws requiring English-language instruction in schools. These laws targeted German immigrants primarily, reflecting prevailing anti-German sentiment particularly during World War I. At the same time, so-called Americanization programs instilled American values in Mexican American schoolchildren, with a major push toward the learning of English.

Gradually, legislators came to value bilingual education—an educational program that recognized the merits of teaching non-English-speaking children substantive subjects in their native language, while usually teaching them English at the same time. The federal Bilingual Education Act adopted in 1968 crystallized this emerging trend by authorizing federal funding for, but not mandating, state bilingual education programs. Some states by statute mandated bilingual education for schoolchildren. Significant litigation in the 1970s brought on behalf of non-English-speaking Chinese students relied on federal antidiscrimination law to challenge the inadequacy of the San Francisco school system that taught them in the English language, which they could not understand. The Supreme Court concluded that failing to accommodate these students constituted discrimination in violation of Title VI of the Civil Rights Act of 1964. Although the Supreme Court was not asked to specify a remedy, it mentioned bilingual instruction as one means to provide a meaningful education to these children with limited English proficiency (*Lau v. Nichols*, 414 U.S. 563 [1974]). The Title VI antidiscrimination provisions applied in *Lau* were boosted by the explicit link between language and race/national origin discrimination in the 1974 federal Equal Educational Opportunity Act, which provides

> No state shall deny equal educational opportunity to an individual on account of his or her race, color, sex, or national origin, by (f) the failure by an educational agency to take appropriate action to overcome language barriers that impede equal participation by its students in its instructional programs. (20 U.S.C. § 1703)

In the wake of the *Lau* decision until the early 1980s, the federal Office for Civil Rights implemented guidelines to impose bilingual education programs in hundreds of school districts with insufficient recognition of the needs of children with limited English proficiency. A federal court in New Mexico subsequently mandated bilingual education in a school district with a large Latino/a student body that had never applied for federal bilingual education funding despite the language barrier its students faced (*Serna v. Portales Municipal Schools*, 351 F. Supp. 1279 [D.N.M. 1972], aff'd, 499 F.2d 1147 [10th Cir. 1974]).

In recent years, however, both the federal government and some key states have adopted laws hostile to bilingual education. The No Child Left

Behind Act of 2001 replaced the Bilingual Education Act with an imperative to develop English-language skills that now requires LEP students to demonstrate yearly progress toward acquisition of English. Voters in the states of California, Arizona, and Massachusetts approved citizen initiatives to eradicate bilingual education (but Colorado voters rejected a similar proposition). For example, California's Proposition 227, adopted in 1998, lambasted the bilingual education model as "experimental language programs" whose "failure" prompted high drop-out rates and low English literacy of many immigrant children. This law requires classroom instruction in all California public schools to be overwhelmingly in English. LEP children must be placed in a temporary English immersion program with instruction in English, but with a curriculum designed for children who are learning English, with the sheltered immersion program not anticipated to exceed one year. The California initiative provides a parental waiver procedure, although it is burdensome and requires the parents to visit the school personally to apply for an annual waiver. In order for parents—likely LEP as well—to secure the waiver, schools may first require that children under age ten undergo a trial period in the English-language classroom and be certified as having physical, emotional, psychological, or educational needs requiring a non-English classroom program.

Court efforts to strike down the California initiative have been unsuccessful—in one federal lawsuit, teachers argued that the initiative restricted their constitutionally protected free speech by giving parents a private right of action to sue teachers who refuse to provide an English-language education. But in-classroom curriculum can be regulated freely by the state so long as it relates to legitimate educational goals. Thus, the court concluded the state could require teachers to teach in English. Although teachers have greater speech rights outside of classroom instruction, the court construed the California law to involve only "instruction" and "curriculum" and not to outlaw Spanish or other non-English languages in other circumstances, such as on the playground, in social settings, or in disciplining students (*California Teachers Association v. State Board of Education*, 271 F.3d 1141 [9th Cir. 2001]). The California law also withstood an equal protection challenge because the court found that racial animus did not motivate its passage (*Valeria v. Davis*, 307 F.3d 1036 [9th Cir. 2002]). Although the U.S. Constitution will not permit voters intentionally to discriminate against a protected class, the court failed to discern any agenda of discrimination on the face of this state law. Still, legislation mandating an English-only classroom, particularly where no exception is made for parental waivers, or where the waiver provision is unduly burdensome, might be suspect under never overruled Supreme Court precedent from 1923 that struck down Nebraska's English-only schooling law on due process grounds. Prompted by anti-German sentiment, that statute prohibited public and private schoolteachers from teaching languages other than English to students in the lower grades. A Nebraska schoolteacher was arrested and fined for offering German instruction during parochial school recess. The Supreme Court found the law did not promote a proper legislative purpose after concluding that the teacher's right to teach and the parents' right to engage him to teach their children fall within the due process guaranty of liberty (*Meyer v. Nebraska*, 262 U.S. 390 [1923]). Additionally, several years after the eradication of bilingual education by a state, it may also be possible to challenge English-only schooling as violating the federal Equal Educational Opportunity Act excerpted above by proof of deficiencies of non-English-speaking students in core academic skills apart from proficiency in English.

What Community Groups and You Can Do to Protect the Rights of Spanish-Speaking Students. States without legal prohibitions on bilingual education tend to decide at the local level whether to accommodate non-English-speaking students. Therefore, Latino/a parents might organize to ensure their school district adequately protects their children's right to learn English while at the same time respecting their Spanish-language culture in the classroom and on the playground. Spanish-speaking candidates also need to seek election or appointment to the school board that sets the local language policies.

Appendix

Resources on Latino/as and the No Child Left Behind Act

- *National Council of La Raza.* Hispanic civil rights and advocacy organization that tracks issues surrounding the No Child Left Behind Act and provides resources. NCLB-related content can be found at http://www.nclr.org/content/policy/detail/998/.
- *The Civil Rights Project/Proyecto Derechos Civiles.* Studies and provides information on several issues connected to the civil rights movement, including NCLB and segregation issues in the nation's schools; www.civilrightsproject.ucla.edu.
- *National Parent-School Partnership Program (Program of the Mexican American Legal Defense and Educational Fund).* Provides a training program for parents and others on several aspects of their children's education, including parent rights and responsibilities, the school structure, and leadership principles. Information on the program can be found on its website, www.maldef.org/psp/ or by calling 213-629-2512. Information on other programs of the Mexican American Legal Defense and Educational Fund can be found at www.maldef.org.

Resources on Affirmative Action and Access to Higher Education

- *Office for Civil Rights, U.S. Department of Education.* Investigates complaints about violations of federal civil rights laws in all schools and colleges that receive federal funding. Many of the Office for Civil Rights investigations are initiated by government agencies, but individuals can also file complaints with the office. Information about how to file a complaint, and the contact information for regional offices, is available at www.ed.gov/ocr. The central office in Washington, D.C., can be reached at 800-421-3481 or by e-mail at OCR@ed.gov.
- *Pew Hispanic Center.* Nonpartisan research organization that studies the role of Latino/as in the United States. Part of the organization's research focuses on education issues affecting Latino/as. See www.pew hispanic.org and click on the "education" link to access this research.
- *Hispanic Scholarship Fund Institute.* Organization that advocates for greater financial assistance for Latino/as to attend college. The institute was founded in 2001 with the goal of doubling the number of Hispanic college graduates by 2010. See www.hsfi.org.
- *The Hispanic Scholarship Fund.* A partner organization with the Hispanic Scholarship Fund Institute. The Hispanic Scholarship Fund is the nation's largest source of financial aid for Latino/as. See www.hsf.net.
- *The Hispanic National Bar Foundation.* The Hispanic National Bar Foundation (HNBF) has teamed up with Ford and the Hispanic Scholarship Fund to provide over $80,000 in scholarships for Hispanic students, including one earmarked for college students who are leaders in their communities and intend to pursue a law degree. The HNBF has partnered with the Princeton Review to provide this Bradshaw Scholarship to needy Hispanic students to enable them to participate in a Law School Admission Test preparation course. See www.hnbf.org. The telephone number to the office in Washington, D.C., is 202-496-7756.

Resources on Bilingual Education

National Association for Bilingual Education, http://www.nabe.org.
Issues in U.S. Language Policy: Bilingual Education, http://ourworld.compuserve.com/homepages/JWCRAWFORD/biling.htm.

Books

Crawford, James, and Stephen Krashen. *English Language Learners in American Classrooms: 100 Questions, 100 Answers.* New York: Scholastic Teaching Resources, 2007.

Notes

1. Charles R. Calleros, "Law, Policy, and Strategies for Affirmative Action Admissions in Higher Education," *Cal. W. L. Rev.* 43 (2006): 151, 152 (noting that private institutions that receive federal aid are subject to Title VI of the Civil Rights Act of 1964, that 42 U.S.C. § 1981 prohibits racial discrimination in contracts between schools and students, and that admissions policies that pass constitutional muster will also likely survive scrutiny under both of these laws).

2. One exception is the mandatory provision of information to the Department of Homeland Security and the Department of State about students with nonimmigrant student visas under the Student and Exchange Visitor Information System (SEVIS). See, e.g., http://www.ice.gov/graphics/sevis/.

3. The Family Educational Rights and Privacy Act (FERPA) (20 U.S.C. § 1232g) barred schools from supplying information to any organization, including immigration agencies, about a student's undocumented status absent parental approval (20 U.S.C.A. § 1232g[b]). After September 11, 2001, Congress passed the U.S. Patriot Act, which created an exception to the FERPA provision, allowing the attorney general or the assistant attorney general to seek court approval to collect otherwise private education records of undocumented students without parental consent. However, the act required certification that the information was relevant to an investigation or prosecution involving terrorism (Patriot Act, § 444).

4. For example, in 2005, the anti-immigrant group, the Federation for American Immigration Reform (FAIR), published a report titled "Breaking the Piggy Bank: How Illegal Immigration Is Sending Schools to the Red," available at www .fairus.org/site/PageServer?pagename=research-researchf6ad. The report alleged that undocumented immigration has more than doubled the cost of public education, causing severe deficits and lowering the availability of services and quality of public school education.

7
Voting Rights

The right to vote is critical to the functioning of a representative democracy. Our republican form of government is based on the principle of consent of the governed. This consent is manifested every time a vote is cast. Most importantly, since elected representatives formulate our governmental policies, voting becomes an indispensable part of selecting representatives who will deliberate and enact legislation that serves the particularized needs of a given community. Such a political process also results in the creation of leadership within the Latino/a community. Given the substantial disparity between Latino/as and the white majority in the areas of economic development, educational attainment, and other socioeconomic indexes, there is a need for leadership that will be responsive to the particularized needs of the Latino/a community. Absent such leadership, the creation of opportunities for advancement within the Latino/a community will be diminished—to the detriment of all of us.

Barriers to Effective Political Participation

The federal Voting Rights Act of 1965 was instrumental in eliminating the more blatant barriers that prevented African Americans from registering to vote. With subsequent amendments in 1975, the act required certain jurisdictions to institute a bilingual election process to provide election materials in a language accessible to Latino/as, Asian Americans, and Native Americans. In 2006 Congress reauthorized and amended certain provisions of the act until the year 2032. Despite this reauthorization, there are still barriers that prevent Latino/as from effective participation in the political process. Perhaps the most significant is the citizenship requirement as a prerequisite to voting. Under our system of government, a state can establish requirements for voting as long as there are no infringements upon any federally protected interests. Presently, most states have state constitutional provisions limiting the right to vote to just U.S. citizens. In some states, such as Maryland, however, certain cities can establish their own voting qualifications and have eliminated the citizenship requirement for voting in municipal elections.

The issue of noncitizen voting is the future civil rights issue of Latino/as. According to the 2000 census, the noncitizen adult population is increasing in many communities across the country. The following represent the percentage of noncitizen adults to the adult population for selected municipalities: Miami, Florida—39.2 percent; Los Angeles, California—32.5 percent; New York City—22.9 percent; Houston, Texas—22.9 percent; and Chicago, Illinois—16.4 percent. In California, there are over 85 municipalities with at least a 25 percent noncitizen adult population ranging from 25.1 percent for the city of Montebello to 63.5 percent for the city of San Joaquin. At this juncture, perhaps the most realistic avenue for eliminating the citizenship prerequisite for voting is through the local initiative process.

Apart from the citizenship voting qualification, the next major obstacle confronting Latino/as is an English-only election process. It was not until the passage of the 1965 Voting Rights Act that meaningful efforts were undertaken to provide an electoral process that was not exclusively English-only. Section 4e of the act prohibited states from requiring a person who had completed the sixth grade in an American flag school where the predominant language of instruction was a language other than English to "read, write, understand, or interpret any matter in the English language" in order to vote (42 U.S.C. § 1973b[e]). This section applied primarily to Puerto Ricans residing in the northeastern part of the United States and was used effectively to establish an election process that was more accessible to Spanish-speaking Latino/a voters. Moreover, the experiences in enforcing Section 4e provided the foundation for the subsequent adoption of the language assistance provisions of the 1975 amendments to the Voting Rights Act.

In 1975 Congress amended the act to require a bilingual election process in covered jurisdictions.[1] When subject to the bilingual election requirements, a covered jurisdiction must implement an election process completely accessible to limited English-proficient (LEP) Latino/as. Such a process includes voter registration, information materials, and ballots printed in Spanish. In addition, the covered jurisdiction should conduct community outreach efforts to register LEP Latino/a eligible voters and provide them election related information.

These federal bilingual election requirements have been instrumental in providing access to limited English-proficient Latino/a voters. However, the effectiveness of these provisions has not been realized. Many jurisdictions simply do not comply with these federal requirements. Accordingly, the U.S. Department of Justice has filed enforcement actions from the 1970s to 2006 in Arizona, California, Florida, Massachusetts, New Jersey, New Mexico, New York, Pennsylvania, Utah, and Washington. These actions have in many instances resulted in fairly comprehensive consent decrees requiring bilingual election materials, bilingual oral assistance at the polling places, and community outreach efforts to Latino/a communities.

Other barriers prevent effective participation of Latino/as in the political process. Varying from state to state, some laws prevent convicted felons from voting while serving a sentence, on parole, or on probation. A recent study concluded that "significant numbers of Latino/as are prohibited from voting by felony disenfranchisement laws."[2] Efforts to challenge these laws on the grounds that they violate the federal Voting Rights Act have not been successful.

A similar discriminatory effect is found in the prohibition barring Puerto Ricans residing in the Puerto Rican islands from voting in presidential elections and from voting for a congressperson or a U.S. Senator. Although U.S. citizens, their voting privileges for these federal offices do not vest until these Puerto Ricans change their residency to one of the fifty states. Once in the states, Puerto Ricans are entitled to all voting privileges and are also protected by the Voting Rights Act from participating in English-only elections. However, based upon the 2000 census, there are 2,716,509 Latino/as who are eighteen years and older residing in Puerto Rico. Such a large number represents the largest concentration of Latino/as in the U.S. and its territories that are disenfranchised.

The barriers described above prevent Latino/as from participating in the political process. However, even when Latino/as are permitted to vote in national, state, and local elections, there are methods of elections and devices that serve to minimize the impact of their vote. The next section will focus on how the electoral process can dilute the voting strength of Latino/a communities and deny them an equal opportunity to participate in the political process and elect candidates of their choice.

Dilution of Latino/a Voting Strength

Dilution of Latino/a voting strength occurs by a method of election that enhances the adverse effect of racially polarized voting to determine the outcome of an election. Racially polarized voting occurs when different racial and ethnic groups vote differently. Such voting patterns can dilute Latino/a voting strength in at-large methods of elections or in election districts that overconcentrate or fragment politically cohesive Latino/a communities.

In an at-large method of election, every voter in the jurisdiction votes for governing board members. In a typical system, a city could be governed by a five-member city council. The city council members are elected citywide. The city council members do not have to reside in any particular area of the city and all of the voters can cast a vote for each office that is the subject of the election. If we assume that all five council members are elected at the same time, then the voter would vote for five candidates. The top five candidates with the most votes are elected. Such an election system is often referred to as an at-large method of election with plurality voting. Under such a system there is no runoff. The candidates receiving the most votes are elected to office even if the candidate does not receive a majority of the votes.

In an at-large method of election with plurality voting, if Latino/a voters are a numerical minority and there are high levels of racially polarized voting, then the candidates preferred by Latino/a voters will be defeated. Such experiences have been well documented by federal court cases considering challenges to at-large methods of election filed pursuant to Section 2 of the Voting Rights Act. Section 2 applies nationwide and permits challenges to any standard, practice, or procedure that based upon a totality of circumstances denies Latino/as, or any minority, an equal opportunity to participate in the political process and elect candidates of their choice.

In the hypothetical at-large method of election described above, Latino/a voters can minimize the dilutive impact by avoiding fielding more Latino/a preferred candidates than there are available vacancies and concentrating their votes on these candidates. However, such an election strategy only works if there are more credible non-Latino/a preferred candidates than there are available vacancies. Only if non-Latino/a voters split their votes among the non-Latino/a candidates can this strategy result in the success of the Latino/a preferred candidates. Such a strategy is often referred to as concentrated, bullet, or single-shot voting. To counter such a strategy, the reigning political power establishment often devises several counterstrategies.

The first strategy usually consists of staggering the terms of the offices. Instead of having all five city council members elected at the same time, the terms are staggered so that two are elected in one election cycle and three are elected in another election cycle. In such a manner the opportunity for splitting the non-Latino/a vote can be minimized and concomitantly the opportunity for maximizing the effect of single-shot voting by Latino/a voters is also minimized. A second strategy is to implement numbered places or numbered posts that are assigned to each elected position. In such an election system, elections are still conducted citywide. However, the candidates must file for a particular office. In this manner incumbent officeholders do not have to compete with each other. The impact on Latino/a voters can be dramatic. Now, a Latino/a preferred candidate must file for a particular office and run against a particular non-Latino/a preferred candidate, usually an incumbent. The adoption of designated places produces a head-to-head contest that serves to disadvantage a numerical minority of Latino/a voters. A third countermeasure may be utilized: the majority vote requirement. If none of the candidates receives a majority of the vote, then there is a runoff between the two candidates receiving the most votes. Thus, the election becomes a contest between one Latino/a preferred candidate and one non-Latino/a pre-ferred candidate where Latino/a voters are a numerical minority and there are significant patterns of racially polarized voting.

Another device used in conjunction with at-large methods of elections that is the functional equivalent of a numbered place system is the use of candidate residency districts. In this method of election, the candidates must reside in a particular district. The district is utilized only for purposes of limiting the number of candidates to a seat assigned to the residency district. Thus, instead of having numbered places assigned to particular offices, there would be a candidate residency district designated by a number that would be assigned to a particular office. Candidates residing in that residency district would then be selected by an at-large method of election or citywide. If the candidates in a given candidate residency district did not achieve a majority of the votes cast then a majority vote requirement could be implemented to determine the successful candidate. Again, if there are patterns of racially polarized voting, a candidate residency district system would have the potential of diluting Latino/a voting strength.

The dilutive effects of at-large methods of election can be minimized by the establishment of election districts or by adopting a method of election where voters can either cast all of their votes for a given candidate or rank their candidate preferences. With respect to district elections within the context of racially polarized voting patterns, Latino/as would have greater access to the political process when they constitute a majority of the voters within an election district. As a majority of the voters, their preferred candidates would receive most of the votes and be declared to be the successful candidate. Clearly if elections are characterized by racially polarized voting, Latino/as would fare better under a district election system where they would constitute 60 percent of the electorate than under an at-large method of election where they would constitute 30 percent of the electorate.

Although district-based election systems can work to the advantage of Latino/a voters, district elections can also discriminate against Latino/a voting strength. This discrimination is accomplished by either drawing district election boundaries that divide politically cohesive Latino/a voting communities or by drawing the boundaries so that Latino/a voters are overconcentrated into one district. A dilutive fragmentation occurs when the boundaries split a predominantly Latino/a community with the resulting effect that Latino/a electoral influence is minimized in each of the election districts. If the election district boundaries were drawn in such a manner that Latino/as constituted a majority of the voters in the district, then Latino/a voters would have a greater opportunity to elect candidates of their choice. In sharp contrast, if the election district boundaries overconcentrate Latino/a voters into one district with the resulting effect that two or more Latino/a voter majority districts could be created if the lines were readjusted, then the redistricting plan will have a discriminatory effect on Latino/a voting strength. In both of these examples, there is a dilution of Latino/a voting strength. This dilution is caused by the presence of racially polarized voting.

Another method for minimizing the effect of at-large methods of elections is through cumulative voting or transferable vote systems. In a cumulative voting system, the elections are still conducted on an at-large basis; however, the voter can cast all of their votes for one or more candidates. For example, if there are three vacancies in an election contest, the voters can usually vote for three persons. In a plurality at-large method of election, the three candidates receiving the most votes will be elected. In a cumulative voting system the voter can cast all three of their votes in favor of a single candidate. This concentrated voting can result in the election of Latino/a candidates. In a transferable voting system, the votes are ranked according to a preference. Although a voter's first preference may not be elected, there is a possibility that the voter's second and third preferences may be successful.

As outlined above, a fairly drawn redistricting plan or the adoption of an alternative form of elections can ameliorate the discriminatory effects of racially polarized voting. However, converting from an at-large method of election to district elections or a cumulative voting system is usually not a voluntary action by the governing body. Such a change will often translate into the loss of political power for governing board members. Consequently, there are usually only two meaningful routes available for Latino/a communities to compel such a conversion: one is through the local initiative process, the other is through litigation.

The local initiative process can be successful even if Latino/as constitute a numerical minority of the voters residing within a jurisdiction. In some communities, there may be significant numbers of non-Latino/a voters who desire local neighborhood representation and thus can participate in a political coalition seeking a dismantling of an at-large method of election. The local initiative process will usually require the collection of signatures of registered voters on a petition requesting that a measure to change the method of election be placed on a ballot for voter approval. However, if the patterns of racially polarized voting are significant, then the possibility of pursuing a change through the local initiative process is minimal.

The next avenue is litigation. There are two options for local Latino/a communities to challenge discriminatory at-large methods of elections. The first option consists of utilizing Section 2 of the Voting Rights Act (42 U.S.C. § 1973). The second option consists of using any state legislation that might enable Latino/as to challenge discriminatory election systems that dilute Latino/a voting strength. Under Section 2, the burden is on the Latino/a community to demonstrate that based upon the totality of circumstances, a given election system operates to deny Latino/as an equal opportunity to participate in the political process and elect candidates of their choice. A variety of devices can function to dilute Latino/a voting strength or deny them equal access to the political process.

As discussed above the device that has the most significant impact in diluting Latino/a voting strength is the at-large method of election. Pursuant to Section 2, Latino/as are not required to demonstrate the presence of a discriminatory intent. Rather, the burden is to demonstrate that the election structure has a discriminatory effect on Latino/a voting strength. Apart from having to prove a variety of evidentiary factors such as a history of discrimination touching upon the right to vote, Latino/a plaintiffs would have to demonstrate that a hypothetical election district can be created that consists of a 50 percent or more Latino/a population base. Once this threshold is met, then elections must be examined to assess the degree of any racially polarized voting. In addition, the extent of Latino/a electoral success must be ascertained. These are then the basic elements to determine whether there is a potential Section 2 violation. To maximize the most efficient use of limited resources, the first factor a local Latino/a community should assess is the extent of minority electoral success. If Latino/a candidates are not successful in elections, then the first threshold has been met. Second, if an analysis of elections shows that Latino/a voters support the Latino/a candidate over the non-Latino/a candidate, and, correspondingly, the non-Latino/a voters support the non-Latino/a candidates, then these elections are probably characterized by racially polarized voting patterns. A preliminary assessment to determine the existence of these voting patterns consists of examining the most heavily concentrated Latino/a voting precincts and the most heavily concentrated non-Latino/a voting precincts to determine if their first preferences are different. If these preferences are different, then the second factor has been met. The third factor consists of performing a demographic analysis to construct a hypothetical geographic compact election district that contains a 50 percent Latino/a eligible voter population threshold. If these three conditions are met, then there is a high probability that there is a potential Section 2 violation. Once these preliminary thresholds are met, then a complete analysis involving all of the factors comprising the totality of circumstances can be undertaken and a decision whether to proceed with a Section 2 case can be made.

Another litigation avenue to protect Latino/a voting rights is state legislation that permits actions filed in state court to address claims of voter dilution. To date only one state has such a statute. In 2002, California adopted the California Voting Rights Act (California Elections Code §§ 14025–14032). That act only applies to challenges to at-large methods of election. As previously noted, at-large elections are the most prevalent system of elections utilized by local governments. In California, a substantial number of municipalities, school districts, and special election districts utilize an at-large method of election to elect members of their governing boards. The state act is a substantial improvement over Section 2 of the federal Voting Rights Act from the perspective of the Latino/a community that seeks to challenge such an election system on the grounds that it dilutes Latino/a voting strength.

First, the state act does not require proof of an ability to create a hypothetical district that contains a majority of Latino/a eligible voters. Second, the state act does not require proof of evidentiary factors such as a history of discrimination touching upon the right to vote, racial appeals in campaigns, and the presence of a candidate slating group that excludes Latino/a candidates. Third, the only requirement under the state act is the demonstration of racially polarized voting that dilutes the opportunity of protected classes to participate in the electoral process and elect candidates of their choice or to influence the outcome of an election. If there are no elections where Latino/as sought elective office, elections involving state and local propositions and measures can be utilized to assess whether elections are characterized by racially polarized voting. Fourth, and most significantly, a case lost by the Latino/a claimants is not subject to any assessment of case expenses known as costs. Unless the case is deemed by the court to be frivolous, unreasonable, or without foundation, the state act does not authorize a winning governmental entity to collect these expenses from claimants that were not successful. Under the federal Section 2 statute, governmental jurisdictions successful in defending their method of election are entitled to recover their costs from the parties initiating the action. These costs can amount to tens of thousands of dollars and can discourage potential plaintiffs from filing an action in federal court.

Section 5 Preclearance

Another protection available only in certain areas of the country involves Section 5 of the federal Voting Rights Act (42 U.S.C. § 1973c), which has been the most effective civil rights law ever enacted by Congress. Section 5 has prevented the implementation of hundreds of voting changes with the potential of discriminating against minority voting strength. Section 5 requires covered jurisdictions to secure federal approval before any voting change can be implemented in elections. The initial 1965 act triggering formula was designed to reach jurisdictions in the South that had engaged in voting discrimination against African Americans. As a result of the 1965 triggering formula only certain states in the South and a small number of other jurisdictions across the country were subject to the Section 5 approval requirements. The next major expansion occurred in 1975 when the triggering formula incorporated an English-only election process in jurisdictions meeting certain criteria. This expanded formula resulted in the coverage of the states of Texas and Arizona and several counties in California.

Under Section 5 a covered jurisdiction is required to submit any voting change enacted after a certain date to either the U.S. Attorney General for administrative approval or preclearance, or to secure judicial preclearance from the U.S. District Court for the District of Columbia. The burden is on the submitting jurisdiction to demonstrate the proposed voting change does not diminish the ability of a minority community to elect a candidate of their choice and that the proposed voting change was not adopted pursuant to an intent to diminish the ability of minority voters to elect candidates of their choice. If a covered jurisdiction cannot secure the requisite Section 5 approval, the voting change cannot be implemented in any elections. Since seeking administrative approval or preclearance from the U.S. Attorney General is less expensive, most of the voting changes are submitted first to the attorney general. If the attorney general concludes that the covered jurisdiction has not met its Section 5 obligation, the attorney general interposes an objection, functionally equivalent to a federal court order, preventing the covered jurisdiction from implementing the voting change in any election.

Section 5 covers any and all changes affecting the right to vote. Changes affecting candidate qualifications; voter registration procedures; the conversion to a bilingual election process; locations of voting precincts; the boundaries of voting precincts; the boundaries of election districts; the boundaries of governmental entities through annexations or deannexations; conversions from district elections to at-large methods of elections or vice versa; the adoption or elimination of majority vote requirements; the adoption or elimination of numbered places; qualifications for independent candidates; the staggering of election terms; the dates of elections; the length of term of office; the elimination of an elected position and the adoption of an appointments system or vice versa; the qualification and placement of initiatives, propositions or measures on the ballot; and the design of ballots, among others, are required to be submitted for Section 5 approval and review.

The impact of Section 5 on Latino/a political empowerment has been dramatic. During the time period from 1965 to July 24, 2004, 223 letters of objection were issued by the U.S. Attorney General against the states of Arizona (21), California (6), New Mexico (1), and Texas (195). A substantial number of these letters of objection involved voting changes affecting the Latino/a community. For example, as noted in a report to Congress, Section 5 prevented the implementation in Texas of a variety of potentially discriminatory changes affecting voting:

- Discriminatory use of numbered posts and staggered terms that ensure that a majority—or even plurality—of non-Hispanic white voters continue to be overrepresented in elected offices.
- Discriminatory implementation of majority vote and/or runoff requirements.
- Polling place or election date changes that deny minorities equal voting opportunities.
- Discriminatory absentee voting practices.
- Discriminatory annexations or deannexations.

- Dissolution of single-member districts, reductions in the number of offices, or revocation of voting rules when minority candidates of choice are about to be elected to office.
- Election procedures that violate Section 203 of the Voting Rights Act.
- Discriminatory redistricting practices that deny minorities an equal opportunity to elect their candidates of choice.[3]

The significance of these letters of objection cannot be overemphasized. Without this Section 5 procedure, Latino/a voters would have had to initiate close to 300 lawsuits challenging all of the voting changes included within these letters of objection. In a traditional lawsuit based on Section 2, the burden is on the Latino/a plaintiffs to demonstrate that a proposed voting change was either adopted pursuant to a discriminatory purpose or had a discriminatory effect on Latino/a voting strength. With Section 5 preclearance, the burden of proof is reversed. The covered jurisdiction has to affirmatively demonstrate that the proposed voting change was not adopted pursuant to a discriminatory purpose and does not have a discriminatory effect on Latino/a voting strength.

In those jurisdictions subject to the Section 5 preclearance requirements, Latino/as must first be aware that a voting change has occurred. Sometimes the voting changes encompass significant changes that are reported in the local media. This type of change may involve a modification to election districts (redistricting) and changes affecting the method of election. However, other changes are not publicized and often are not known until the day of the election. These changes may involve a reduction in the number of polling places. When the voting change is submitted for Section 5 approval the U.S. Department of Justice (DOJ) includes this submission on its website (http://www.usdoj.gov/crt/voting/overview.htm#vra). Typically there is a sixty-day time period for local communities to provide comments to the proposed voting change. These comments have in the past played a critical role in securing a letter of objection.

What Community Groups Can Do to Protect Section 5 Rights. For those instances where the covered jurisdiction does not submit the voting change and the public is not aware that such a voting change has occurred, there are various actions local Latino/a communities can take. First, the Latino/a community, pursuant to state public record laws, can request copies of any documents relating to changes affecting voting. The request can reference the federal regulations governing the application of Section 5. These regulations list the type of changes affecting voting that must be submitted for Section 5 approval (28 C.F.R. § 51.13). Once the information is received, it can be reviewed and forwarded to the DOJ to determine if any voting changes listed in the information provided have been submitted for Section

5 approval. Second, if there is a suspected voting change, the DOJ can be notified. The DOJ can then investigate to determine whether in fact such a voting change has occurred. Third, members of the local Latino/a community can review actions taken by the governing board of the covered jurisdiction to determine if any ordinances, resolutions, or other actions involve changes affecting voting. If such changes are found, they can be forwarded to the DOJ for additional review and possible compliance action. In addition, an action can be filed in either federal or state court to require the covered jurisdiction to comply with Section 5. If such compliance is not forthcoming prior to an election, Latino/a plaintiffs can secure an injunction prohibiting local election officials from implementing the voting change in the upcoming election.

Invisible Government Boards

A major obstacle to Latino/a political empowerment consists of the nearly invisible special election districts. These special election districts range from water districts, mosquito abatement and vector control districts, to hospital districts, among others. Many of these districts do not conduct elections because no candidates file for office. If no one is aware of the presence of these special election districts and no one is aware that the governing board is an elective body then for all practical purposes these districts remain invisible to local communities. Such invisibility prevents any meaningful public oversight, thereby precluding any public accountability.

These special election districts are especially important to Latino/a communities. First, these districts have taxing authority and can collect taxes from Latino/a communities. Second, these districts enact resolutions and policies that have a direct bearing on the well-being of a Latino/a community. For example, water districts could adopt regulations that could significantly improve the water quality of farming communities. In these communities the drinking water may be derived from underground water contaminated with pesticide and fertilizer residue. Third, these districts hire personnel. Having public accountability could result in a diverse workforce. Fourth, these districts often award contracts for construction projects and the rendition of services. These contracts could be awarded to Latino/a businesses. Fifth, the elective boards of these special election districts can serve as an entry point for the development of Latino/a elected political leadership. This political leadership often serves as the training ground for other elective city, school district, state legislative, and federal congressional offices.

For these reasons, local Latino/a communities should determine whether these special districts exist within their county or other regional form of government and whether an elected governing board governs these special districts. Usually the county or other regional form of governments will have information on these districts. Another source for this information can be found in the governmental department that conducts elections. A review of previous election returns for the past ten years will reveal elections for special election districts. Also, there may be a regional agency that requires certain governmental actions by special election districts to be approved by the regional agency before the actions can be finalized. These regional agencies are usually required by state law to keep this information archived. For example, in California, there are Local Area Formation Commissions that require cities and special election districts meeting certain criteria to submit any modification to the district's boundary for approval. These modifications involve annexations and deannexations that change the boundaries of the special election district. A review of the approvals by this commission will reveal the existence of special election districts. Finally, since most of these special election districts have the authority to assess taxes and fees, the tax assessor either at the state level or at the regional level should have a list of these special election districts. Once the list is obtained, the special districts can be contacted to determine whether their governing body is elected or appointed. Armed with this information, local Latino/a communities can then strategize to target these jurisdictions for electoral campaigns. Since governmental agencies usually do not keep this information in a centralized location, local Latino/a communities will need to engage in aggressive efforts to ferret out this information. Only by engaging in a proactive strategy to secure this basic information on special election districts will these important governmental entities lose their cloak of invisibility and become a critical component of a local Latino/a community's effort to politically empower their communities.

Appendix

For securing information on the protection of the right to vote as it affects Latino/as there are governmental agencies, civil rights organizations, and members of the private bar.

Governmental Agencies

For a comprehensive overview of the existing federal laws that protect the right to vote visit the website for the Voting Section, Civil Rights Division, United States Department of Justice: http://www.usdoj.gov/crt/voting/overview.htm#vra.

For additional information regarding applicable state laws that affect the right to vote and general election information visit the websites for the individual secretaries of state and those governmental entities that conduct local elections. For example, in California go to http://www.sos.ca.gov/elections/elections.htm. For Los Angeles County, California, go to http://regrec.co.la.ca.us/.

Civil Rights Organizations

The premier Latino/a civil rights litigation organization is the Mexican American Legal Defense and Educational Fund (MALDEF). The organization has been litigating voting rights cases on behalf of the Latino/a community since the early 1970s. These cases have ranged from challenging discriminatory methods of election that dilute minority voting strength, to enforcement of the special provisions of the federal Voting Rights Act, and to the removal of obstacles that deny the Latino/a community equal access to the political process; visit http://www.maldef.org/index.cfm.

Another organization engaged extensively in litigation to protect the right to vote has been the League of United Latin American Citizens (LULAC). The organization and its local chapters have served as plaintiffs in numerous voting rights cases across the country. For example, the San Benito County and Monterey County, California, local chapters have been at the forefront of protecting the right to vote in Northern California. In addition, local chapters in Texas have also participated as plaintiffs in many voting rights cases. See http://www.lulac.org/civicparticipation.html.

An organization that represents the interests of Latino/a elected officials and has an excellent research component is the National Association of Latino/a Elected and Appointed Officials (NALEO; http://www.naleo .org/). Although the organization is not engaged in litigation, it works on legislative advocacy efforts to advance the voting rights interests of the Latino/a community and has a national network of elected officials that have a vested interest in making the electoral process more accessible to Latino/a voters.

In the area of voter registration and voter participation there are the Southwest Voter Registration and Education Project, http://www.svrep.org/, and the William C. Velasquez Research Institute, http://www.wcvi.org/. The Southwest Voter Registration and Education Project has been directly responsible for increasing voter registration and participation rates within the Latino/a community across the country. The William C. Velasquez Research Institute has been involved in many research efforts that document the levels of voter registration and voter turnout rates among Latino/a voters.

Some states have other organizations involved in litigation and advocacy efforts in the political access area. For example in California there is the Lawyers Committee for Civil Rights of the San Francisco Bay Area: http://www.lccr.com/. This organization has been involved in numerous voting rights cases filed pursuant to the federal Voting Rights Act, including actions challenging discriminatory at-large methods of election that dilute

Latino/a voting strength and are filed under the California State Voting Rights Act of 2001. In addition, the Mexican American Political Association (MAPA), http://www.mapa.org, has served as a plaintiff in numerous voting rights actions in California. These cases have ranged from challenging discriminatory at-large elections that dilute Latino/a voting strength to enforcement of the special provisions of the federal Voting Rights Act.

Private Attorneys

Private attorneys in Texas and California have played a critical role in the enforcement of the federal Voting Rights Act and the California State Voting Rights of 2001. Although there is no formal listing of these attorneys, information regarding these attorneys can be secured through MALDEF or LULAC.

Additional Reading

For an excellent overview of the right to vote in the United States, see Alexander Keyssar, *The Right to Vote: The Contested History of Democracy in the United States* (New York: Basic Books, 2000).

For a comprehensive review of voting rights litigation up to the early 1970s, see Armand Derfner, "Racial Discrimination and the Right to Vote," *Vand. L. Rev.* 26 (1973): 523.

For articles discussing the issue of a language other than English in the electoral process, see James Thomas Tucker and Rodolfo Espino, "Government Effectiveness and Efficiency? The Minority Language Assistance Provisions of the VRA," *Tex. J. on C.L. & C.R.* 12 (2007): 163; Jocelyn Friedrichs Benson, "Su Voto Es Su Voz! Incorporating Voters of Limited English Proficiency into American Democracy," *B.C. L. Rev.* 48 (2007): 251; Lupe S. Salinas, "Linguaphobia, Language Rights, and the Right of Privacy," *Stan. J. Civ. Rts. & Civ. Liberties* 3 (2007): 53; JoNel Newman, "Ensuring that Florida's Language Minorities Have Access to the Ballot," *Stetson L. Rev.* 36 (2007): 329; James Thomas Tucker, "Enfranchising Language Minority Citizens: The Bilingual Election Provisions of the Voting Rights Act," *N.Y.U. J. Legis. & Pub. Pol'y* 10 (2006–2007): 195; Terry M. Ao, "When the Voting Rights Act Became Un-American: The Misguided Vilification of Section 203," *Ala. L. Rev.* 58 (2006): 377.

For articles discussing the impact of redistricting on the Latino/a community in Texas, see Symposium, "Drawing Lines in the Sand: The Texas Latino/a Community and Redistricting," *Tex. Hisp. J.L. & Pol'y* 6 (2001): 1.

For an article discussing the merging of remedies to address minority vote dilution claims and election administration issues, see Joaquin G. Avila, "The Washington 2004 Gubernatorial Election Crisis: The Necessity of Restoring Public Confidence in the Electoral Process," *Seattle U. L. Rev.* 29 (2005): 313.

For articles dealing with Latino/as and Section 5 of the Voting Rights Act, see Alvaro Bedoya, "The Unforeseen Effects of *Georgia v. Ashcroft* on the Latino Community," *Yale L.J.* 115 (2006): 2112; Juan Cartagena, "Latinos and Section 5 of the Voting Rights Act: Beyond Black and White," *Nat'l Black L.J.* 18 (2004–2005): 201; Victor Andres Rodríguez, "Section 5 of the Voting Rights Act of 1965 After Boerne: The Beginning of the End of Preclearance?" *Cal. L. Rev.* 91 (2003): 769. For an article involving the impact of proposed legislation on Latino/a voter turnout, see Alvaro Bedoya, "Backlash at the Booth: Latino Turnout After H.R. 4437," *Yale L.J.* 115 (2006): 116.

For a comprehensive annotated bibliography, see Terrye Conroy, "The Voting Rights Act of 1965: A Selected Annotated Bibliography," *Law Libr. J.* 98 (2006): 663. For a comprehensive article on cases filed pursuant to Section 2 of the federal Voting Rights Act, see Ellen Katz, Margaret Aisenbrey, Anna Baldwin, Emma Cheuse, and Anna Weisbrodt, "Documenting Discrimination in Voting: Judicial Findings Under Section 2 of the Voting Rights Act Since 1982, Final Report of the Voting Rights Initiative, University of Michigan Law School," *U. Mich. J.L. Reform* 39 (2006): 643. For articles involving the issue of noncitizen voting, see Joaquin Avila, "Political Apartheid in California: Consequences of Excluding a Growing Noncitizen Population," UCLA Chicano Studies Research Center, Latino Policy and Issues Brief No. 9, Los Angeles, Calif., Dec. 2003, http://www.chicano.ucla.edu/press/siteart/LPIB_09Dec2003.pdf; Tara Kini, "Comment: Sharing the Vote: Noncitizens' Voting Rights in Local School Board Elections," *Cal. L. Rev.* 93 (2005): 271; Gabriela Evia, "Consent by All the Governed: Reenfranchising Noncitizens as Partners in America's Democracy," *S. Cal. L. Rev.* 77 (2003): 151.

For articles focusing on the disenfranchisement of Latino/a felons, see Marisa J. Demeo and Steven A. Ochoa, "Diminished Voting Power in the Latino Community: The Impact of Felony Disenfranchisement Laws in Ten Targeted States," Mexican American Legal Defense and Educational Fund (2003); Damian J. Martinez, "Felony Disenfranchisement and Voting Participation: Considerations in Latino Ex-Prisoner Reentry," *Colum. Hum. Rts. L. Rev.* 36 (2004): 217. For an article focusing on the necessity for a diverse judiciary, see Kevin R. Johnson and Luis Fuentes-Rohwer, "A Principled Approach to the Quest for Racial Diversity on the Judiciary," *Mich. J. Race & L.* 10 (2004): 5. For a discussion regarding the potential of Latino/a voter coalitions with other racial and ethnic groups, see Sylvia R. Lazos Vargas, "The Latina/o and APIA Vote Post-2000: What Does It Mean to Move Beyond "Black and White" Politics?" *Or. L. Rev.* 81 (2002): 783. For an article dealing with the political implications of providing Mexican citizens in the United States with dual nationalities, see Jorge A. Vargas, "Dual Nationality for Mexicans," *San Diego L. Rev.* 35 (1998): 823. For an article touching on the difficulties encountered in a redistricting plan in accommodating two or more racial or ethnic groups, see Deborah Ramirez, "Forging a Latino Identity," *La Raza L.J.* 9 (1996): 61. See also

Steven Bender, Sylvia R. Lazos Vargas, and Keith Aoki, "Race and the California Recall: A Top Ten List of Ironies," *Berkeley La Raza L.J.* 16 (2005): 11; Jonathan Nagler and R. Michael Alvarez, "Latinos, Anglos, Voters, Candidates, and Voting Rights," *U. Pa. L. Rev.* 153 (2004): 393.

Sampling of Congressional Testimony

When the Voting Rights Act was amended in 1975, 1982, 1992, and 2006, there was extensive testimony presented by various organizations and individuals attesting to the persistent and pervasive presence of voting discrimination against Latino/as. The various congressional reports document this voting discrimination: 1975, Senate Report 94-295 (Public Law 94-73); 1982, Senate Report 94-417 (Public Law 97-205); 1992, House Report 102-655 (Public Law 102-344); 2006, House Report 109-478 (Public Law 109-246).

Notes

1. Generally, a jurisdiction is subject to the bilingual election requirements under two provisions of the Voting Rights Act: Section 203, 42 U.S.C. § 1973aa-1a, and Section 4(f)(4), 42 U.S.C. § 1973b(f)(4). Under Section 203, a jurisdiction is subject to the bilingual election requirements of Section 203, "if more than 5 percent of the voting age citizens are members of a single-language minority group who do not 'speak or understand English adequately enough to participate in the electoral process' and if the rate of those citizens who have not completed the fifth grade is higher than the national rate of voting age citizens who have not completed the fifth grade." Under Section 4(f)(4), a jurisdiction is subject to the bilingual election requirements if "(1) over five percent of the voting age citizens were, on November 1, 1972, members of a single language minority group, more than 5 percent of the voting age citizens on November 1, 1972, consisted of members of a single language minority group, (2) registration and elections were provided only in English on November 1, 1972, and (3) fewer than 50 percent of the voting-age citizens were registered to vote or voted in the 1972 Presidential election," 28 C.F.R. § 55.5. For a listing of jurisdictions subject to the bilingual election requirements of Section 4(f)(4), see 28 C.F.R. Appendix to Part 55. The term *language minority group* includes persons of Spanish heritage or Latino/as.

2. Mexican American Legal Defense and Educational Fund, "Diminished Voting Power in the Latino Community: The Impact of Felony Disenfranchisement Laws in Ten Targeted States" (December 2003).

3. Nina Perales, Luis Figueroa, and Criselda G. Rivas, *Voting Rights in Texas, 1982–2006*, A Report of RenewTheVRA.org, (June 2006): 14–15.

8
Criminal Justice System

Racial Profiling

Most Latino/as expect that their "Latino/a" appearance is likely to get them noticed by police or immigration officials. If you look "Mexican" or "foreign," for example, the immigration official or customs agent might decide to ask you a few more questions when you return from a trip abroad or are passing through an immigration checkpoint. But can the same immigration official also stop you as you walk the streets of your neighborhood to ask you for your immigration status? And what if the person who stops you in the street is not an immigration agent but a police officer who decides that your youthful Latino/a appearance might mean you are a gang member? And is it legal when police disproportionately stop Latino/as when they drive and search their cars for drugs?

The answer to these questions depends on several factors. The Fourth Amendment to the U.S. Constitution generally prohibits racial profiling in law enforcement. However, the definition of racial profiling is narrow and courts have permitted law enforcement to engage in certain uses of race to conduct law enforcement, including relying on "Mexican" or "foreign" appearance to stop or search persons. This is particularly true in immigration proceedings, where law enforcement agents have greater flexibility to discriminate than in traditional criminal enforcement because its purpose is considered administrative. Moreover, in immigration enforcement, the remedy to suppress the evidence is generally not available. Therefore, immigration agents are more likely to engage even in prohibited racial profiling. Additionally, certain types of administrative enforcement allow the state to engage in racial profiling to conduct a criminal investigation, as long as the administrative function also validates the seizure or search. In other words, the administrative function becomes a "pretext" for the criminal enforcement function.

114

In this chapter, we first explain racial profiling in the context of traditional criminal law enforcement to understand the basic doctrine. We then apply that doctrine to two special cases, both of an administrative nature, which have a disproportionate effect on Latino/as as compared to whites. The first is the "driving while brown" phenomena, which has permitted law enforcement to use traffic violations as a pretext to stop Latino/as suspected of criminal activity. The second is racial profiling as part of immigration enforcement.

What Is Racial Profiling?

Racial profiling occurs when a state agent targets a person solely because of race for a stop or search with the purpose of conducting a law enforcement function. The Fourth Amendment protects the "people" against racial profiling by public but not private actors. A public actor includes all federal and state employees. Usually a public actor is a police officer but can also be a public school teacher, a government employer, or an immigration officer, to name a few. In contrast, racial profiling by a private security guard at a store will not trigger Fourth Amendment protections. This is true even if the private actor turns over to police evidence that is used to prosecute the person. One exception is when there was significant collaboration with the investigation between the public and private actor throughout so that the racial profiling can be attributed to the state.

A seizure or a search must occur before Fourth Amendment limits apply to state uses of race. Not all encounters with state employees, including police, result in a seizure or search, as courts have defined these terms, however. In the racial profiling context, the most relevant encounters that do not receive Fourth Amendment protection are those considered consensual.

For example, a police officer could stop a young Latino on the street on a hunch that the Latino is carrying drugs. Usually, the officer would have to articulate specific facts that led him to reasonably suspect that the Latino possesses drugs in order to stop him, question him, or pat him down (see below). If the officer lacks reasonable suspicion, however, he can still ask the youth whether he can speak to him and search his jacket or pants pockets. A court could find that the youth voluntarily stopped, answered questions, and allowed the search, even if the officer stopped the youth based solely or primarily for his Latino appearance. Any evidence seized as a result of this encounter, then, could be introduced at trial.

But when would such an encounter be considered consensual? The doctrine of consent during "seizures" asks whether a reasonable person similarly situated would have felt free to leave. In answering the question, courts consider the surrounding facts that might indicate coercion, such as the demeanor and actions of police, and the environment. These are measured against a so-called reasonable person standard; that is, what matters is not the actual perception of the encounter by the targeted person but what a "reasonable" person similarly situated would have perceived. Notice of a right to refuse cooperation, though not required, is relevant to assess voluntariness. As applied, the doctrine has provided law enforcement great flexibility to engage in consensual encounters. The Supreme Court, for example, has considered bus sweep encounters consensual, even when the officer sought consent of passengers while blocking the aisle (*Florida v. Bostick*, 501 U.S. 429 [1991]), and during airport encounters, when the passenger was asked to accompany Drug Enforcement Agents to a small room for further investigation (*United States v. Mendenhall*, 446 U.S. 544 [1980]).

Consensual searches similarly occur when a person voluntarily assents to a state actor's request to search, regardless of whether the person knew or was notified that he could refuse. The doctrine also takes into account the totality of circumstances and asks whether a "reasonable person" similarly situated would have felt coerced to consent. Courts have allowed consent searches even when the person is seized, including in the context of traffic stops. In addition, it matters whether the state actor reasonably searched only those places that could contain what he specifically sought. Thus, an officer should specify what he is seeking. Usually, consent to search for drugs or weapons accords officers flexibility as to scope of search, as these items could be small.

Finally, the Fourth Amendment does not entirely preclude targeting on the basis of race. What the amendment actually prohibits is for race to be the sole factor for a stop or search. Race, however, can be among several other factors law enforcement uses to conduct a criminal investigation.

Consider, for example, an allegation that police targeted a few Latino/a youths to conduct a *Terry* stop and frisk to detect drugs. *Terry* stops and frisks are brief investigative encounters between police and individuals who are suspected of criminal activity. In the case *Terry v. Ohio*, 392 U.S. 1 (1968), the Supreme Court held that police need to possess reasonable suspicion that a crime was committed or was about to be committed and fear for their or the public's safety in order to briefly question and pat the suspect down for weapons.

Reasonable suspicion requires police to have specific facts, which in light of the totality of the circumstances, would lead a reasonable police officer to conclude that a crime is being committed. Police can rely on certain characteristics, such as race or type of neighborhood, to develop reasonable suspicion, but not as the sole criteria, as doing so raises equal protection concerns. Similarly, a person's refusal to cooperate with law enforcement when approached cannot be the sole factor to establish reasonable suspicion, as doing so would run afoul of the doctrine that a person can refuse to "consent" to be seized or searched.

Thus, a drug courier profile could include "Latino" as a characteristic, among others, that supports a finding of reasonable suspicion (or probable cause)[1] to justify a seizure or search. In addition, the "just don't look right" deduction to assess reasonable suspicion (or probable cause) can also include race. Returning, then, to our example, police could justify the *Terry* stop and frisk of the Latino/a youths, even if police targeted them, in part, for being Latino/a, if they can point to other factors that overall give rise to reasonable suspicion. These additional factors might include that the Latino/a youths were in a predominantly white neighborhood or that they avoided police, such as by walking faster, running away, looking nervous, or looking away.[2] How many additional factors police need to justify their actions would depend greatly on the judge.

"Driving While Brown"

Traffic enforcement has disproportionately targeted blacks and Latino/as. Roving traffic stops require that police have at least reasonable suspicion. However, any traffic violation, including a broken tail light or driving five miles over the speed limit, provides probable cause, or more than reasonable suspicion, to stop a driver. The civil rights complaint has been that police resort to traffic violations as a pretext to stop persons, especially blacks and Latino/as, not because they violated traffic laws, but because police have a hunch that they committed another crime, usually involving drugs.

Pretextual stops, however, are permitted. In the case *Whren v. United States*, 517 U.S. 806 (1996), the Supreme Court upheld the constitutionality of traffic stops, even if racial profiling was used, as long as the stop was also justified by suspicion of a traffic violation. The Court reasoned that attempting to guess if police stopped a car primarily for a traffic violation or another law enforcement reason would require the court to read the officer's mind. Furthermore, the Court considered that existing Fourth Amendment doctrine provided drivers with sufficient protection against unreasonable traffic stops because police would need further justification to search the vehicle or arrest them.

Fourth Amendment doctrine on car searches grants law enforcement the discretion to conduct searches of cars to discover crimes unrelated to the traffic violation. Even before *Whren*, police could ask passengers to exit the vehicle, detect anything in plain view, seek consent to search the vehicle, or search the passenger compartment for weapons if they feared for their safety. Since *Whren*, the Supreme Court has upheld the use of dog sniffs during routine traffic stops (*Illinois v. Caballes*, 543 U.S. 405 [2004]) and arrests based on minor traffic infractions (*Knowles v. Iowa*, 525 U.S. 113 [1998]). Once a person is arrested, the whole vehicle can be searched pursuant to an arrest or as part of an inventory search. In fact, studies show that a greater number of blacks and Latino/as are searched than whites during *Whren* stops, usually through consent.

The *Whren* doctrine is followed in about forty states, but the rest have looked to their own constitutions to disallow or limit pretextual stops. Some states, for example, examine the totality of the circumstances of the stop to determine whether police stopped the vehicle to issue a traffic infraction or to investigate a different crime. Other states have adopted legislation or policies disallowing certain types of searches, such as those based on consent. For this reason, advocacy in this area should involve state courts and legislatures. Police-gathered statistics offer a starting point for evaluating racial profiling during traffic stops in each community.

What You Can Do as a Victim of Racial Profiling. If you feel you have been a victim of "driving while brown," even if you are not arrested, file a formal complaint with the police department and/or with the citizens' review board, which oversees civil sanctions against police officers. Information on filing a complaint is usually available on the police department's webpage. Make sure to get the name and identification of the police officer. You should also contact a local or national civil rights group, such as the American Civil Liberties Union for help. If you have been criminally charged, make sure your public defender raises the issue of racial profiling in a motion to suppress the evidence based on the state constitution.

Racial Profiling in Immigration Enforcement Cases

Racial profiling is also generally permitted in immigration enforcement. Immigration enforcement is the investigation, arrest, detention, and removal of foreign nationals. Enforcement may be conducted by federal immigration officials and by local police and other law enforcement officers, although the latter may not have constitutional or departmental authority. Immigration officials—either employees of U.S. Immigration and Customs Enforcement (ICE) or U.S. Customs and Border Patrol (CBP)—enforce immigration laws at the border, including airports, fixed checkpoints near the border, and in the interior of the country, including workplaces and homes. Local police generally enforce immigration laws as part of their investigative routines, such as when an officer reports a driver suspected of unlawful immigration status to ICE after a routine traffic stop. Sometimes, immigration enforcement can lead to criminal prosecution, either because the immigration violation is also an immigration crime or because the foreign national has committed a separate crime.

Racial profiling during immigration raids occurs when enforcers target groups or individuals because of their foreign appearance. Racial profiling also occurs when law enforcement investigates leads based solely on citizen complaints motivated by biases against certain groups or persons based on their "foreignness." Both practices intensified greatly post-9/11 and resulted in the removal of a greater number of targeted persons, including Latino/as. Most of these practices, for which there are few remedies, go unchallenged in immigration removal proceedings (see below).

The nature and scope of Fourth Amendment protections against racial profiling vary, depending on who conducted the seizure or search, and whether the foreign national faces criminal or immigration consequences. For example, if an immigration officer discovers evidence that is later used to prosecute a foreign national in a criminal trial, courts apply Fourth Amendment doctrine on racial profiling related to the administrative function. That function is statutorily defined and is also circumscribed by the Fourth Amendment. Specifically, the Immigration and Nationality Act (INA) grants immigration officers the power to question any person they believe to be unlawfully in the country to ascertain their immigration status and to arrest any person if "there is reason to believe that the alien so arrested in the United States is in violation of the immigration laws" (INA § 287[g]). The Supreme Court, moreover, has required officers to have reasonable suspicion to effectuate roving traffic stops (*United States v. Brignoni-Ponce*, 422 U.S. 873 [1975]) and probable cause is also required for immigration arrests.

There are, however, several special circumstances that occur in the immigration context worth mentioning. First, the doctrine of consent has granted great flexibility to immigration agents to target Latino/as in the workplace, or during the execution of warrants against persons not the target of the arrest, to inquire about their immigration status. In *INS v. Delgado*, 466 U.S. 210 (1984), the Court held that persons questioned during an immigration workplace raid were not "seized" for purposes of the Fourth Amendment. There, the INS moved systematically through a garment factory, asked employees to identify themselves and asked them from one to three questions about their citizenship. During the survey, armed INS agents were stationed near the exits, as other agents moved throughout the factory and questioned workers at their work areas. The agents showed badges, had walkie-talkies, and carried arms, though they never drew their weapons. More recently, in *Muelher v. Mena*, 125 S.Ct. 1465 (2005), police officers, armed with a search warrant based on probable cause that Raymond Romero had been involved in a gang-related drive-by shooting, executed the warrant and detained respondent Iris Mena in handcuffs and asked her about her immigration status. The Court considered the handcuffing a reasonable seizure under the Fourth Amendment as a necessary measure to protect officer safety. The officers, however, then proceeded to ask Mena about her immigration status, and the Court held there is no requirement of particularized reasonable suspicion for purposes of inquiry into citizenship status. Instead, the Court expanded the questionable doctrine of consent, even though Mena had been handcuffed for more than two hours, and allowed ICE's inquiry into her immigration status without reasonable suspicion to stand. In essence, the Court did not consider Mena's immigration inquiry an additional seizure under the Fourth Amendment, which would have required independent justification.

Second, certain types of racial profiling disallowed in criminal enforcement are permitted in immigration enforcement. Usually, for example, engaging in racial profiling to stop persons at vehicular checkpoints violates the Fourth Amendment. Immigration agents, however, can target persons on the basis of "Mexican" appearance alone at fixed immigration checkpoints near or at the border. The Supreme Court's rationale for allowing racial profiling in this context is related to the Court's view on the importance of immigration and border enforcement, which justifies some degree of greater individual intrusion. Nevertheless, the Court made clear that the scope of immigration checkpoints should be limited to asking the driver and passengers about their immigration status or any suspicious circumstances (*United States v. Martinez-Fuerte*, 428 U.S. 543 [1976]). However, law enforcement may seek consent from motorists for further questioning or to conduct car searches, activities that can "voluntarily" delay the motorists without triggering a Fourth Amendment problem. In addition, law enforcement may use trained dogs to detect drugs or bombs in vehicles, as dog sniffing is not considered a "search" under the Fourth Amendment.

Third, more commonly ICE is conducting immigration raids with easily accessed civil warrants. These warrants expand ICE's law enforcement scope of legality beyond consent into forceful tactics. ICE has access to employee immigration records collected by employers and is statutorily able to subpoena these to conduct immigration investigations and procure warrants. Moreover, ICE has easy access to more than 600,000 civil warrants to enforce against persons with prior removal orders, labeled absconders or fugitives, who appear on their dated databases. As such, ICE has entered the workplace and people's homes with warrants, which ICE then uses to ask everyone to declare their immigration status and arrest those who cannot provide proper documents. Most arrested are placed in removal proceedings, but some have been criminally charged with identity theft for using someone's else social security number.

Fourth, the absence of an exclusionary remedy for Fourth Amendment violations in immigration proceedings leaves most immigrants without a remedy, even when a violation has occurred. The most common judicial remedy against racial profiling is a motion to suppress evidence in court. If the racial profiling, for example, results in criminal charges, then the defendant may challenge the legality of the seizure and search and seek to exclude the "fruit of the poisonous tree"—that is, any statement or evidence that resulted from the illegal seizure or search. The exclusionary remedy for Fourth Amendment violations is meant to deter against future racial profiling by police officers. When the racial profiling places the foreign national in immigration removal proceedings, however, a motion to suppress is not available. The only exception the Supreme Court has recognized is when immigration officials commit an "egregious" violation of the Fourth Amendment or other liberties that might "transgress notions of fundamental fairness and undermine the probative value of the evidence obtained" (*INS v. Lopez-Mendoza*, 468 U.S. 1032 [1984]). Interpreting this language, the Ninth Circuit, with jurisdiction over nine states and two U.S. territories, has held that immigration officers commit an "egregious violation" when they target persons solely on the basis of race or national origin, a transgression that warrants the use of the exclusionary rule in removal proceedings.[3] However, in practice, if a foreign national is detained, in the absence of a Fourth Amendment remedy in removal proceedings, there is little he can do to challenge the violation. Moreover, most foreign nationals in removal proceedings are not represented by counsel, know very little about their rights, and have few remedies to challenge removal. As a result, overwhelmingly, foreign nationals agree to voluntarily leave the U.S. rather than request an immigration hearing.

What You Can Do in an Immigration Raid. If you ever encounter immigration authorities, keep in mind the following (for ICE raids in the workplace, see also Chapter 2 for tips):

- *Keep silent.* You do not have to answer any questions about where you were born or about your immigration status, nor be required to show proof of immigration status or other identification documents. It is quite common in Latino/a culture to answer questions from authority figures. Please, do not follow the custom; in this case it is more important to exercise your right to remain silent. The officers questioning you are simply doing their job; it does not mean *you* have to answer their questions.

    In some states, state police (not ICE) may require you by law to provide your name (not your identification) and could arrest you if you refuse. Providing a false name could lead to charges of fraud if you are discovered. Moreover, your family could have a difficult time locating you if you are arrested.

    Even if you are in custody, you have a right to remain silent. Be especially mindful that anything you say can be used against you and that immigration violations, including having a false identity, carry criminal consequences.

    ICE has to prove all the answers to these questions before it can deport you. You will damage your own case by answering their questions.

- *Do not open the door to your house.* You do not have to open the door to your house unless immigration authorities have a warrant with the correct name of a person who lives in the house and with the correct address. It is better that you do not open the door until after you have seen the warrant (ICE should slip under the door). If ICE refuses, do not open the door. The same right to remain silent applies in this context.

- *Do not consent to a search.* If you do open the door to your house, tell ICE or the police you do not consent to a search of your house without a search warrant. Write down the names and badge numbers of each officer, and the names, addresses, and numbers of witnesses. If ICE has a warrant, and you are not the person named in the warrant, keep silent. Make a list of everything ICE seizes.

- *Do not carry fake documentation.* Fake documents, someone else's identity documents, or even your identification from another country can become evidence against you in an immigration removal or in a criminal proceeding against you for document fraud.

If you are arrested, in addition to remaining silent, keep in mind the following:

If you are placed in removal proceedings, ask the immigration judge for a list of legal services providers. You have the right to call a family member, an immigration lawyer, and your consulate for help. Consider asking the immigration judge for more time to find a lawyer before deciding what to do with your case.

Do not sign any paper agreeing to voluntarily depart the country, especially if you are a victim of domestic violence or human trafficking, have been in the U.S. for at least ten years and have U.S. or lawful permanent resident children or a spouse, or are afraid to return to your country of origin.

Ask for bail. You have to show you are neither a danger to society nor a flight risk. It helps if you are the principal caretaker of your children.

Raise the issue of racial profiling and other ICE abuses with your lawyer, especially if you have been criminally charged. You might be able to suppress any evidence seized against you.

The Right to Remain Silent

Most people associate the Fifth Amendment with the *Miranda* warning that police must give to suspects before interrogating them. The Fifth Amendment doctrine regulating police interrogations, however, involves three separate doctrines: the Due Process clause, the privilege against self-incrimination, and the *Miranda* warning. The Due Process clause in the Fifth Amendment of the U.S. Constitution provides that "no person . . . shall be deprived of life, liberty, or property, without due process of law."[4] Courts have interpreted this clause to protect persons from making involuntary statements that could be used against them in a criminal trial. In addition, the Fifth Amendment's privilege against self-incrimination provides that "no person . . . shall be compelled in any criminal case to be a witness against himself." The privilege against self-incrimination has one principal purpose, which is to protect defendants in a criminal trial from being "compelled" to testify or be witnesses against themselves. The role of the Fifth Amendment privilege in the pretrial context, most particularly in the interrogation room, however, should be treated as an entirely separate doctrine known as *Miranda*. In *Miranda v. Ari-*

zona, 384 U.S. 436 (1966), the Supreme Court required police to issue a warning to a suspect in custody before he was interrogated, in order to protect the right against compelled self-incrimination. Thus, *Miranda* was understood to expand the privilege against self-incrimination beyond the confines of the criminal trial itself and to declare that interrogations without the *Miranda* warning while in custody violate the Fifth Amendment privilege against self-incrimination.

In essence, these three doctrines provide distinct yet interrelated protections to persons when they are interrogated or questioned as witnesses. In this chapter, we discuss first *Miranda* protection, as it is often the starting place for determining the legality of an interrogation. We then discuss the Due Process clause, which invalidates any "involuntary" statement made by a suspect during interrogation. Lastly, we discuss the privilege against self-incrimination, which operates as an automatic prohibition against persons' being compelled to be a witness against themselves at trial.

Miranda

Miranda has become familiar thanks to the media and cop shows. Almost anyone can recite the typical warning by heart: "You have the right to remain silent. If you give up that right, anything you say can and will be used against you in a court of law. You have the right to an attorney. If you cannot afford an attorney, one will be provided to you at no cost." But what rights does this warning actually contain and when do these rights apply? As it turns out, the answers to these questions are quite complex, and most people, not understanding what these rights mean, overwhelmingly waive them. In fact, partially because of confusion and partly because of human nature—i.e., a tendency to confess—few people exercise any of the rights *Miranda* confers.

Miranda holds that any statement obtained as the result of custodial interrogation may not be used against a suspect in a criminal trial unless the prosecutor proves that the police provided certain procedural safeguards to secure the suspect's privilege against compulsory self-incrimination. Understanding *Miranda*, therefore, requires knowing when and what procedural rights *Miranda* confers and how suspects can exercise them.

First, a suspect must be in "custody" and must be "interrogated" before *Miranda* is even triggered, factors that are not always present when police question suspects. The Court defined "custodial interrogation" as "questioning initiated by law enforcement officers after a person has been taken into custody or otherwise deprived of his freedom of action in any significant way" (*Miranda*, 384 U.S. at 444).

To ascertain custody, courts apply a "reasonable person" test and ask whether a suspect under the same totality of circumstances would reasonably believe they were in custody. To be in custody, the suspect must either be under arrest or otherwise deprived of freedom beyond a classic *Terry* or traffic violation pullover (see discussion above on racial profiling). Many factors like the location of the interrogation, the suspect's reasons for being there, the number of officers present, and the officers' conduct during the interrogation are relevant to the test. Being compelled to appear before a grand jury or a probation officer, however, is not considered custodial. Suspects should also remember that if they voluntarily submit to detention—that is, the consensual stop doctrine—the custodial element is not present.

An interrogation requires that police initiate either direct questioning or engage in words or actions that the police "should know are reasonably likely to elicit an incriminating response from the suspect" (*Rhode Island v. Innis*, 446 U.S. 291 [1980]). Taunting by the police to uncover the suspect's emotional vulnerabilities usually does not meet the test. There are also administrative or public safety exceptions when police can interrogate a suspect in custody without triggering *Miranda* requirements. For example, police can ask routine booking questions, such as name, date of birth, and current age, that are necessary to process the detainee, even if some of the answers are incriminating. Similarly, police can ask a "dangerous" suspect in custody questions related to public safety. In all cases, if a suspect blurts out information without being asked by police, that is not an interrogation.

If and only when a suspect is to be subjected to a custodial interrogation must police issue the *Miranda* warning. The warning does not have to be in writing but must make reference to the basic rights to remain silent and to an attorney. As a matter of policy and routine, police usually issue the warning before initiating an interrogation, and some police departments require a written warning. When the warning is not issued, statements by the suspect may be excluded in a criminal trial, subject to some exceptions, which we discuss in the exclusionary remedy section below.

If police issue the warning, the responsibility shifts to the suspect to invoke the right to remain silent or the right to counsel. The federal government and the majority of states require suspects to make a clear and unequivocal statement to invoke *Miranda* rights so that any ambiguity is resolved in favor of the state—ambiguity is interpreted as a waiver of the right. A small number of states take the opposite position and resolve any ambiguous invocation of *Miranda* rights in favor of the suspect—ambiguity is not a waiver but an invocation. Another number of states take a middle approach and require police to seek clarification from the suspect about the meaning of the ambiguous statement. The questions then become: what constitutes a clear and unequivocal invocation of *Miranda,* and conversely, what is ambiguous invocation? Generally, anything short of the suspect's asserting that he wishes to remain silent or to see an attorney will be considered ambiguous. For example, a person who asks police, "Should I get an attorney?" rather than stating, "I want an attorney," is making an ambiguous invocation.

Suspects, therefore, can waive the right to remain silent or the right to counsel simply by omission—that is, failing to invoke the right. In addition, suspects can waive the rights by choice or through ambiguous statements or actions. Courts do not require an explicit statement of waiver from the suspect to support a finding that he waived the right to remain silent or the right to counsel. That is, courts allow police to imply that a suspect waived *Miranda* rights through ambiguous conduct or statements. This could be as simple as a suspect's refusing to answer any direct question but discussing the case with the interrogating officer on his own. A suspect might also refuse to sign a statement waiving his *Miranda* rights yet still answer questions posed by the interrogator. If the suspect simply remains silent after the warning, however, courts may exclude a statement if police did not first seek acknowledgement from the suspect that he understood his rights. In all cases, prosecutors must prove that the suspect's waiver was voluntary and that the suspect had the capacity to waive his rights. Some courts have treated language barriers as one circumstance that might contribute to a finding of incapacity (see discussion below), along with the suspect's education level, emotional state, and mental health.

Finally, if a suspect invokes his *Miranda* rights, the effect will depend on whether he invoked the right to remain silent or the right to counsel. The right to counsel adopts a more definitive approach, so that once a suspect invokes the right police cannot interrogate him until he has a meaningful opportunity to consult with counsel and even then, only if counsel is present. Of course, at any time, the suspect can waive the invocation if he initiates "further communication, exchanges, or conversations with the police" before he has a chance to consult with counsel.[5] This further communication includes any comments or inquiries that can fairly be said to open up a generalized discussion relating to the investigation but excludes routine questions or comments related to the custodial relationship. Regarding the right to remain silent, however, prosecutors need only show that police "scrupulously honored the right."[6] This means the right is not indefinite. Police can come back and question the suspect at a later time. How much later depends on several factors, including whether a different police officer conducts the subsequent interrogation, whether the interrogation is about a separate crime, or whether the *Miranda* warning was reissued.

What You Should Do If You Are in Police Custody. Based on the foregoing, persons who find themselves in the custody of police or other law enforcement officers should remember that it is their responsibility to assert their *Miranda* rights. In all cases, detainees should do the following:

- Ask to see a lawyer immediately and refuse to answer any question other than their name and address. Be unambiguous about your request and simply state, "I want to speak to my lawyer and I want to remain silent."

- Never initiate a conversation with law enforcement officers, even after you have asked to see a lawyer.
- Resist the urge to answer any question posed to you, including by persons you think are not law enforcement. Sometimes, they may be undercover agents and anything you say to them may be used against you.

The Due Process Clause

The Due Process clause renders inadmissible in a criminal trial a suspect's involuntary statements to police. The rationale is that such statements cannot be reliable, are unfair, or undermine human dignity. The key question in these cases is whether a statement is "involuntary."

The general relationship between "involuntary" and "compelled" as it relates to *Miranda* is worth noting first. As explained above, the *Miranda* doctrine is born out of the privilege against self-incrimination, not the Due Process clause. Moreover, the Due Process clause prohibits the admissibility of "involuntary" statements, whereas the privilege against self-incrimination clause uses the word "compelled." Despite the different terminology, courts have conflated the meaning of "involuntary" and "compelled," at least when scrutinizing police interrogations. In terms of *Miranda*, this means that courts look to whether police complied with *Miranda* as one factor to determine whether the statement was "voluntary" or "noncompelled." Various holdings post-*Miranda* suggest, however, that violations to the *Miranda* warning will not automatically mean the statement was "compelled" or involuntary. Conversely, the fact that a *Miranda* warning was issued often helps police claim that the confession was voluntary or noncompelled. It is also true, however, that issuing the *Miranda* warning does not make every statement "voluntary," if other factors, such as physical or emotional abuse, are present during the interrogation.

In general, there is no definitive distinction between voluntariness and involuntariness. Rather, a voluntary confession is determined by the totality of the surrounding circumstances and a consideration of the character of the accused and the details of the interrogation. As a practical matter, the typical confession case is one in which the court provides a lengthy factual description of the facts because every factor is relevant but hardly any factor is determinative on its own. This is true also of the *Miranda* warning. As is explained in more detail below, the issuance or nonissuance of the *Miranda* warning during an interrogation becomes relevant to the assessment of "voluntariness." Other relevant factors include the behavior of law enforcement officers, and the length, tactics, and location of interrogation.

In addition, when assessing "voluntariness," courts purport to determine under which circumstances a person was in fact "willed to confess" (*Cu-*

lombe v. Connecticut, 367 U.S. 568 [1961]), but in practice, courts make a normative assessment of whether the pressure placed on a person is morally reprehensible. Admittedly, the moral assessment changes in response to circumstances, especially extraordinary ones. For example, post-9/11, the U.S. government has attempted not only to narrow the definition of "torture," but to question whether "torture" is even an absolute prohibition in terrorism cases in order to justify interrogation techniques used against the 9/11 detainees. Some of these techniques include sleep deprivation, use of strobe lights and loud music, shackling suspects and holding them in painful positions, sexual taunting and humiliation, and intimidation through the use of dogs. What remains to be seen is whether post-9/11 interrogation techniques will bleed over into nonterrorism cases to alter the conception of "voluntariness" in Fifth Amendment cases. The question is made more difficult considering the vagueness of what crimes constitute acts of terror or who is a terrorist. To date, courts have not considered the substance of these questions because the executive branch of the federal government has made every effort to curtail judicial jurisdiction over the post-9/11 detainees and has asserted the power to detain such persons without charging them with a crime.

Many post-9/11 interrogation techniques would not have met previous standards of Fifth Amendment "voluntariness." The closest the U.S. Supreme Court has come to a definitive rule in interrogation cases is that actual or threatened use of violence to obtain a statement from a suspect violates the Fifth Amendment. Courts, in fact, consistently condemn such police practices as whipping or slapping a suspect in order to obtain a confession. Courts also invalidate confessions if the suspect was threatened with mob violence, deadly attacks from fellow prisoners, or was subjected to a painful medical procedure if he did not confess. Confessions given by a suspect deprived of food, water, and sleep for an extended period of time are also suppressed.

Other types of psychological pressures can also render a confession "involuntary." Among the factors relevant to an assessment of whether psychological pressures are too great are the length of the custodial detention; the length of the interrogation itself; the time and location of the interrogation; delay in presenting a suspect to a judicial officer; whether the suspect was kept incommunicado; and the personal characteristics of the suspect, such as youth, education level, and prior experience with police. For example, as early as 1944, the U.S. Supreme Court declared that nearly thirty-six hours of nonstop incommunicado interrogation was "inherently coercive" (*Ashcraft v. Tennessee*, 322 U.S. 143 [1944]). Also, a suspect who is especially young or who is suffering from illness or injury will be more likely to succeed in claiming that a confession was involuntary.

In addition, police promises of lenience can sometimes become grounds for "involuntariness." Courts, for example, often hold that a confession is involuntary when police obtain it after promising that the result will be nonprosecution or lesser punishment. Police, can, however, promise to seek leniency from the prosecutor on behalf of the defendant if he confesses. By the same token, courts have considered police threats of harsh treatment as a basis of identifying involuntary confessions. For example, the Supreme Court suppressed a confession because it was secured in response to a police threat to take the suspect's wife into custody (*Rogers v. Richmond*, 365 U.S. 534 [1961]).

Finally, in limited circumstances, certain types of police lies during interrogation to obtain confession can sometimes result in a finding of involuntariness. This depends, however, on what police lie about. In practice, police can and often do use deception to obtain confessions without violating due process. Generally, permissible lies pertain to or are intrinsic to the type of evidence police have linking a suspect to the crime, including confession from other suspects, witness statements, or physical evidence. Police lies are only problematic when these are extrinsic or unrelated to the evidence, such as lying that nonconfession will result in children being taken away or being subjected to painful medical procedures to obtain physical evidence.[7]

The Self-Incrimination Clause at Trial

Generally speaking, any person testifying in any proceeding, if the testimonial evidence might incriminate the speaker at any time then or later in a criminal proceeding, may assert the privilege against self-incrimination. Therefore, in addition to a criminal defendant, any witness in a trial can also invoke the personal privilege, provided the statement is "compelled" and the person is a "witness against himself."

The required compulsion occurs when the holder of the privilege is forced by subpoena to testify at trial or to produce incriminating documents. Having to testify at trial in order to avoid being fired from a government job (not private) also meets the compulsion element. The self-incriminating clause applies to any proceeding, civil or criminal, formal or informal, where the answers might incriminate the person testifying in a criminal proceeding, even when the language of the self-incriminating clause suggests that the right may be asserted only in a criminal trial.

The word "witness" against himself requires that the communication be both "testimonial" and incriminating. Distinguishing testimonial communication from physical evidence is difficult and not always clearly done. Most obviously, trial testimony, oral confessions to the police, and statements expressed in personal documents satisfy the requirement. Certain uses of the human voice or written words, however, are not protected. For example, a person may lawfully be compelled at a lineup to utter words or to write words on a piece of paper, if the purpose is to use the voice or the handwriting as identifying physical characteristics, and not to admit guilt. In addition, some physical evidence has not been considered "testimonial," such as a blood sample to test alcohol levels. When a communication is testimonial, the next inquiry is whether it is incriminating. Here, the privilege extends anytime the testimony could expose the person to a criminal charge. Thus, it embraces not only answers that would themselves support a conviction, but likewise those that would furnish a link in the chain of evidence needed to prosecute the claimant. In all cases, the risk of incrimination must be substantial and real, and not merely trifling or imaginary (*Marchetti v. United States*, 390 U.S. 39, 53 [1968])—not a very precise standard.

The Exclusionary Remedy

It is important to note that the nature and scope of the exclusionary rule as applied to pretrial interrogations depends on whether the violation is to the Due Process clause or to *Miranda*. In terms of the Due Process clause, the exclusionary rule is part of the right enforced, not just a remedy. By contrast, for a *Miranda* violation, the exclusionary rule functions as a remedy that the U.S. Supreme Court has at times characterized as constitutionally mandated (higher legal status) or simply a "prophylactic" rule or judicially created remedy (lower legal status).[8] This matters because the scope of the exclusionary rule depends on its nature. Generally speaking, the rule has broader application if the violation is to the Due Process clause, not just to *Miranda*.

A confession obtained involuntarily—that is, a violation of the Due Process clause—is inadmissible at trial for all purposes. This means that a prosecutor cannot introduce an involuntary statement to prove the defendant's guilt, for impeachment purposes, or for any other reason. The remedy of exclusion would also apply to any evidence collected as a result of the involuntary statement, unless police can identify an independent source. When an involuntary confession is erroneously introduced at trial, the conviction must be reversed unless prosecutors can prove beyond a reasonable doubt that the confession did not affect the trial outcome. In addition, for the Due Process clause to be violated, it is not necessary for the statement to be used in a criminal trial. A person compelled to make an involuntary statement could still sue police for civil damages, even if the statement is never used in a criminal trial.

The exclusionary rule for confessions obtained in violation of *Miranda's* procedural safeguards is more limited. For example, a prosecutor may still use a *Miranda*-tainted statement to impeach a defendant who testifies inconsistently at trial. In addition, the "fruit of the poisonous tree" protection—in which exclusion extends also to evidence resulting from the tainted statement—is more limited in the *Miranda* context and depends on the nature of the *Miranda* violation. For example, prosecutors may use witnesses whose names were obtained from a statement without a proper *Miranda* warning. More recently, the Supreme Court also allowed prosecutors to introduce physical evidence resulting from *Miranda*-tainted statements (*U.S. v. Patane*, 542 U.S. 630 [2004]). Finally, police may "cure" their *Miranda* violation in a subsequent interrogation. For example, police may give the warning in a second interrogation after no warning was given in the first, as long as failing to follow *Miranda* was not a purposeful strategy to "break down the witness."[9]

Pretrial Language Rights

The following sections discuss language rights of Latino/as in the criminal justice system. The first addresses the rights of non-English-speaking Latino/as in traffic stops and other detentions where their vehicle or luggage is searched. This discussion also revisits the *Miranda* rights given a suspect upon arrest. The next sections discuss the right to an interpreter at trial as well as language issues in the composition of the jury. Finally, the last section addresses the language rights of the incarcerated Latino/a who wants to communicate with friends and relatives in a language other than English, as well as receive prison services such as health care in that language.

Consent to Search

Searches by police of a suspect's car or luggage are invalid unless accomplished with a search warrant or undertaken pursuant to a recognized exception to the warrant requirement under the Fourth Amendment of the U.S. Constitution—such as consent. Often, the authorities will rely on the suspect's consent to the search to justify a warrantless search. In order to be effective under Fourth Amendment protection against unreasonable search and seizure, consent must be given freely and voluntarily. Where the suspect has no understanding or a limited understanding of English, consent is sometimes not effectively given. For example, in one federal case for heroin possession with intent to distribute, narcotics agents confronted a monolingual Spanish-speaking Latino defendant in a Utah train station and asked him in English for identification. The suspect understood this command because the Spanish word is very similar. One of the agents then made hand motions while speaking English indicating he wanted to look in the suspect's bags. The suspect opened the first bag for the officer. The narcotics officer then used gestures to indicate he wanted to look into the other bag, and the suspect handed the bag to him that contained a tube filled with heroin. At a later court hearing, the Latino defendant contended he did not understand he had the right to deny the officer permission to search the bag. The court found the search was not consensual, as no clear and unequivocal permission was given—the pantomime gestures of the officer, who tried to overcome the language barrier, were insufficient to obtain consent and convey the suspect's right to refuse consent (*United States v. Benitez-Arreguin*, 973 F.2d 823 [10th Cir. 1992]).

In another federal case, federal drug agents at an airport confronted a Latino with extremely limited English skills. One of the agents pointed to his bag and asked, "Drogas? (drugs)." The suspect responded no and handed the bag to the officer, who asked in English if it was okay for him to look. The suspect responded, "sí." Finding no evidence of drugs, the agent pointed to the jacket the suspect was carrying and asked to look. The agent pointed from his eyes to the jacket, as he had done for the bag. The Latino suspect shrugged his shoulders, turned his head, and nodded his head up and down twice. The agents found two packets of cocaine in the jacket and arrested him. The federal court rejected this combination of short English sentences and pantomime. The suspect's response was one of resignation, rather than an expression of free and voluntary approval. Further, the agents failed to communicate that the suspect could refuse the search (*United States v. Gallego-Zapata*, 630 F. Supp. 665 [D. Mass. 1986]).

Even where police request consent to search in Spanish, the language barrier and translation shortcomings can prevent effective consent. For example, in an Arkansas case, police officers brought a Spanish-speaking city employee to interpret their request to search a Latino rape suspect's residence for a gun. The employee testified he told the suspect in Spanish that the officer "got a permit to go search his apartment where he lives." The suspect said "okay," or "go ahead." The court found the interpreter failed to communicate effectively the request to search the residence. Rather, his misleading translation suggested the officer already had permission to search the residence (*Lobania v. State*, 959 S.W.2d 72 [Ark. Ct. App. 1998]).

Occasionally, a court disagrees with the Latino/a suspect's contention that his or her English is insufficient to permit consent to a search in English. A defendant does not need perfect command of the English language in order to give voluntary consent; "it is enough that he understand English well enough to comprehend the situation" (*United States v. Verduzco*, 996 F.2d 1220 [7th Cir. 1993] [unpublished opinion]).

Interrogation

In addition to concerns with consent to search, language issues surround the interrogation process after arrest. Although rights in this situation derive from the federal constitution's Fifth Amendment privilege against self-incrimination, the standard for waiver is similar to the standard for consent to an otherwise nonpermitted search under the Fourth Amendment. Upon arrest a suspect is entitled to receive the *Miranda* warnings (explained above) in a language he or she is able to understand; any waiver of the right to remain silent must be voluntary, knowing, and intelligent (*Miranda v. Arizona*, 384 U.S. 436, 478–479 [1966]). Courts have held that the arresting officers need not use the suspect's native language if the suspect has sufficient command of the English language (*Companeria v. Reid*, 891 F.2d 1014 [2d Cir. 1989]). As in the consent to search cases, the court must determine if the suspect's ability to comprehend English is sufficient to permit him to understand the *Miranda* warning.

In dealing with a Spanish-speaking suspect who does not sufficiently comprehend English, the arresting officers are well advised to deliver the *Miranda* warnings by means of an officially prepared Spanish-language card, which the officer is trained to pronounce. Still, the Spanish card could have translation errors and not effectively convey the *Miranda* rights. In one case, the Spanish *Miranda* card contained egregious errors, such as implying that the defendant had to be completely without money in order for the court to appoint an attorney, rather than being unable to afford the attorney (*United States v. Higareda-Santa Cruz*, 826 F. Supp. 355 [D. Or. 1993]). Where an officer attempts to deliver the warnings in Spanish, sometimes the officer fails to correctly translate the *Miranda* rights. For example, in a Wisconsin case, the Spanish-speaking officer told the Latino suspect the suspect had the right to "apuntar un abogado," which means "to point a lawyer" rather than "to appoint a lawyer." He also apparently failed to convey in Spanish the potential right to have a lawyer appointed without cost (*State v. Santiago*, 542 N.W.2d 466 [Ct. App. 1995], aff'd, 556 N.W.2d 687 [Wis. Sup. Ct. 1996]).

Courts also require police to conduct the interrogatory process in a language the defendant understands. For example, a federal court struck down the conviction of a Latino for importing marijuana based in part on incriminating statements he made during an English-language interrogation. Although the Spanish-speaking defendant replied affirmatively to the question whether he understood English, the interrogating agent had to rephrase questions the defendant did not seem to comprehend. The court record showed the defendant understood little in English; although he attended an English-language high school in the United States, he received D+ grades in eleventh- and twelfth-grade English. There was testimony too that when under stress and in dealing with persons of authority, the defendant would claim he understood English despite his inadequate fluency (*United States v. Garibay*, 143 F.3d 534 [9th Cir. 1998]). Some states, such as Oregon, by statute compel police to provide an interpreter when interrogating a suspect who speaks limited English (Or. Rev. Stat. § 133.515).

Breathalyzer Warnings

Unlike the constitutional underpinning of *Miranda* warnings and consents to searches that may compel Spanish-language accommodation, nonconstitutionally grounded warnings like those given when administering a breathalyzer test may not require a translation. For example, the Georgia Supreme Court rejected a constitutional equal protection and due process challenge against the police practice of giving an implied consent warning in English even to non-English-speaking drunk driving suspects. This warning addresses the impact of failing to submit to the blood alcohol test, resulting in license suspension and the refusal being used as evidence in the drunk driving trial. Georgia law required interpreters to explain the warning to hearing impaired drivers, but failed to accommodate non-English speakers. Although government policies that discriminate on the basis of national origin are subjected to strict scrutiny and rarely upheld, the Georgia court refused to view language discrimination as national origin discrimination and therefore applied the more lax rational basis standard to uphold the government's refusal to translate. The court looked to the expense to government and the potential delay in administering the blood alcohol test as rational grounds for denying translation. It then rejected a due process claim, treating the blood alcohol–implied consent warnings as a matter of legislative grace in contrast to the constitutional underpinning of the right to silence warnings contained in *Miranda* (*Rodriguez v. State*, 565 S.E.2d 458 [Ga. 2002]).

Language Inability Causing Crime

Can monolingual Spanish-speaking Latino/as be charged with and convicted of crimes resulting from their failure to understand English? This question often stems from notices suspending driver's licenses delivered to Spanish-speaking drivers in English. Challenges relying on the constitutional guarantees of due process and equal protection typically fail on the reasoning that the Spanish-speaker should have obtained a translation of the important-appearing papers from the government. For example, the New Mexico Supreme Court upheld the revocation of a driver's license when the Spanish-speaker driver failed to request a hearing within the requisite ten days as specified in the English-language notice of revocation he was given when arrested for drunk driving. The court felt a reasonable person in the driver's situation, when given a hand-delivered notice by the arresting officer, would obtain a translation. Therefore, the English-language notice fulfilled the due process obligation that requires notice and an opportunity for a hearing before the state can revoke a driver's license (*Maso v. State Taxation and Revenue Dept.*, 96 P.3d 286 [N.M. 2004]). Appellate courts in Colorado and Indiana have reached comparable conclusions. Applying similar reasoning, the Supreme Court of Massachusetts upheld the criminal convictions of Spanish-speaking Latino/as for ignoring a city housing department order in English condemning their apartments as unfit for habitation. The relevant statute punished reckless offenses, and the court viewed their failure to obtain translation of the official notice delivered to them in hand by a constable as reckless. In addition to the due process challenge, the Latino/a defendants claimed their prosecution violated equal protection that guards against action discriminatory to Latino/as as a class. Although regulation targeting Latino/as implicates a suspect class that requires a compelling government interest to justify the unfair treatment, the court found no suspect class implicated because the English-notice policy burdened not just Latino/as, but all persons illiterate in English. Therefore, the government policy only had to withstand a challenge as not rationally related to a permissible governmental purpose, and the court relied on its view of English as the country and the state's "official" language to shield English governmental notices as "patently reasonable" (*Commonwealth v. Olivo*, 337 N.E.2d 904 [Mass. 1975]).

Language Rights During a Criminal Trial

Spanish-speaking Latino/as unable to effectively understand English are entitled to interpreters in criminal trials either by statute or under constitutional requirements ensuring the right to confront adverse witnesses. If the criminal defendant is indigent, the government will provide the interpreter at no cost. In 2002, there were 174,405 interpreted events in federal district courts, 94 percent of those involving Spanish. Despite the general authorization of interpreters in criminal trials, many potential uncertainties and shortcomings in the criminal prosecution of language minorities remain that are addressed below.

Although the Supreme Court has not ruled on the issue, both federal and state courts widely recognize a constitutional right to an appointed interpreter for criminal defendants who cannot understand English. In a leading case, the federal Second Circuit appeals court so ruled in a case involving the murder conviction of a native Puerto Rican who came to New York as a young adult and could not understand any English. His court-appointed lawyer spoke no Spanish. The trial court supplied an interpreter only sporadically during the proceedings—for twenty minutes before the trial to allow the Latino defendant to confer with his lawyer. At trial, the defendant's testimony and that of other Spanish-speaking witnesses were translated into English for the jury's benefit. That translator also met with the defendant twice during the four-day trial for ten to twenty minutes to summarize the testimony of the many English-speaking witnesses against him. The translator never translated English testimony against the defendant while the trial was in progress, other than these brief summaries, which the court found insufficient. The court recognized that to the defendant "most of the trial must have been a babble of voices." Basing its ruling under the constitutional guarantee of the right to confront adverse witnesses, as well as the more general requirement of due process, the court felt that, "not only for the sake of effective cross-examination [of witnesses], however, but as a matter of simple humaneness, [the defendant] Negron deserved more than to sit in total incomprehension as the trial proceeded" (*United States ex rel. Negron v. State of New York*, 434 F.2d 386, 390 [2d Cir. 1970]). The court ruled that a criminal court, if on notice of a severe language difficulty, must make clear to the defendant that he is entitled to a competent translator to assist him throughout the trial, at state expense if necessary.

Eventually, Congress adopted the Court Interpreters Act that established the right to a certified court interpreter in any criminal action and even civil actions brought by the federal government when a defendant or witness is unable to comprehend the proceedings due to a language barrier (28 U.S.C. § 1827). California's Constitution establishes the right to an interpreter in criminal proceedings (Cal. Const. art. I, § 14) and most other states now authorize interpreters by statute.

Because the Supreme Court has not addressed this area and the relevant statutes are sometimes unclear or nonexistent, several uncertainties still surround the Spanish-speaking Latino/a defendant's right to a court-appointed translator. Among them is whether the right to a translator covers proceedings before (such as the preliminary hearing and the setting of bail) and after the trial (such as sentencing and parole board hearings). The federal interpreter statute extends to "all proceedings . . . including pretrial and grand jury proceedings" (28 U.S.C. § 1827[j]), and presumably covers such proceedings as sentencing. Answers under state law for state criminal proceedings turn similarly on the wording of any state statute or other law. For example, a California appeals court held the state's constitution authorizing interpreters in all criminal "proceedings" does not extend to a presentence interview by a probation officer because that interview is not a court "proceeding" (*People v. Gutierrez*, 222 Cal. Rptr. 699 [Ct. App. 1986]).

After sentencing, recognition of language rights is sporadic. The Texas Court of Criminal Appeals concluded a Latino unable to understand English was not protected under the federal or Texas constitutions from imprisonment due to his language barrier. The Latino defendant was convicted for driving while intoxicated. If able to speak English, he would have been sentenced to a state-run alcohol education program and given probation rather than jail. Because the judge believed there was no adequate Spanish-language program, he sentenced the Latino driver to jail. Although equal protection guarantees protection against discrimination on the basis of race or national origin, the court did not view this language discrimination as race or national origin discrimination. Because no suspect class was harmed, the court had to decide simply whether the trial court's actions were rationally related to a legitimate government interest—hardly an obstacle for most government policies. Here, the possible expense of setting up alcohol education programs in languages other than English justified denying probation to the Spanish-speaking driver. Although the state could have accommodated the language barrier by appointing an interpreter for the Latino driver attending English-language classes, the court believed requiring translation was untenable for a cash-strapped government and was a decision best left to the legislature. In the absence of legislation, then, there was no right to an interpreter or to a court-mandated Spanish-language alcohol education program as an alternative to jail (*Flores v. State*, 904 S.W.2d 129 [Tex. Ct. Crim. App. 1995]). The Texas legislature responded to the abhorrent *Flores* decision by enacting law prohibiting denial of community supervision (e.g., drunk driving diversion programs) solely because of the defendant's inability to understand English (Tex. Code Crim. Proc. § 42.12).

Some judges impose their English-only views on Spanish-speaking defendants during sentencing. For example, a Washington State judge routinely asked Latino/a defendants if they were "legal," and ordered them to enroll in English classes. Two Latinos who pled guilty to drug dealing charges were sentenced by a Pennsylvania judge to jail and ordered to learn English.

Focusing on the criminal trial itself, it is uncertain whether the right to an interpreter encompasses just hostile witness testimony or extends to include rulings from the judge, instructions to the jury, and dialogue between the (presumably) court-appointed lawyer and the non-English-speaking Latino/a client. The federal Court Interpreters Act cited above refers to the need for an interpreter to help the defendant understand witnesses but also to facilitate communication with counsel and the judge. Interpreting its state constitution, the California Supreme Court identified three essential roles of court-appointed interpreters in criminal proceedings:

> (1) They make the questioning of a non-English-speaking witness possible; (2) they facilitate the non-English-speaking defendant's understanding of the collo[q]uy between the attorneys, the witness, and the judge; and (3) they enable the non-English-speaking defendant and his English-speaking attorney to communicate. . . . An interpreter performing the first service will be called a "witness interpreter," one performing the second service, a "proceedings interpreter," and one performing the third service a "defense interpreter." (*People v. Aguilar*, 677 P.2d 1198, 1201 [Cal. 1984])

In this case, the trial court allowed the prosecutor to "borrow" the court-appointed interpreter to translate for the judge and jury the Spanish testimony of a prosecution witness. The appeals court decided this violated the Latino defendant's state constitutional right: "The 'borrowing' of the interpreter, the accused's only means of communicating with defense counsel and understanding the proceedings, was a denial of a constitutional right." Other courts disagree with the need for multiple interpreters (see *People v. Avila*, 797 P.2d 804 [Colo. Ct. App. 1990]). For example, a federal appeals court rejected the need for multiple interpreters in a trial with several codefendants, some of whom were native English speakers and others who were Spanish speaking and not fluent in English. The court appointed one interpreter for the three non-English-speaking Latino/as. The interpreter fed translations of English language witnesses to the three defendants by means of headsets they wore. One of the Latino/a defendants had an attorney who spoke Spanish, but the other two had English-speaking lawyers. These two Latino/a defendants contended they were prejudiced by their inability to communicate with their counsel during the trial as the other defendants could. But the appeals court concluded the federal Court Interpreters Act was satisfied and did not require separate interpreters to allow communication between the Latino/a defendants and their non-Spanish-speaking counsel. Further, there was no constitutional right to multiple interpreters. The appeals court reasoned that the Latino/a defendants had ample opportunity to consult with their attorneys—the trial court offered to recess the proceedings any time they needed to consult their attorneys using the witness interpreter (*United States v. Bennett*, 848 F.2d 1134 [11th Cir. 1988]).

It is also unclear to what extent the constitutional or statutory right to an interpreter extends outside the courtroom to out-of-court communications and strategizing between the non-English-speaking defendant and English-only counsel, with some courts suggesting that providing an interpreter at trial is enough. Presumably these courts might similarly reject any constitutional argument that a monolingual Spanish-speaking Latino/a is entitled to a court-appointed bilingual lawyer to represent him or her (see *United States ex rel. Torres v. Brierton*, 460 F. Supp. 704, 705 [N.D. Ill. 1978]).

Additional uncertainties include the extent to which the indigent non-English-speaking defendant is entitled to translations at government expense of documents introduced by the prosecution or those relevant to his or her defense. Recognizing that the federal Court Interpreters Act does not address translation of court documents, a federal court invoked federal constitutional guarantees under the Sixth Amendment to order translation of court documents at government expense for monolingual Spanish-speaking criminal defendants in a complex drug and money laundering trial, including the right to assist in one's own defense, to effective assistance of counsel, and to confront government witnesses on cross-examination (*United States v. Mosquera*, 816 F. Supp. 168 [E.D.N.Y. 1993]). But federal and state courts are sometimes unwilling to recognize a right to translation of criminal trial documents at government expense.[10]

Because a defendant's understanding of the criminal charges is a crucial part of the court's acceptance of a guilty plea, courts will entertain challenges by non-English-speaking defendants who pled guilty to untranslated (or poorly translated) charges. For example, a Latino defendant pled guilty to charges of burglary and racketeering. He signed a guilty plea statement that listed the names of the crimes in English. The court interpreter described the charges against him using the Spanish term "ratero," which the defendant perceived to mean "burglary." The state appeals court sent the case back to the trial court to determine if the defendant understood the elements of the racketeering offense, which involves a pattern of unlawful activity (*Prieto v. State*, 573 So. 2d 398 [Fla. Dist. Ct. App. 1991]).[11]

Even when constitutional or statutory grounds exist for interpreters, the trial judge enjoys wide discretion to determine the criminal defendant's degree of fluency in the English language. Providing a translator does not ensure the non-English-speaking defendant a clear understanding of the proceedings. Sometimes the interpreter is unqualified, although states are increasingly requiring certification of interpreters. Even skilled interpreters can make errors given the variations of language from place to place. For example, Spanish words in one part of the world or even the United States may have a different meaning elsewhere, and some words in English cannot be exactly translated.

Spanish Speakers on Criminal Juries

A Latino/a standing trial on criminal charges likely desires a jury of his or her peers that may include other Latino/as. However, the courts have ensured this often will not be the case, as they have allowed prosecutors to exclude Latino/as from the jury if the prospective jurors are unable to understand English or even if they can speak English but also understand Spanish.

Latino/as have long suffered discrimination in the jury pool. A 1969 prosecutor training manual included a warning from a Texas prosecutor against letting "Jews, Negroes, Dagoes and Mexicans" serve on a criminal jury. Litigation that reached the U.S. Supreme Court in the 1950s revealed that although 14 percent of a Texas county's residents had Latino/a surnames, for the previous twenty years not a single county resident with a Latino/a surname served on a grand jury or criminal jury. The Supreme Court struck down the murder conviction in that county of a Latino defendant, concluding this systematic exclusion from the county jury pool of those of Mexican origin denied his constitutional equal protection rights (*Hernandez v. Texas*, 347 U.S. 475 [1954]). Legendary Chicano lawyer Oscar "Zeta" Acosta later challenged as unconstitutional the grand juror selection process in California that relied on judges to nominate suitable candidates, a system that led to a disproportionately small number of Mexican American jurors but which passed constitutional muster because of the absence of any proven intent to discriminate.

Non-English-Speaking Jurors

In addition to unlawful discrimination keeping Latino/as out of the jury pool, courts will exclude many Latino/as by tolerating English-only requirements for jury service. In federal trials, juror fluency in English is required by federal statute (28 U.S.C. § 1865). Even in a federal drug trial in Puerto Rico, a federal appeals court rejected the Latino defendant's contention that the English-only requirement for jury eligibility violated his Fifth (due process in federal trial) and Sixth (right to jury trial) Amendment constitutional rights because the restriction excluded two-thirds of the Puerto Rican population. The court believed the overwhelming national interest served by requiring English in a federal court justified conducting Puerto Rican proceedings in English and requiring jurors to be proficient in English (*United States v. Flores-Rivera*, 56 F.3d 319 [1st Cir. 1995]). Although in theory an interpreter could translate the proceedings for a non-English-speaking juror, a Washington appeals court rejected this accommodation in enforcing state law that rendered persons incompetent to serve as jurors if they cannot communicate in English (*State v. Marsh*, 24 P.3d 1127 [Wash. Ct. App. 2001]).[12] Contrast the enlightened approach in New Mexico, whose state constitution ensures the right to sit on juries, as well as to vote or hold political office, regardless of the inability to speak, read, or write English (or Spanish) (N.M. Const. art. 7, § 3).

Bilingual Jurors

Prosecutors can permissibly exclude for cause even those potential Latino/a jurors fluent in English if they are also fluent in Spanish and the trial will involve Spanish-language evidence. The U.S. Supreme Court upheld this outrageous conduct by a prosecutor because he offered a race-neutral basis for striking Latino/as from the jury pool—the prosecutor relied on prospective juror responses to questions and their demeanor in refusing to trust that bilingual juror candidates would accept English translations of the court interpreter over their own understanding of the testimony of Spanish-speaking witnesses for the prosecution (*Hernandez v. New York*, 500 U.S. 352 [1991]). Because the prosecutor did not rely on Spanish-language fluency alone, but rather on demeanor and responses of prospective jurors to his questioning that caused the prosecutor to doubt their ability to accept the official translation of Spanish-speaking witnesses, the Supreme Court did not have to confront the more difficult question of whether a prosecutor can strike potential jurors for their Spanish fluency alone without questioning and observing them on this issue. A federal appeals decision authored by Supreme Court Justice Samuel Alito provides a strong indication the Supreme Court would approve such prosecutor conduct under the Equal Protection clause. Alito's opinion regarded prosecutor elimination of potential jurors based on language as different from race or national origin discrimination and therefore permissible unless the prosecutor used language as a proxy to discriminate on the basis of race or national origin. Because the drug trial was to involve significant evidence presented in Spanish to be translated for the jury, and the prosecutor also struck potential jurors who were not Latino/a but understood Spanish, the court accepted the finding of a state court that this prosecutor was not motivated by race in striking the Spanish-speakers (*Pemberthy v. Beyer*, 19 F.3d 857 [3d Cir. 1994]). Therefore, in a trial where Spanish-language evidence is expected, which is particularly likely in prosecutions of Latino/as, the prosecutor apparently might lawfully exclude any prospective juror who understands Spanish.

Apart from this potential to lawfully exclude jurors who understand Spanish when Spanish testimony is expected, the prosecutor's striking of jurors who appear Latino/a or have Spanish surnames, without legitimate grounds, may violate the defendant's constitutional right to a trial of his peers. For example, in a murder case that reached the California Supreme Court, the prosecutor struck all the Spanish surnamed individuals from the jury. When required to justify the juror disqualifications to overcome the defendant's constitutional challenge, the prosecutor offered inconsistent and pretextual explanations—for example, contending that some of the Latino/a jurors were too young and lacked maturity but leaving a youthful non-Latino/a on the jury. Using group stereotypes as the sole reason for striking the jurors violated the defendant's constitutional rights. The court treated this impermissible discrimination against jurors with Spanish surnames as equivalent to discriminating against Latino/as on the basis of national origin, race, or color (*People v. Trevino*, 704 P.2d 719 [Cal. 1985]).

Prisoners' Language Rights

Language rights of Spanish-speaking prisoners often conflict with safety prerogatives and funding concerns in prisons. Areas of conflict have included prison English-only rules governing inmates in their prison conversations with other inmates or visitors and in their incoming and outgoing communications by mail or phone. Latino/as and other inmates for whom English is not a first language have also challenged such shortcomings as a lack of translators in the delivery of prison medical services. Prisoners rely primarily on the federal constitutional guarantees of free speech and protection from cruel and unusual punishment in protesting these policies and practices. Success has been mixed as the applicable legal standards take account of the safety and economic justifications prisons assert in adopting these policies. Another important factor is the prisoner's ability to communicate in English as an alternative to the native language; as in the workplace, English-only restrictions in prisons are more likely to be upheld when applied to bilingual prisoners with communicative alternatives.

In a Wisconsin prison, the staff would instruct inmates to speak in English if the staff felt it necessary for security concerns. In an action by a bilingual Latino prisoner challenging this policy under the federal First Amendment free speech protections, the court had to decide whether the policy was reasonably related to legitimate penal concerns and whether alternate means to exercise the denied right of speech remained available. The court recognized as legitimate the security concerns over Spanish-language conversations in the presence of staff that included the potential for escape, assault, hostage-taking, riot, and gang activity. It also noted the Latino prisoner had a record of gang involvement and retained the option to speak in English, in which he was also fluent. Thus, the court affirmed dismissal of the prisoner's lawsuit (*State of Wisconsin ex rel. Velez v. Litscher*, 680 N.W.2d 833 [Wis. Ct. App. 2004] [unpublished opinion]).

English-language policies governing external communications of prisoners are of uncertain validity. Federal courts in Iowa have upheld prison policies that allow written communications with inmates in languages other than English only if that language is the sole language in which the inmate is able to communicate. Thus, bilingual prisoners would be unable to write or receive letters in Spanish, although a monolingual Spanish-speaker would be so permitted. Originally from Mexico, a bilingual Latino prisoner challenged this policy under the First Amendment as applied to his communications with his mother and other family members in the United States. The prison identified legitimate security interests reasonably related to the policy—the risk that an escape plot or smuggling scheme could be hatched by mail. The Latino prisoner also had sufficient alternative means of communication available—he could call his family or receive them in person (*Ortiz v. Fort Dodge Correctional Facility*, 368 F.3d 1024 [8th Cir. 2004]). Some federal courts have been more receptive to prisoner challenges to language rules. A federal appeals court confirmed that a Laotian inmate's First Amendment rights were violated where the prisoner established that an in-state refugee service center was available to translate all correspondence from Lao to English cost-free to the prison (*Thongvanh v. Thalacker*, 17 F.3d 256 [8th Cir. 1994]). A federal court also struck down a Pennsylvania prison's English-language rule that prohibited a prisoner from communicating in Hungarian with his only living relative, a sister in Hungary (*United States ex rel. Gabor v. Myers*, 237 F. Supp. 852 [E.D. Pa. 1965]).

Prisoners' rights to language accommodation may not apply to other aspects of daily prison life. Because prison housing determinations and prisoner classifications (for example, whether the prisoner should be kept in maximum security cells) generally do not implicate constitutional liberty interests of due process, a federal appeals court held that prisoners are not entitled to government-provided interpreters for prison hearings to determine these classifications (*Franklin v. District of Columbia*, 163 F.3d 625 [D.C. Cir. 1999]). Still, the court noted that interpreters may be required when the prisoner is subjected to extraordinary treatment such as transfer to a mental hospital. Further, the court found that the prison's failure to supply interpreters to prisoners seeking medical care did not violate constitutional protection against cruel and unusual punishment, nor did the prisoners have a constitutional right to privacy that would force the prison to hire bilingual medical personnel to save non-English-speaking prisoners from seeking translation help from bilingual prisoners in obtaining medical care.

Immigration Crimes

Increasingly, the United States has imposed criminal penalties against foreigners who violate the immigration laws. Many of what were originally considered solely civil immigration offenses are now crimes. Almost 90 percent of defendants charged with immigration crimes are Latino/a. Moreover, Mexican nationals continue to make up the largest group of persons—over half—of those investigated for immigration offenses. Although it is true that undocumented immigration originates heavily from Latin America, disparate enforcement of immigration laws, including the overenforcement of the Mexican border and the underenforcement of the Canadian border, also explains the statistics. In fact, much of the increase in immigration crime has been restricted to a number of judicial districts, largely those bordering Mexico.

Immigration crimes fall within four broad categories: unlawful entry or reentry into the United States; harboring or smuggling the undocumented; immigration document fraud and false statements; and employment-related crimes. For most immigration crimes, noncitizen ("alien") status is a necessary element of the crime; however, U.S. citizens are also chargeable with certain types of immigration offenses. Neither sanctuary nor humanitarian reasons are valid defenses for violations of immigration crimes; nor can the First Amendment's free speech provision protect actions that help undocumented immigrants enter or reside in the United States.

Certain immigration crimes constitute felonies, others are misdemeanors, and penalties vary widely. Statutes prescribe a maximum penalty for each type of immigration crime, ranging from two to twenty years, while the federal sentencing guidelines establish minimums, allowing for upward and downward departure depending on several factors, including prior criminal history. However, prosecutorial discretion to negotiate pleas in immigration cases often leads to wide variation in actual penalties. The average time served by an immigration offender in 2000 was twenty-one months.

Unlawful Entry and Reentry

Unlawful entry or reentry constitutes the most common type of immigration offenses prosecuted. Priority is given to repeat entrants who have criminal histories or outstanding warrants and those previously removed from the United States.

Unlawful entry includes entering or attempting to enter the United States without inspection or through misrepresentation. Unlawful entry is a criminal misdemeanor, punishable by a fine and up to six months in prison (INA § 275[a]). Subsequent or multiple illegal entries or attempted entries, however, constitute felonies and are punishable by up to two years imprisonment (INA § 275[a]). In addition, a person previously removed who again enters or attempts to enter may also be punished with up to two years imprisonment (INA § 276).[13] This sentence can increase up to ten years if the person who enters or attempts to enter was removed because of the commission of three or more misdemeanors or one nonaggravated felony, and to twenty years if the removal was for the conviction of an aggravated felony (INA § 276), as the term is defined by immigration law (INA §101[a][43]).

Smuggling and Harboring

Smuggling and harboring are the second most common types of immigration offenses and encompass crimes associated with assisting undocumented persons to break immigration laws. The most common felony of this type occurs when any person, including a U.S. citizen, knowingly brings or attempts to bring a person, regardless of immigration status, through an unauthorized border crossing. The offense is punishable by up to ten to twenty years imprisonment and/or fines, depending on past violations, commission of the offense for personal financial gain, and bodily harm to any person during the offense. A misdemeanor charge, punishable by up to five years imprisonment, can attach even if the person acted only in reckless disregard—something less than actual knowledge of the fact that the noncitizen lacked authority to enter the United States (INA § 274[a][1][A][1]).

Harboring includes conduct that tends to substantially help a foreign national remain in the country unlawfully, regardless of whether the conduct relates to actual entry. This can include assistance with housing, employment, obtaining legal status, use of a false name, or attempting to prevent detection by immigration authorities. It can also include transporting or attempting to transport an undocumented person within the United States, knowingly or in reckless disregard of the person's status, with the intent to further that person's unlawful stay (INA § 274[a][1][A][ii]). The intent to further the person's unlawful stay can be shown though indirect evidence. An offer of employment plus voluntary transportation or payment for transportation plus lodging or other arrangement can satisfy the court's intent requirement.

Furthermore, simply encouraging or inducing a foreign national to enter or reside in the United States, whether knowingly or recklessly disregarding the illegal nature of the action, is also a felony. The action is punishable by up to five, ten, or twenty years, or even life imprisonment or death, depending on whether the crime was committed for personal gain, whether previous violations were committed, and whether bodily injury or death resulted (INA § 274[a][1][A][iv]). Felonious inducement of unlawful immigration includes such acts as advising undocumented persons to continue working in the United States and assisting with the completion of immigration applications that involve false statements or obvious errors or omissions (*U.S. v. Oloyede*, 982 F.2d 133, 137 [4th Cir. 1993]).

In addition, conspiring to commit smuggling or harboring crimes is a felony. Again, punishment depends on prior violations, violations for personal gain, and resultant injury or death and can range from a maximum of five years to life imprisonment or even death. This felony may be treated as a separate charge (INA § 274[a][1][A][v][I]). The three elements of criminal conspiracy are (1) an agreement by two or more persons to engage in illegal activity; (2) an overt act by at least one person taken in furtherance of the agreement, and (3) the intent to commit the illegal activity.

Immigration Document Fraud and False Statement Crimes

The third type of immigration crime is document fraud. This crime includes the use or attempted use of false immigration documents as evidence of authorized stay or employment in the United States; the possession and distribution of such documents; and the possession of materials to forge immigration documents (8 U.S.C. § 1546[a]). Immigration documents include visas, work permits, or border crossing cards. While not immigration crimes, falsely representing a social security number or procuring or distributing a counterfeit social security card are also crimes (42 U.S.C. § 108[a][7]). Impersonating another or falsely using the name of a dead person to evade or attempt to evade immigration laws is another type of fraud-related immigration crime (42 U.S.C. § 1546[a][4]). Furthermore, knowingly and falsely claiming U.S. citizenship or forging any document to establish U.S. citizenship, such as a birth certificate or passports, can also result in felony conviction (8 U.S.C. §1015[c], [e], and [f]; 8 U.S.C. § 1425; 8 U.S.C. § 1426[a]–[c], [h]).

Fraud crimes can also encompass making false statements or representations to immigration officers, either in person or in written submissions, for the purpose of procuring an immigration benefit. Assisting a foreign national in preparing an application or immigration document knowingly or with reckless disregard of the fact that the application or document contains false information may also be criminal (INA § 274[e]).

While rarely prosecuted, marriage fraud is a type of immigration-related crime. Marriage fraud occurs when a couple knowingly enters into a marriage for the "purpose of evading the immigration laws" and is punishable by up to five years imprisonment (8 U.S.C. §§ 1154[c], 1186b[b][1][A]). Both spouses may be criminally prosecuted (8 U.S.C. § 1325[c]). Therefore, immigration officials often subject couples procuring a marriage-based visa to interrogations about intimate aspects of the marital relationship, in an effort to determine the "good faith" nature of the marriage. What constitutes a "good faith" marriage for immigration purposes hinges on particular notions of marriage and preferences, namely the establishment of a joint domicile and commingling of funds, usually for the purpose of raising a family.

Employment-Related Offenses

A fourth type of immigration crime holds both employees and employers criminally liable for seeking or providing unauthorized work in the United States. However, rarely is the law enforced against employers, particularly when employers assert good-faith compliance. Before the mid-1990s, criminal penalties applied only to employers who engaged in a pattern of violation practices involving the hiring, referring for a fee, and/or recruiting of a person known to be unauthorized to work in the United States, or for failure to complete the Employment Eligibility Form (I-9) for all employees. Since 1996, employers also face felony charges for knowingly hiring more than ten illegally smuggled undocumented persons (8 U.S.C. § 1324[a][3]) or for operating a sweatshop of undocumented workers (8 U.S.C. § 1325[d]).

Undocumented workers can also be charged criminally for forging immigration documents to procure employment. Indeed, every year since

1990, the first year for which such statistics are available, more employees than employers have been prosecuted for working without authorization. National security concerns post-9/11, for example, resulted in a large number of indictments when the federal government arrested during Operation Tarmac many airport employees, mainly screeners and luggage handlers, who used forged documents to procure employment. Most recently, worksite immigration raids have resulted in thousands being criminally charged with document fraud for using someone else's social security number.

Immigration Consequences for the Commission of Crime

Every year, tens of thousands of foreign nationals, including lawful permanent residents (LPRs), face harsh immigration consequences for the commission of crimes. Especially since 1996, immigration enforcement has prioritized the detention and removal of "criminal aliens," including foreign nationals who have committed or been convicted of low-level misdemeanor offenses. In 1996, Congress not only expanded the list of crimes that could become grounds for removal, but it stripped judges of any discretion by making removal mandatory in all cases, even when removal separated families. These laws also applied retroactively to persons who committed crimes before the law's enactment. Overwhelmingly, criminal removal grounds have affected Mexicans and other Latin American nationals because immigration enforcement as a whole targets this population.

The Admitted/Nonadmitted Distinction

All foreign nationals, whether legal or undocumented, are subject to removal for the commission of crimes, but their treatment differs. The different treatment turns on whether the foreign national is considered to have been *admitted* to the United States as the term is defined under immigration law. The definition can be very technical but understanding it is the first step to knowing what consequences will fall on a foreign national who has committed crimes.

Since 1996, the Immigration and Nationality Act (INA) has distinguished between foreign nationals who have and those who have not been admitted into the United States. Admitted persons include those granted a visa, whether permanent or temporary (even if expired) (INA § 101[a][13][A]). Nonadmitted persons include parolees (persons granted permission to enter, usually for humanitarian reasons); those applying for a visa; and persons who enter without authorization, such as the undocumented (INA § 101[a][13][B]). Admitted persons seeking to adjust their status—usually from a temporary visa to a permanent one (INA § 245[a])—and certain LPRs, including those returning from a trip abroad for longer than six months or who committed any offense abroad, are also treated as seeking admission (INA § 101[a][13][C]).

The first principal distinction between admitted and nonadmitted persons is that the INA contains separate provisions defining criminal-related grounds for their removal. Provisions for admitted persons are in INA § 237(a)(2) and are known as deportation grounds. Provisions for nonadmitted persons are in INA § 212 (a)(2) and are known as exclusion or inadmissibility grounds. Both sections share categories of crimes that subject foreign nationals to removal, although the elements may differ. The most common shared category includes crimes involving moral turpitude (INA §§ 212[a][2][A] and 237[a][2][A]).

The second major distinction that favors admitted persons is that whenever crime becomes the basis of removal, with few exceptions,[14] first there must be a criminal conviction. By contrast, for nonadmitted persons, an admission to facts constituting a crime or a reasonable belief by the immigration official that a crime has been committed or attempted generally suffices for removal. In such cases, records in civil trials or information provided in an immigration application or to an immigration officer, such as at an airport, may be sufficient for removal.

The definition of criminal conviction under immigration law requires an adjudication of guilt and the apportionment of punishment, whether in a U.S. or foreign criminal process (INA § 101[a][48]).[15] Punishment is the court's actual sentence, regardless of time suspended. Punishment also need not include jail time but includes probation or community service, a rehabilitative program, or fines (INA § 101[a][48][B]). Adjudication of guilt does not require a formal pronouncement of guilt by a judge or jury at a trial; rather, the defendant can simply plead guilty or *nolo contendere* (no contest) or admit sufficient facts. Courts also presume a conviction when a judge offers probation without rendering a guilty verdict and the defendant successfully completes the probation. In such a case, the judge may withhold or defer judgment. By contrast, if the defendant obtains probation prior to the start of trial, such as through a pretrial diversion scheme, and the defendant does not plead guilty, then there is no conviction. A juvenile delinquency process, moreover, will not result in a conviction for immigration purposes, and a juvenile who is a permanent resident, for example, would not be deportable for that crime. Postconviction relief will only cease to be a conviction for immigration purposes if it is vacated on the merits due to a procedural or constitutional defect.[16] By contrast, in most jurisdictions, a conviction that is expunged, dismissed, canceled, vacated, discharged, sealed, or otherwise removed pursuant to a postconviction rehabilitative state procedure is still a conviction.

The third distinction that favors admitted persons is the burden of proof during removal proceedings. The government has to prove that the admitted person is removable by "clear and convincing" evidence (INA § 240[c][3]). By contrast, a nonadmitted person in removal proceedings or a person seeking admission must establish that she is clearly and beyond a doubt entitled to be admitted or is not inadmissible, and, if the person is already in the United States, that she is lawfully present pursuant to a prior admission (INA § 240[c][2]).

The Harshness of Criminal-Related Grounds

Criminal-related removal grounds often result in worse consequences for the foreign national than other grounds for removal. In addition, it matters greatly what criminal-related grounds get charged in the removal proceedings, as some carry the worst results.

First, relief from removal may be unavailable for persons removable on the basis of crime. Congress, for example, created exceptions or authorized discretionary waivers for many exclusion or removal grounds—often to allow for family reunification. Such waivers, however, are less available for certain crimes or not at all for others. In addition, crime may bar eligibility for other types of relief from removal, including cancellation of removal and asylum, which are discussed in Chapter 10 in the section on relief from removal and Chapter 11 in the section on legalization, respectively.

Second, criminal-related grounds could mean longer exclusion from the United States or ineligibility to seek legal readmission. Once ordered removed, a person is generally barred from readmission for at least five years if removal occurred immediately upon apprehension when trying to cross the border. The bar exists for at least ten years for persons removed who were already inside U.S. territory (INA § 212[a][9][A]). If removal was ordered on the basis of crime, however, the person becomes subject as well to the criminal-related inadmissibility grounds, some of which have no exceptions or waivers.

Third, criminal-related grounds may result in fewer due process guarantees for the foreign national in removal proceedings, including limited to no judicial review. For example, except for LPRs, foreign nationals convicted of aggravated felonies are not eligible for immigration hearings before an independent judge and are subject to administrative removal based solely on the findings of a designated DHS officer (INA § 238[b]). In addition, the INA strips federal courts of judicial review of most cases involving removal of foreign nationals on criminal-related grounds (INA § 242[a][2][C]). Still, the Supreme Court has preserved habeas corpus review in such cases (*INS v. St. Cyr*, 533 U.S. 289 [2001]), while the Ninth Circuit retained jurisdiction on determining whether a foreign national was deportable as charged (*Coronado-Durazo v. INS*, 123 F.3d 1322 [9th Cir. 1999]). These holdings have permitted challenges concerning the alleged erroneous interpretation of statutes or their constitutionality, but not to review the administrative factual findings. Then in 2005, Congress passed legislation that purports to overrule these decisions by eliminating all habeas corpus review of all final orders of removal (REAL ID Act, 119 Stat. 231). Congress, however, also added a new provision (INA § 242[a][2][D]), which allows judicial review of "constitutional claims or questions of law raised upon a petition for review," which must now be filed with the courts of appeals. Thus, while federal district courts no longer retain jurisdiction, the various courts of appeals can still hear legal and constitutional challenges in cases involving criminal removals.

Fourth, criminal-related grounds may mandate detention of the foreign national during removal and postremoval, possibly indefinitely. All persons subject to removal on the basis of crime must be detained, except those previously admitted who are removable only for one crime involving moral turpitude, for which the sentence imposed was less than a year (INA § 236[c]). In 2003, the Supreme Court upheld the constitutionality of this mandatory detention requirement (*Demore v. Kim*, 123 S. Ct. 1708 [2003]). Depending on whether the foreign national contests his removal, the detention can last from three weeks to three years. Usually, mandatory immigration detention begins upon completion of the criminal sentence, but the person may also be detained if already released from prison. Postremoval detention, according to the Supreme Court, is only authorized for up to six months, unless DHS can show that the person is likely to be removed to a third country in a "reasonably foreseeable future" (*Zadvydas v. Davis*, 533 U.S. 678 [2001]). When a third country refuses to accept them, however, few foreign nationals with criminal convictions are released based on national security reasons.

Finally, criminal-related grounds could substantially increase the penalty and likelihood that a person would be prosecuted for illegal reentry.

Two Major Categories of Criminal-Related Grounds for Removal

There are several categories of criminal-related grounds for removal,[17] although the most common charges are for crimes involving moral turpitude and aggravated felonies. Crimes involving moral turpitude, in fact, cover such a breadth of crimes that the category subsumes a more specific category of criminal-related grounds. Whenever possible, immigration agencies elevate the charge to an aggravated felony to effect harsher consequences.

Generally, the INA definition of a crime consists of three parts: the elements that must be present to establish removal; exceptions to the application of the crime; and any waivers that are only discretionary under the INA. The burden of proving elements and exceptions rests with the government in the case of persons who are deportable and with the foreign national in cases where the person is inadmissible (INA § 240[c][1]–[3]). For all waivers in all cases, the burden of proof rests with the foreign national (INA § 240[c][4]) and is not subject to judicial review (INA § 242[a][2][B]).

Generally, the Board of Immigration Appeals (BIA) and the federal circuit courts decide whether a crime should be grounds for removal. The decisionmaker usually consults only the statute under which the foreign national was convicted or charged, unless the statute is divisible, and the record of conviction is available. The record of conviction includes the charging document, the defendant's plea, the verdict, and the judgment and sentence, as well as any factual admissions made by the defendant during any plea and/or sentencing.[18] The BIA and the federal circuit courts do not always agree with each other. Nor do the federal circuit courts always agree with one another when deciding whether a crime should be grounds for removal. In such instances, foreign nationals could rely on the disagreement to argue against removal.

Crimes Involving Moral Turpitude

The category of crimes involving moral turpitude applies as both an inadmissibility and deportation ground, with some statutory variation in its elements, exceptions, and waivers. This category encompasses a breadth of crimes that carries for most foreign nationals the harsh immigration consequences described above, including disqualification of nonpermanent residents from cancellation of removal relief as discussed in Chapter 11.

The INA does not define the phrase "involving moral turpitude." Judges have therefore defined the phrase through their decisions. Generally, the BIA has held that moral turpitude refers to conduct that is inherently base, vile, or depraved, and contrary to the accepted rules of morality and the duties owed to persons, or to society in general. For example, judges normally view larceny, theft, fraud, and serious violence as moral turpitude crimes. Also, the offense will generally include specific intent to do harm or knowledge of the act's illegality. In personal injury cases, however, the BIA has held that gross recklessness—a conscious disregard of a substantial and unjustifiable risk—may still meet the definition. For example, simply driving under the influence is not a crime of moral turpitude, unless aggravating factors that contain the element of knowledge, like driving with a suspended license, are present (*Matter of Lopez-Meza*, 22 I&N Dec. 1188 [BIA 1999]). Furthermore, neither the seriousness of the criminal offense nor the severity of the sentence imposed determines whether a crime involves moral turpitude, unless the INA itself requires a minimum sentence. Moreover, aiding in the commission of a crime or acting as an accessory is enough to constitute acts of moral turpitude if the underlying offense involves moral turpitude. In addition, offenses that are regulated, not penalized, are generally found not to involve moral turpitude. Thus, for example, most immigration law violations are not considered to involve moral turpitude unless they involve fraud.

To become inadmissible, the person need only have admitted to acts that constitute the essential elements of the crime involving moral turpitude. Only two exceptions are allowed to the crimes involving moral turpitude. The first is the "youthful offender exception," in which the offender was under eighteen years of age and acted more than five years before the date of application for admission. The second is the "petty offense exception," in which the maximum penalty possible in case of a conviction did not exceed one year, and the actual prison time did not surpass six months (INA §212[a][2][A][ii]). The only authorized discretionary waiver applies to a single charge of crime involving moral turpitude if more than fifteen years have passed between the commission of the crime and the time of the application for admission; or if removal would result in extreme hardship to a U.S. citizen or LPR spouse, parent, son, or daughter; or if the foreign national is a battered spouse (INA § 212[h]).

As a deportation ground, a statute of limitation applies, but only for a single conviction of a crime involving moral turpitude. The person must have been convicted of a single crime involving moral turpitude within five years after the date of admission (or ten years for persons who held S visas),[19] where a sentence of one year or longer was possible. However, a conviction or convictions at any time with more than one crime of moral turpitude, not arising out of a single scheme, will also result in removal (INA § 237[a][2][A][i] and [ii]). This definition allows no exceptions, and the only possible waivers are presidential or gubernatorial pardons (INA § 237[a][2][A][v]) or an INA § 212h waiver for family unification if extreme hardship would result to a U.S. citizen or LPR spouse, parent, son, or daughter, or if fifteen years have passed since conviction of the crimes, but only for LPRs who have lawfully resided continuously in the United States for at least seven years immediately preceding the initiation of removal.

"Aggravated Felonies"

The harshest criminal removal ground affecting foreign nationals is that of the "aggravated felony." A conviction for an aggravated felony may trigger mandatory detention, precludes almost all relief from removal, may trigger administrative removal, and may result in permanent exclusion from the United States.

"Aggravated felony" is a term defined under INA §101(a)(43), under which the crime can be state, federal, or foreign.[20] Under the definition, the crime also need not be a felony, nor an aggravated crime. For example, a conviction of simple battery or for shoplifting with a one-year suspended sentence—either of which could be a misdemeanor or a violation in most states—can be deemed an aggravated felony. The list of aggravated felonies encompasses hundreds of crimes. The interpretation of the aggravated felony provision by the BIA and federal courts has been nuanced and complex, requiring careful study of the case law. Generally, the term applies to convictions of crimes that are punished by one-year terms of incarceration, such as theft, violent crime, burglary, counterfeiting/forgery, commercial bribery, obstruction of justice, trafficking in vehicle ID numbers, receipt of stolen property, document fraud, or perjury. It can also include crimes whose financial interest is greater than $10,000, such as crimes involving fraud or deceit, money laundering, and tax evasion. Yet a few other crimes are aggravated felonies, regardless of sentence, including drug and firearm trafficking, murder, rape and sexual abuse of minors, and several other offenses related to operating a business of prostitution, slavery, or peonage.

Since 1996, an expanded definition of "aggravated felony" has been applied retroactively such that long-term permanent residents convicted of crimes years ago could suddenly face permanent removal from the United States. In addition, nonpermanent residents charged with aggravated felonies are subject to expedited removal wherein DHS will issue them virtually unreviewable administrative orders of removal (INA § 238 [b]). Interestingly, LPRs convicted of an aggravated felony are not eligible for any waivers from removal, save if the LPR procures a pardon for the crime (INA § 237(a)[2][A][v]). In contrast, non-LPRs who commit an aggravated felony (except murder or torture) may seek a § 212(h) waiver for family unification or if fifteen years have passed since the commission of the crime (see above). Additionally, if aggravated felons return to the United States postremoval and become subject to federal prosecution for illegal reentry after deportation, they could face up to twenty years in prison (18 U.S.C. § 1326).

Crime and Naturalization

The commission of crime could also disqualify a person from naturalization. In fact, LPRs with criminal convictions might risk removal when applying for naturalization and should be careful when applying. An LPR who is in removal proceedings and who has not been denied naturalization, however, should still request that a judge grant her leave to file for naturalization, which could provide relief from removal (8 CFR § 1239.2[f]). In such cases, the LPR must still establish that she is eligible for naturalization, a factor that could be hindered by the commission of crimes.

One of the requirements for naturalization is that the person be of "good moral" character (INA § 316[a], as defined under INA § 101[f]). The definition excludes, among others, persons who within the three or five years of U.S. legal residence, which is required for naturalization, have simply committed (even if there is no conviction) crimes involving moral turpitude or drug-related crimes, except if the crime is only possession of thirty grams of marijuana or less (INA § 101[f][3]); have been convicted of two or more gambling offenses (INA § 101[f][5]); or who have been confined, as a result of a conviction, to a penal institution for an aggregate period of 180 days or more for an offense committed at any time (INA § 101[f][7]). If the conviction is for an aggravated felony at any time, the person becomes permanently barred from establishing good moral character (INA § 101[f][8]).

Appendix

Tips for Criminal Defense Lawyers

In some criminal cases, it may be possible to avoid removal for your client through smart plea bargaining or appeals to judges during sentencing. The possibilities for successful plea bargaining depend on the facts of each case, and defense attorneys should exercise creativity in negotiating alternative charges or lower sentences to avoid the removal of their clients, whenever possible. To do this, defense attorneys must understand the substantive requirements of each of the criminal-related grounds for removal under the INA, and, for that purpose, there are useful state guides that list the immigration consequences that attach to criminal charges that are usually provided online for free by the state criminal defense bar (see list of web pages below). There are also training seminars available, including one provided by a leading immigration legal publisher (www.ilw.com).

These are only a few basic options, concepts, and methodologies that defense counsel should employ when weighing the options, preferably in consultation with an immigration attorney:

- *Pretrial diversion schemes.* Pretrial diversion schemes that do not require a formal plea before the court and result in the ultimate dismissal of the charges can help an LPR avoid a criminal conviction for immigration purposes. However, an admission to the essential elements of the crime in the context of a pretrial diversion scheme could still result in removal under inadmissibility grounds, which do not require a conviction.
- *Deferred adjudication.* Deferred adjudications of guilt are not effective in avoiding a conviction for immigration purposes.
- *State First Offender Programs in the Ninth Circuit.* Only under the Ninth Circuit jurisdiction, adjudication under the Federal First Offender statute (or state counterpart) does not result in a conviction for immigration purposes.
- *Juvenile adjudications.* Adjudications of juvenile delinquency are not considered criminal convictions under immigration law.
- *Avoiding a sentence imposed of one year or more.* For crimes that require a sentence of up to a year, a 364-day sentence can avoid its application.
- *Keeping restitution under $10,000.* For crimes that require a sentence of restitution of $10,000 or more, keeping restitution under that amount can avoid its application.
- *Raising an ineffective assistance challenge.* Defense counsel might seek to undo a prior state criminal plea agreement based on an ineffective assistance of counsel challenge if trial counsel either misinformed or failed to inform the client on the immigration consequences of the plea.

This challenge is generally based on the foreign national's statutory or state constitutional right, which exists only in some states, to receive information about the immigration consequences of the crime.[21]

Additional Resources

Organizations and Persons That Could Help You in Case of Racial Profiling or Miranda Rights Violations

- The American Civil Liberties Union, http://www.aclu.org/affiliates/ (lists state office contacts for filing a complaint).
- Your public defender's office
- Your criminal lawyer

Organizations That Could Help You in Case of an Immigration Raid

- The American Civil Liberties Union, http://www.aclu.org/affiliates/ (lists state office contacts for filing a complaint).
- The Mexican American Legal Defense and Educational Fund, http://www.maldef.org/about/offices.cfm (provides a list of regional offices).
- Puerto Rican Legal Defense and Education Fund, http://www.prldef.org/Contacts/Contactus.htm (contains a list of contacts).
- Union representatives in your place of employment for what to do in case of a raid.
- Your consulate.

Selected Publications

Kesselbrenner, Dan, and Lory D. Rosenberg (under the auspices of the National Lawyers Guild). *Immigration Law and Crimes.* West Group, 2002.

Kramer, Mary E. *Immigration Consequences of Criminal Activity: A Guide to Representing Foreign-Born Defendants,* 3rd. ed. Waldorf, MD: AILA Publications, 2008.

McWhirter, Robert James. *The Criminal Lawyer's Guide to Immigration Law: Questions and Answers.* Chicago: ABA, Criminal Justice Section, 2006.

Rosenberg, Lory Diana. *Immigration Defense for Defense Counsel: An Elementary Resource and Training Guide for Defenders* (2003–2004), available at http://www.fd.org/pdf_lib/LRosenberg_Immigration_Consequences_2004.pdf.

Rosenberg, Lory Diana. *Understanding the Immigration Consequences of Convictions: An Essential Practice Guide and Training Manual for Defense Counsel* (2003), available at http://www.fd.org/pdf_lib/ImmigConsequences.pdf.

Tooby, Norton. *Criminal Defense of Immigrants.* 4th ed. Oakland: The Law Offices of Norton Tooby, 2007.

Tooby, Norton. *Safe Havens: How to Identify and Construct Non-Deportable Convictions.* Oakland: The Law Offices of Norton Tooby, 2005.

Tooby, Norton. *Post-Conviction Relief for Immigrants.* Oakland: The Law Offices of Norton Tooby, 2004.

Tooby, N., J. J. Rollin, and J. Foster. *Aggravated Felonies,* 6th ed. Oakland: The Law Offices of Norton Tooby, 2006.

Tooby, N. , J. J. Rollin, and J. Foster. *Crimes of Moral Turpitude.* Oakland: The Law Offices of Norton Tooby, 2005.

Resources on Language Issues in Criminal Proceedings

National Association of Judiciary Interpreters and Translators: http://www.najit .org/faq.html.

Moore, Joanne I., and Margaret Fisher, eds. *Immigrants in Courts.* Seattle: University of Washington Press, 1999.

Fleming, Thomas M. "Right of Accused to Have Evidence or Court Proceedings Interpreted, Because Accused or Other Participant in Proceedings Is Not Proficient in the Language Used," *American Law Reports* 32, no. 5 (1995): 149.

Pamphlets About Your Rights in Case of Immigration Raids

Atención, Protéjase de las Redadas de Inmigración, http://www.casademaryland .org/docs-pdfs/redadas.pdf.

Warning, Protect Yourself Against Immigration Raids, http://www.casade maryland.org/docs-pdfs/raids.pdf.

Selected Organizations and Other Web Resources

The American Immigration Law Foundation, www.ailf.org.

The American Immigration Lawyers Association, http://www.aila.org.

The Defending Immigrants Partnership, http://www.nlada.org/Defender/ Defender_Immigrants.

The Immigrant Legal Advocacy Project, www.immigrantlegaladvocacy.org/ crimes.html.

The National Immigration Project of the National Lawyers Guild, www.national immigrationproject.org.

The National Legal Aid and Defender Association, Defender Resources, www .nlada.org/Defender/Defender_Immigrants/Defender_Immigrants/Defender.

New York State Defenders Association, Immigrant Defense Project, http://www .nysda.org/idp/index.html.

The Law Offices of Norton Tooby, http://www.criminalandimmigrationlaw.com/ Free_verified.asp.

The Law Offices of Norton Tooby, Criminal and Immigration Law E-Newsletter (free), http://www.criminalandimmigrationlaw.com/CILU_current_issue.asp.

National Immigration Project of the National Lawyer's Guild, Criminal and Deportation Defense, http://www.nationalimmigrationproject.org/CrimPage/CrimPage .html.

The Public Defender Service for the District of Columbia, www.pdsdc.org/ CriminalLaw/Database/ImmigConsequences.asp?DocMode=Print.

The Washington Defenders Immigration Project (WDIP), http://www.defensenet .org.

Notes

1. Probable cause, which is required for all arrests and full searches, is a higher standard than reasonable suspicion and essentially requires state actors to have a fair

probability that the person arrested has committed a crime. See, e.g., *Brinegar v. United States,* 338 U.S. 160 (1949).

2. See, e.g., *Illinois v. Wardlow,* 528 U.S. 119 (2000).

3. *Gonzales-Rivera v. INS,* 22 F.3d 1441, 1452 (9th Cir. 1994); *Orhorhaghe v. INS,* 38 F.3d 488, 501 (9th Cir. 1994). The states are Alaska, Arizona, California, Hawaii, Idaho, Montana, Nevada, Oregon, and Washington. The two territories are Guam and the Northern Mariana Islands.

4. The Due Process clause of the Fifth Amendment clause applies to federal agents. The Fourteenth Amendment, which applies to state and local governments, has a similar Due Process clause.

5. *Oregon v. Bradshaw,* 462 U.S. 1039 (1983).

6. *Michigan v. Mosley,* 423 U.S. 96 (1975).

7. *Lynumn v. Illinois,* 372 U.S. 528 (1963); *Leyra v. Denno,* 347 U.S. 556 (1954).

8. Contrast *Michigan v. Tucker,* 417 U.S. 433 (1977) and *Dickerson v. United States,* 530 U.S. 428 (2000).

9. *Oregon v. Elstad,* 470 U.S. 298 (1985); *Missouri v. Seibert,* 542 U.S. 600 (2004).

10. See *Canizales-Satizabal v. United States,* 73 F.3d 364, 1995 WL 759472 (7th Cir. 1995) (unpublished opinion); *Calderon-Palomino v. Nichols,* 36 P.3d 767 (Ariz. Ct. App. 2001) (neither due process nor equal protection guarantees provide indigent Latino defendant with right to government translation of court documents in criminal proceeding; finding rational government interest in avoiding cost and delay of translation).

11. See also *State v. Orozco,* 609 So. 2d 1043 (La. Ct. App. 1992) (vacating guilty plea by Spanish-speaking defendant from El Salvador who lacked understanding of elements of drug charges against him); *Eristma v. State,* 766 So. 2d 1095 (Fla. Dist. Ct. App. 2000) (Haitian national not fluent in English failed to understand the concept of "going to trial" that his defense counsel did not adequately explain to him; court calls for an evidentiary hearing to decide whether he had ineffective assistance of counsel in rejecting a plea offer from the state).

12. The court found the English-only juror requirement satisfied the rational basis standard under the equal protection guarantee by allowing the government to forego the substantial additional expense of interpreters. It is not clear whether this rationale would hold true where the defendant is unable to understand English and thus the court proceedings would need to be translated for his or her benefit anyway. Still, an interpreter would be necessary for juror deliberations.

13. Previously removed persons can include not only those ordered removed by an immigration judge, but, in some cases, also those who signed a form to voluntarily depart or who were detected and sent back by a border patrol agent.

14. The few exceptions, known as conduct offenses, include the removal of persons who after admission have been drug abusers or addicts (INA § 237[a][B][ii]) and perpetrators of domestic violence who have violated a protection order (INA § 237[a][E][i]).

15. For a foreign judgment to qualify as a conviction, the underlying criminal conduct must also be prohibited under U.S. law. *Matter of McNaughton,* 16 I&N Dec. 569 (BIA 1978). In addition, U.S. criminal law governs the treatment of foreign crimes as felonies or misdemeanors, as well as degree of punishment for equivalent crimes. *Matter of De La Nues,* 18 I&N 140 (BIA 1981).

16. *Matter of Rodriguez-Ruiz,* 22 I&N Dec. 1378 (BIA 2000). A more recent BIA decision, *Matter of Pickering,* 23 I&N Dec. 621 (BIA 2003) appears to limit

Rodriguez-Ruiz by potentially disallowing relief where the conviction is vacated for purposes of avoiding removal.

17. These include provisions addressing controlled substance offenses, money laundering, firearm offenses, crimes of domestic violence, smuggling of unauthorized persons into the United States, and visa/passport violations. See INA §§ 212(a)(2) and 237(a)(2).

18. *Matter of Madrigal-Calvo,* Int. Dec. 32774 (BIA 1996); *Matter of Pichardo,* Int. Dec. 3275 (BIA 1996). It does not include the police report unless it is considered part of the plea agreement.

19. S visas are available to witnesses or persons possessing information relevant to a crime who collaborate with law enforcement. INA §101(a)(15)(S).

20. If the offense involves a law of a foreign country, the definition applies if the term of imprisonment was completed within the previous fifteen years.

21. These states include California, Connecticut, Florida, Georgia, Hawaii, Maryland, Massachusetts, Minnesota, New Mexico, North Carolina, Ohio, Oregon, Rhode Island, Texas, Washington, Wisconsin, and the District of Columbia.

9

Immigrants Choosing Lawyers and Filing Taxes

Choosing Legal Representation

Persons are not required to hire a lawyer for immigration law matters, such as filing a petition for immigration benefits or seeking removal relief. However, legal representation is highly recommended. Immigration laws in the United States are becoming more complex, and more immigrants are being removed, sometimes as a result of filing petitions for immigration benefits that lack merit, are not well-substantiated, or contain information that render the applicant subject to removal.

Under U.S. immigration law, legal representation is a privilege, not a right. Therefore, unlike criminal law proceedings in which the state must provide free legal counsel to indigent clients, U.S. immigration laws do not guarantee access to free legal representation, and it is the person seeking the immigration benefit or relief from removal who must hire and pay for the service. Unfortunately, legal representation can be expensive and to some, unaffordable and unattainable.

Free legal representation is quite limited, in part because U.S. law prohibits federal funds being used to offer free legal services to undocumented persons. Not-for-profit organizations, law school legal clinics, or private attorneys provide free legal representation to indigent persons usually with family-based or asylum and refugee petitions or to assist victims of domestic violence or human trafficking. Even so, there are many more clients than there are services available.

Can You Hire or Seek Nonlawyers to Help You with Immigration Matters?

Immigrants who cannot afford lawyers' fees sometimes hire nonlawyers to handle their legal matters. Usually, persons seek the services of public notaries (*notarios*), family members, or friends. In the United States, public notaries, unlike notarios in Latin America, are not attorneys. A notario's power is limited to witnessing and notarizing a signature on important documents, including immigration-related papers. Notary training consists of taking a simple test and paying a nominal fee. Accordingly, notary publics (notarios) or immigration consultants are forbidden by law to offer immigration legal advice, act as lawyers, or provide legal representation in immigration court or agencies for any purpose, unless certified. In fact, nonattorneys giving legal advice are engaging in the unauthorized practice of law (UPL).

The only persons authorized to offer legal representation under federal immigration law are

- Lawyers licensed to practice law in the United States (as defined in 8 C.F.R. § 1.1[f]). This does not include lawyers with a foreign degree or foreign license who are present in the United States. An attorney who is licensed to practice law and is in good standing in a court of general jurisdiction of her country of residence may represent an undocumented person provided that the attorney represents persons only in matters outside the geographical confines of the United States. Additionally, the service official before whom the attorney wishes to appear has discretion to allow such representation.
- Law students and law graduates not yet admitted to the bar but who are certified to appear before the Immigration Court (as defined in 8 C.F.R. § 292.1[a][2]). To appear in immigration proceedings, law students must be supervised by an immigration attorney, usually a law professor.
- Accredited representatives (who can be nonlawyers) (as defined in 8 C.F.R. § 292.1[a][4]), such as representatives of nonprofit organizations certified by the Board of Immigration Appeals. Under 8 C.F.R. § 292.2, qualifying organizations must charge only nominal fees; collect reasonable membership dues of persons giving assistance; and have at their disposal adequate knowledge, information, and experience related to immigration law and procedure.
- Reputable individuals (who can be nonlawyers) (as defined in 8 C.F.R. § 292.1[a][3]) of good moral character who appear on an individual case basis at the request of the person entitled to representation; appear without any remuneration or pay and file a declaration to that effect; have a preexisting relationship with the person entitled to representation; and receive permission from the presiding official at the appearance.
- Federal immigration law used to allow nonattorneys to provide assistance under special laws, as when Congress granted amnesty to the undocumented in 1986. Since then, however, Congress designated Qualified Designated Entities to provide legalization assistance.

Despite their lack of legal training, most notarios do more than simply notarize papers, and many file immigration petitions on behalf of clients. Does this mean they are engaging in UPL? Under federal standards, the answer is yes under most circumstances. Federal regulations define the practice of law as "the act or acts of any person appearing in any case, either in person or through the preparation or filing of any brief or other document, paper, application, or petition on behalf of another person or client" before any immigration agency (8 C.F.R. § 1.1[i]). Furthermore, the term *preparation* means the study of the facts of a case and the applicable laws, coupled with giving advice and auxiliary activities (8 C.F.R. § 1.1[k]). Thus, notarios or immigration consultants may help an individual fill in blank spaces on forms. However, they cannot advise or tell clients what information to enter on the form. In fact, under federal standards, a notario who selects a form for filing is engaging in UPL.

Despite this expansive definition of UPL and the fact that each year, tens of thousands of immigrants seeking legal assistance become victims of bad legal representation, federal standards are rarely, if ever, enforced. Even well-intentioned notarios wreak irreparable harm on foreign nationals, due to the complexities of immigration law. Some notarios intentionally exploit vulnerable immigrants who are desperate to become legal residents. There are horrific stories of notarios who fail to perform the immigration services for which they are paid; forge or alter government documents to deceive consumers; and misinterpret aspects of immigration law and proceedings to file petitions that have little to no chance of success. Unfortunately for immigrants, the costs of bad legal representation are high—liberty, family and community relationships, property, jobs, and other opportunities can all be severed or lost as a result.

In addition to federal standards, state laws often limit UPL. Some states simply bar nonlawyers from providing immigration services or restrict their advertising, as by disallowing the use of the term *notario*. Others restrict the type of services that notarios may provide. These allowances include (1) completing a form provided by a federal or state agency but not advising a person regarding answers on these forms; (2) translating a person's answer to questions on the forms; (3) securing supporting documents, such as birth certificates that must accompany the forms; (4) submitting completed forms on a person's behalf at their request to the immigration agencies; and (5) making referrals to persons who could undertake legal representation. Some states also mandate that notarios provide a written contract to clients with a description of the services to be performed, the cost, and a statement that the consultant is not an attorney. Some states even require notarios to post a bond or show proof of malpractice insurance.

How Do You Find Trustworthy Legal Representation?
Whenever possible, retain a lawyer to handle all your immigration matters. Doing so does not provide 100 percent protection against legal malpractice.

However, lawyers have legal training, are governed by a professional code of ethics, usually carry legal malpractice insurance, and are generally subject to greater accountability standards and mechanisms in case of wrongdoing.

At a minimum, retain a lawyer, whether free or paid, when you need representation for yourself, a family member, or employee who:

- Entered the United States illegally and/or resides or has resided in the country undocumented, including with an expired visa, and is seeking legalization.
- Has a criminal history, no matter how small, and is seeking legalization or naturalization.
- Has been ordered deported in the past and is seeking legalization.
- Has certain medical conditions, including contagious diseases, a mental illness, or a disability.
- Has been arrested or charged with a crime and is not or cannot prove U.S. citizenship. Here, you should seek separate immigration legal representation, even if you have a public defender or private criminal counsel in the criminal proceeding because of the immigration consequences that attach to crime. Few criminal lawyers understand immigration law and most are not required by law to advise clients about the immigration consequences.
- Is in immigration detention or in removal proceedings, regardless of immigration status.
- Has a fear of remaining or being returned to the home country and is considering applying for refuge or asylum.
- Is applying for visas with difficult qualifying and procedural requirements, including marriage, student, employment-based petitions, or those under special legislation such as the Nicaraguan Adjustment and Central American Relief Act (NACARA).
- Is a victim of human trafficking, a battered spouse or a child of a U.S. citizen or lawful permanent resident, or is cooperating with law enforcement in an investigation, which may allow for certain types of visas.

If you cannot afford a lawyer, try finding a reputable not-for-profit agency that provides free legal representation. If no free legal services are available, retain only those nonlawyers who have been certified by the relevant immigration agencies. Find out also about your state's regulation of nonlawyers, including notarios, and resist hiring persons who offer services that are beyond the scope of those state regulations or who do not otherwise comply with state requirements.

When shopping for legal representation or assistance, be sure to look for these qualifications:

- Active, current, unrestricted license to practice law, preferably in the state where the person has an office, and in U.S. Federal Court, *or* proof of DHS accreditation and any of the other requirements listed above.
- Experience in current immigration law.
- Substantial *courtroom* experience in complex immigration issues, especially if you need help with removal (deportation) proceedings.
- Recommendations from other people, nonprofit organizations, corporations, embassies, and consulates.
- Honesty, professionalism, and respect.

Ask *a lot* of questions, such as:

- What percentage of your practice involves immigration law?
- Do you have a written contract I can sign?
- In a written contract, look for an explanation of your and your legal representative's rights and responsibilities to each other. For example: costs, payment deadlines, work deadlines, and for nonlawyers, restrictions on scope of services and a statement that they are not lawyers.
- Has anyone complained against you to the state bar or any agency responsible for receiving complaints for the legal services you provide? If yes, what was the date of the complaint and what were the results?
- Do you have the time and resources to fully address my case?
- Do you have any current clients with immigration issues similar to mine?
- What is your strategy to help me with my case?
- Can you guarantee me success?
  If they answer a very enthusiastic yes, beware *because* no one *can guarantee success in any immigration law matters.* Be especially careful if someone else you may have consulted was not as enthusiastic about your case. If your case is too risky, difficult, or lacks merit, you must accept the reality that you may not be successful to pursue it.

To ensure more effective and efficient legal assistance or representation in your case, take the following steps:

- Make sure you have a written contract and you understand its terms before paying for any legal services. Keep a copy of the contract for your files.
- Make copies and get receipts for all payments you make. Do not pay in cash.
- Get copies of all documents that you sign and always keep your originals, unless originals must be submitted with the application.

- Get copies of all documents your legal representative files before an immigration agency or in court.
- Call the office periodically to check on the status of your case. If you do not hear back, go in person. If you still do not hear back, consider taking the case to a different attorney and filing a complaint. Immigration cases take a long time to be resolved, and you cannot fault your legal representative for the delay. Make sure, however, that the delay is due to the agency, and not to your representatives' omission or errors.

What You Can Do If Your Legal Representation Is Bad. In most cases, unfortunately, there is little the affected persons can do to reverse the worst harm, namely removal. This is especially the case when the original petition lacked merit (e.g., did not qualify for visa or the person was inadmissible or deportable) and no waiver or exception existed to the removal. The best remedy, then, is always preventative. Be very careful at the outset when choosing legal representation for immigration matters.

In a few cases, filing a motion to reopen the case is possible, especially when the bad legal representation pertained to failing to raise a defense, such as exceptions to exclusion or deportation grounds, or to assert a remedy, such as cancellation of removal, that might have been available to the foreign national. Motions to reopen, however, are difficult and generally only granted when the immigration judge has overlooked significant facts. The motion to reopen is often used to present new facts. Thus, an undocumented person who is seeking a review of administratively noticed facts would use a motion to reopen since the underlying facts may have changed but the underlying law has remained unchanged. Filing a motion to reopen is a difficult process and must be supported with a legal memorandum and evidentiary materials. Given the formalities and expertise necessary to draft the motion to reopen, a person without an attorney will not be capable to challenge the administrative notice through a motion to reopen. In fact, the Supreme Court has held that the INS has wide discretion in deciding whether to grant motions to reopen and has insisted that motions to reopen be granted sparingly.[1] In addition, some persons who have been removed could request a family reunification waiver and reapply for admission prior to the ten-year bar that generally attaches to removal orders (see Chapter 11 on legalization).

Irrespective of whether the foreign national is able to return to the United States or if legalization is obtained, the injured foreign national or his family and friends should also consider pursuing an administrative, civil, or criminal complaint against the legal representative, particularly in egregious cases before federal or state agencies. The deterrence effect of these sanctions depends on how well they are enforced, which varies widely. Lawyers and accredited representatives are subject to suspension and disbarment from practicing immigration law by federal immigration agencies. State laws, including professional codes of ethics, regulating lawyers or immigration consultants, in addition, may impose fines or remedies that enjoin or bar the wrongdoer from practice or impose criminal penalties. Most states have also enacted statutes that make it a misdemeanor to engage in UPL.

At the federal level, lawyers and accredited representatives who provide immigration representation may be suspended or barred from further practice by the Board of Immigration Appeals (BIA) if it is in the public interest to do so (8 C.F.R. § 292.3[a]). At least the following activities can be the basis for sanctions: charging excessive fees, fraud, bribery, threats, willfully misinforming, unethically soliciting business, practicing or aiding another to practice law without authorization or during suspension or disbarment by another court or agency, contemptuous conduct, failing to return a record to the government, a felony conviction or sentence to one year of imprisonment, falsely certifying a copy or a document, or willfully making false representations regarding qualifications or authority to represent others in a case (8 § C.F.R. 292.3[a]).

To file a complaint, a written document must be submitted with the Office of the General Counsel of the Service. Disciplinary complaints must state in detail the information that supports the basis for the complaint, including, but not limited to, the names and addresses of the complainant and the practitioner, the date(s) of the conduct or behavior, the nature of the conduct or behavior, the individuals involved, the harm or damages sustained by the complainant, and any other relevant information. The Office of the General Counsel of the Service will notify the Office of the General Counsel of the Executive Office for Immigration Review (EOIR) of any disciplinary complaint that pertains, in whole or in part, to a matter before the BIA or the immigration courts.

The procedures that states have established for pursuing legal malpractice or UPL complaints vary greatly. When the penalty is administrative or civil in nature, the process begins by someone filing a complaint with the local state bar association that regulates lawyers and in some cases nonlawyers engaging in UPL. The outcome in an administrative proceeding can result in informal or published communications of reprimand to the wrongdoer, and, when particularly egregious, can lead to disbarment—that is, the loss of a lawyer's license to practice law—or a cease and desist order against nonlawyers that bars them from providing immigration services. In some states, victims can seek private remedies in a tort action in court, but in other states, the state prosecutorial agencies are charged with pursuing UPL cases or criminal cases against lawyers, usually those involving criminal fraud or deceptive trade practices.

Finally, sometimes civil rights groups may bring high impact litigation to protect immigrants against bad legal representation. Usually, however, these civil rights groups will only take the case when there is a pattern of abuse and if the remedy is likely to be effective and benefit a large group of people. In 2003, for example, the Mexican American Legal Defense and Educational Fund (MALDEF) filed a lawsuit against Attorney General John Ashcroft, then in charge of Immigration and Naturalization Service (INS, now U.S. Citizenship and Immigration Service [USCIS]), for the INS Chicago District Office's practice between 1997 and 2001 of accepting untimely applications prepared by notarios, retaining the processing fees for their applications, and using information from the documents as a means to institute removal proceedings against many of the applicants, a practice that affected up to 5,000 undocumented immigrants. A final decision in the case is still pending.

Paying Taxes in the United States

The Internal Revenue Code (IRC) mandates that all foreign nationals who work or earn all or part of their income in the United States must pay income taxes. In addition, the United States has entered into tax treaties with approximately seventy countries around the world, including Mexico. Such treaties should be considered if applicable since they sometimes modify the general rules described in this section. Discussion of those treaties is beyond the scope of this section. Foreign nationals include all persons who are not U.S. citizens, either by birth or through naturalization. This definition includes undocumented persons who earn an income in the United States, even though they are not authorized to work, nonimmigrants or those who hold temporary visas, and LPRs. According to recent census statistics and other studies, there are an estimated 10.4 million LPRs, 1.2 million temporary legal residents, 2.5 million refugee arrivals, and 10.3 million undocumented foreign nationals who work in the United States who must pay taxes on any income they earn. Indeed, many do. Studies show that immigrants pay their fair share of taxes, and, in some cases, substantially more than they receive in public services and benefits.[2] Most foreign nationals do not qualify for most state or federal public benefits and are unable to claim any social security benefits, despite having to pay social security payroll taxes.

For federal income tax purposes, foreign nationals are classified as either residents or nonresidents. A foreign national who is a "resident for tax purposes" is generally subject to tax in the same manner as a U.S. citizen. He or she must report all interest, dividends, wages, or other compensation for services, income from rental property or royalties, and other types of income, whether from sources within or outside the United States. Taxing of nonresident foreign nationals is more complicated and generally depends on whether the income source is connected to trade or business in the United States or is passive and "fixed or determinable annual or periodical income." A nonresident foreign national usually is subject to U.S. income tax only on U.S. source income.

At first glance, it appears more advantageous to be a nonresident than a resident for tax purposes because resident foreign nationals must report their "worldwide," not just their U.S. income. Neither status, however, is uniformly preferable to the other because nonresidents cannot take certain deductions allowed to resident filers. For example, only resident foreign nationals qualify for the standard deduction and are able to file joint returns or qualify as dependents. Not all tax benefits are available to all resident foreign nationals as for U.S. citizens. Only LPRs who are also residents for tax purposes, for example, qualify for the earned income tax credit. This credit is a federal tax benefit for low-income or moderate-income working people in the form of a refund of all or some of the federal income tax deducted from the worker's paycheck during the year.

Under the IRC, residency does not turn on legal status alone, so that most undocumented persons who have lived and worked in the United States would still be considered residents for tax purposes. In this section, we focus on which foreign nationals qualify as residents. We also explain the process for filing taxes by resident foreign nationals. We then discuss how failure to file a tax return and pay taxes can result in civil or criminal penalties. Finally, we explain the consequences of tax violations to foreign nationals in immigration proceedings.

Which Foreign Nationals Are Treated as Residents?

Most foreign nationals living and working in the United States qualify as residents under the IRC. For foreign nationals who are LPRs, "residency" for tax purposes turns solely on their LPR status. For the undocumented and many who hold temporary work visas, "residency" turns, rather, on the number of days they have been physically present in the United States.

More specifically, federal tax law classifies a foreign national as a resident if

- *He or she is an LPR of the United States at any time during the calendar year for which the person files a tax return.* An LPR will continue to be considered a U.S. resident until such time as his status is revoked or abandoned (IRC §7701[b][6][B]). In fact, if an LPR files as a nonresident, immigration agencies could consider it an admission that they have abandoned their LPR status.
- *He or she meets the "substantial presence" test.* A foreign national generally meets the substantial presence test in any calendar year if (1) he or she is present in the United States at least thirty-one days during the taxable year and (2) the sum of the number of days on which he or she is present in the United States during the taxable year and the two preceding calendar years equals or exceeds 183 days (IRC § 7701[b][3][A]). In the calculation, each day of presence in the current year is counted as a full day; each day of presence in the first preceding calendar year is counted as one-third of a day; and each day of

presence in the second preceding year is counted as one-sixth of a day (IRC § 7701[b][3][A][ii]). Thus, a foreign national who is present in the United States for at least 183 days during the taxable year is a resident for tax purposes. If present for less than 183 days during the taxable year, he is still a "resident," if he has been present for at least thirty-one days during the taxable year and has spent substantial portions of his time in the United States during the three-year period ending with the taxable year. To be present in the United States means that the foreign national is physically present in U.S. territory at any time during the day, regardless of the length of time. There are exceptions to the physical presence test, including when presence is due to a medical emergency that obstructed travel or when persons are exempted because of their immigration status (IRC §§ 7701[b][3][D] and 7701[b][7]). Exempted persons include certain persons who have been admitted temporarily (nonimmigrants) as students, professional athletes, teachers, and trainees (IRC §§ 7701[b][5]).

- *He or she makes the "first year" election* (IRC § 7701(b][1][A]). The "first year" election allows a foreign national to elect to be treated as a U.S. resident when he or she is not an LPR and does not meet the "substantial presence" test, which the foreign national may wish to meet if he or she expects a refund. To qualify, the foreign national must still have met the substantial presence test for the calendar year immediately following the election year and the minimum presence requirement for the election year. Minimum presence means that the foreign national was present for a period of at least thirty-one consecutive days in the election year and at least a period equal to or exceeding 75 percent of the number of days included in the "testing period." The "testing period" refers to the period beginning with the first day of the thirty-one day period of presence and ending with the last day of the election year (IRC §§ 7701[b][4][A][iv][I] and [II]).

How Should You File a Tax Return
If You Do Not Have a Social Security Number?

Anyone (including a foreign national) who files a U.S. federal tax return must have a taxpayer identification number, which is used by the Internal Revenue Service (IRS) in the administration of tax law. For most taxpayers, this number is the social security number (SSN), issued by the Social Security Administration. Except for LPRs and other legal foreign nationals authorized to work in the United States, however, foreign nationals do not qualify for SSNs and must request an individual taxpayer identification number (ITIN) directly from the IRS.

An ITIN is a tax processing number available only for certain nonresident and resident foreign nationals, their spouses, and dependents, who are ineligible for an SSN. It is a nine-digit number, beginning with the number

"9," formatted like an SSN (NNN-NN-NNNN). To obtain an ITIN, a person must complete IRS Form W-7. Form W-7 requires documentation substantiating foreign status and true identity for each individual. Foreign taxpayers may either mail the documentation, along with the Form W-7, to the Philadelphia Service Center, present it at an IRS walk-in office, or process the application through an Acceptance Agent authorized by the IRS. The IRS has reduced to thirteen the number of documents the agency will accept as proof of identity to obtain an ITIN. An original, or a certified or notarized copy, of an unexpired passport is the only document that is accepted for both identity and foreign status. In the absence of a passport, foreign nationals must provide a combination of current documents that contain expiration dates. The documents must also show name and photograph and support the claim of foreign status. The IRS will also accept certified or notarized copies of a combination (two or more) of the following documents, in lieu of a passport:

- National identification card (must show photo, name, current address, date of birth, and expiration date)
- U.S. driver's license
- Civil birth certificate
- Foreign driver's license
- U.S. state identification card
- Foreign voter's registration card
- U.S. military identification card
- Foreign military identification card
- Visa
- U.S. Citizenship and Immigration Services photo identification
- Medical records (dependents under fourteen years old only)
- School records (dependents and/or students under twenty-five years old only)

The ITIN, unlike the SSN, is not to be used for identification purposes or to procure a job. Thus, many undocumented workers usually possess an invalid SSN for employment purposes and an ITIN for tax filing purposes. Consequently, every year, hundreds of thousands of tax returns are filed with ITINs and W-2 forms (the form provided by employers that show wages) with invalid SSNs. The discrepancy, in essence, is an admission that the worker is not authorized to work in the United States. This is preferable, however, to filing taxes using only the invalid SSN, which constitutes an additional violation of U.S. tax and social security laws.

When the taxpayer files with an ITIN that does not match the SSN on the W-2 form, the IRS will process the return under the ITIN but will notify the taxpayer in writing that a corrected W-2 must be filed with the ITIN. Since this request cannot be executed, the IRS will resolve the mismatch by verifying that taxpayer's information provided in the W-2 and will process the return either to assess the tax liability or to issue a refund. Of course, the ITIN cannot be used as the SSN, which is used to calculate social security retirement benefits. As a result, unauthorized workers who pay social security taxes will not likely receive any benefits for their payments as long as they are not authorized to work in the United States.

What Are the Civil or Criminal Consequences for Tax Violations?

Every year, hundreds of thousands of taxpayers avoid paying some or all of their taxes by failing to file altogether or sometimes fraudulently. Tax evasion can result in civil or monetary tax liability, often with penalties imposed by the IRS or the courts, and sometimes in criminal charges.

The IRS learns about tax return inaccuracies in a number of ways. For example, the agency matches information reported by others to information on filed returns, investigates information provided by informants, checks self-reporting by the taxpayer, and conducts audits.

In general, the IRS must determine any additional tax due within three years of when the return was due or actually filed, whichever is later. However, there are many situations in which this limitations period is extended (I.R.C. §§ 6501 & 6503). After the IRS determines the additional tax, it has a further period of time in which to actually collect from the taxpayer. This period for collection is at least ten years or longer (I.R.C. §§ 6502 & 6503).

If the taxpayer fails to file a required return, or files it late, or fails to pay the tax shown on the return as due, the IRS is likely to impose delinquency penalties. A penalty of 5 percent of the tax due is imposed for each month or part of a month that the return is late, up to a maximum of 25 percent of the tax due (I.R.C. § 6651[a][1]). If the failure to file is motivated by fraud, the penalty amount rises to 15 percent per month, capped at a 75 percent maximum (I.R.C. § 6651[f]).

If the return is filed on time, but the tax shown as due is not paid on time, a .05 percent penalty is imposed for each month or part of a month of the lateness, again up to a maximum of 25 percent (I.R.C. § 6651[a][2]). A late payment of additional tax properly determined by the IRS to be due results in a similar penalty (I.R.C. § 6651[a][3]). These penalties may be excused if the delinquency was "due to reasonable cause and not due to willful neglect," but reasonable cause is defined fairly strictly under the Internal Revenue Manual (I.R.M. 20.1.1.3).

If the taxpayer has already fully paid the tax, such as through tax withholding from his or her wages, late filing of the income tax return will not lead to a delinquency penalty. There are still good reasons to file the return, however, even if it is late. For example, if withholding has exceeded tax liability, the taxpayer is entitled to have that excess refunded. Failure to make a timely claim results in inability to claim at all. In general, refund claims must be filed within two years of when the tax was paid, although various special rules can affect this period (I.R.C. § 6511).

Insufficient withholding is subject to a penalty for failure to pay estimated tax (I.R.C. § 6654). Even if the return is late and some penalties are due, late filing and late payment may still be desirable because they could prevent imposition of additional and possibly more severe penalties.

If the return is filed on time but inaccurate, the consequences depend on the cause and magnitude of the errors. If the taxpayer made an honest mistake despite taking reasonable care, the taxpayer will have to pay the extra tax due plus interest. The interest rate is tied to general economic interest rates and thus varies quarterly (I.R.C. §§ 6601 & 6621). At this writing, the interest rate on tax underpayments was around 8 percent compounded daily.

If the return is inaccurate because of negligence on the taxpayer's part or other factors set out in the statute, the taxpayer may have to pay, in addition to the additional tax and interest, a penalty equal to 20 percent of the part of the underpayment attributable to the negligence (I.R.C. § 6662[a] & [b]). For this purpose, negligence "includes any failure to make a reasonable attempt to comply with the provisions" of the IRC and also includes "any careless, reckless, or intentional disregard" of those provisions (I.R.C. § 6662[c]). The penalty will not be imposed if there was reasonable cause and "the taxpayer acted in good faith" (I.R.C. § 6664[c][1]). Reasonable cause can include reliance on the advice of a tax professional as long as the professional was well qualified and the reliance was reasonable (Treas. Reg. § 1.6664-4[b][1]).

If the return is fraudulent, a penalty equal to 75 percent of the underpayment attributable to fraud can be imposed (I.R.C. § 6663). Taxpayers commit tax fraud when they intentionally engage in wrongdoing with the specific intent to evade tax that they knew was owed.

In addition to the above civil penalties, a taxpayer may be subject to criminal sanctions, although these are much less commonly applied. The IRC defines many tax crimes, and some overlap occurs among the sections. The most serious of the tax crimes applies to "any person who willfully attempts in any manner to evade or defeat any tax imposed by (the IRC) or the payment thereof." Doing so constitutes a felony punishable by imprisonment of up to five years, fines of up to $100,000, and the costs of prosecution (I.R.C. § 7201). These are "per count" figures. Because, in general, each tax year is a separate count, fraud over multiple years can multiply the punishment totals.

Other criminal tax offenses in the IRC include willful failure to file returns, pay estimated tax or tax, and/or keep or supply required information (I.R.C. § 7203); failure to supply required information to an employer or other person, or supplying false information (I.R.C. § 7205); making false declarations under penalties of perjury (I.R.C. § 7206[1]); aiding or assisting tax evasion (I.R.C. § 7206[2]); removing or concealing property to defeat tax collection (I.R.C. § 7206[4]); delivering or disclosing to the IRS any false "list, return, account, statement, or other document" (I.R.C. § 7207); and failing to collect or to pay to the IRS tax amounts that the person was required to collect or truthfully account for (I.R.C. § 7202).

A key element of tax crime is willfulness. Criminal tax penalties can be imposed only if the taxpayer or other defendant acted willfully, that is, voluntarily, knowingly, and intentionally. Willfulness suffices. The government need not prove evil intent or bad faith on the part of the taxpayer.

How Do Tax Violations Affect Immigration Proceedings?

Either failing to pay taxes or committing tax fraud could have adverse immigration consequences. These consequences include impediments to legalization or naturalization and even removal. Usually, a foreign national's failure to file and pay taxes when the person has not been charged with or convicted of a crime can be remedied by filing back taxes. The worst situation, however, is when the tax violation has resulted in criminal liability.

Therefore LPRs should vigilantly stay current on tax payments, both local and federal, before applying for naturalization. Form N-400, the application for naturalization, specifically asks in Question 5, Part 10A whether the applicant owes any federal, state, or local taxes that are overdue. A yes reply could result in denial of the application, as the person could be viewed as lacking oath and allegiance to the United States, one of the requirements for naturalization. A false no could also constitute immigration fraud, which could affect a finding of good moral character, a requirement for naturalization.

Moreover, a charge or conviction resulting from failure to file taxes or for committing fraud when filing could be considered a crime involving moral turpitude or even an aggravated felony. Immigration cases have held that a charge or conviction for willfully failing to file a return or to supply information with intent to evade taxes constitutes a crime involving moral turpitude.[3] Thus, a charge or even an admission to facts of willful tax evasion could render a person applying for a visa ineligible for legalization. For a person already holding a visa, even as an LPR, a conviction for willful tax evasion could result in removal. Also, when the conviction for tax fraud has resulted in a loss to the government greater than $10,000, an LPR or other visa holder could face permanent removal as an aggravated felon (under INA § 101[a][43][M][ii]).

Additionally, LPRs and U.S. citizens who are considering sponsoring their relatives for a visa will be required to file an affidavit of support on behalf of their family member. An affidavit of support serves as evidence that the family member seeking legalization is not likely to become a public charge, in part because the sponsor's income will count against the family member's eligibility for public benefits until that person becomes a U.S citizen or for up to ten years. In filing an affidavit of support, the sponsor must submit tax returns for the three most recent years as evidence of income

(Immigration Form I-134). Persons who do not have income and have not filed taxes may procure the affidavit of support from a third person.

Appendix

Choosing an Immigration Attorney or Representative

- If you want to verify whether a person (nonattorney) or agency is authorized to provide immigration legal services, then check the website of the Executive Office for Immigration Review (EOIR), at http://www.usdoj.gov/eoir/statspub/raroster.htm.
- For a list of low-cost or free immigration legal service providers in your state, go the American Bar Association (ABA) Commission on Immigration's website at www.abanet.org/publicserv/immigration/probono.shtml and click on your state in the map.
- Catholic Legal Immigration Network, Inc. (CLINIC) has offices throughout the country, and their website is www.cliniclegal.org.
- If you are able to pay for a lawyer, good immigration lawyers generally join the professional organization for immigration lawyers known as the American Immigration Lawyers Association. You can find a lawyer by going to http://www.ailalawyer.com.

Filing Complaints If You Are a Victim of Bad Legal Representation

- If you have been a victim of an immigration notario or consultant, file a complaint with the state attorney general's office or the state Consumer Affair's Office in your state. If enough complaints are filed, the state agency might investigate them for fraud or deceptive practices.
- If you have a complaint about your attorney, contact your local state bar association to make a complaint.
- For both attorneys and accredited representatives, you can also file a complaint with DHS or the Executive Office of Immigration Review. For details, visit http://www.usdoj.gov/eoir/press/00/profcondfaks.htm. The complaint form is available at http://www.usdoj.gov/eoir/eoirforms/eoir44.pdf.
- Read the following website for more information about filing complaints: http://www.cliniclegal.org/Legalization/resources/FilingcomplaintsagainstNotariosandImmigrationConsultants.pdf.

Paying Taxes

For more information on tax identification numbers (TINs), visit, http://www.irs.gov/businesses/small/article/0,,id=98350,00.html.

Notes

1. In *INS v. Abudu*, 485 U.S. 94 (1988), the Supreme Court directed the Board of Immigration Appeals not to reopen unless certain showings are made and did not affirmatively require reopening under any particular condition. More recently, the Supreme Court held in *INS v. Doherty*, 498 U.S. 1081 (1991), that "the granting of a motion to reopen is . . . discretionary . . . and . . . disfavored."

2. See, e.g., Immigration Policy Report, *Immigrants Pay Their Fair Share*, available at www.ailf.org/ipc/policy_reports_2002_pay.asp (discussing the 2001 study conducted by the Bureau of Economic and Business Research at the University of Florida); James P. Smith, *The New Americans: Economic, Demographic, and Fiscal Effect of Immigration* (Washington, D.C.: National Academy Press, 1997) (finding that due to contributions by immigrants, the total net benefit to the social security system will be nearly $500 billion).

3. *Carty v. Gonzales*, 2005 WL 2413944 (9th Cir. 2005).

10
Documented Immigrants

Government Benefits

Prior to 1996, all immigrants were eligible for most federal public benefits. The Personal Responsibility Act and Work Opportunity Reconciliation Act of 1996 (PRWORA), however, removed or restricted immigrants' eligibility for federal aid programs and authorized states to deny several federal and state benefits, including to documented immigrants. The stated policy goals for these reforms were to promote self-sufficiency among immigrants and to discourage immigration (PRWORA § 402[a][1] & [a][3]). These reforms, however, were founded on erroneous assumptions of immigrants' dependence on public benefits and resulted in increased stigmatization of immigrants and the denial of a basic safety net and health services to them.

PRWORA classified all foreign nationals into two categories of eligibility for federal, state, or local public benefits: "qualified aliens" and "not-qualified aliens" (PRWORA § 431). "Qualified aliens" included, among others, LPRs, those granted refugee or asylum status, and certain battered spouses or children (PRWORA § 431). PRWORA further categorized "qualified aliens" into two groups: those who arrived before and after the date President Clinton signed the law, which was August 22, 1996 (PRWORA § 431). "Not-qualified aliens" included not only the undocumented but also those holding temporary legal status (nonimmigrants) or those awaiting legalization.

In general, PRWORA did three things. First, it restricted the eligibility of "qualified aliens" to receive several federally funded public benefits. Second, it authorized state and local governments to deny locally funded benefits to "qualified aliens," despite Supreme Court precedent (*Graham v. Richardson*, 403 U.S. 365 [1971]) requiring states to treat citizens and legal immigrants alike in terms of public benefits eligibility. Third, the legislation tightened restrictions on the few public benefits once available to certain persons now considered "not qualified."

In this section, we discuss the major provisions of PRWORA affecting documented immigrants' access to public benefits. Congress has also adopted post-PRWORA federal legislation conferring broader immigration and public benefits to certain foreign nationals who have been victims of violence, including victims of domestic violence.[1] We also discuss what a few states have done to restore documented immigrants' access to some of these benefits based on strong public policy or rights-based reasons.

PRWORA, SSI, and Food Stamps

PRWORA barred "qualified aliens" from receiving supplemental security income (SSI) and food stamps, at least until those eligible attain citizenship or meet additional requirements (PRWORA §§ 401 and 402[a][][1]). SSI is a federally funded, need-based program that provides cash assistance to low-income persons who are over sixty-five years old, blind, or disabled (Social Security Act, 42 U.S.C. §§ 1381–1383). Food stamps are coupons provided to needy families for the purpose of buying food (Food Stamp Act, 7 U.S.C. §§ 2017[a], 2014[d], [e] and 2012[o]).

Certain classes of "qualified aliens" were exempted from SSI and food stamps restrictions: (1) refugees, asylees, and individuals granted withholding of deportation, but only for the first five years after being granted that status; (2) active duty service members, veterans, and their direct family members; and (3) LPRs who could prove they had worked at least forty qualifying quarters, or ten years, for social security purposes (PRWORA § 402[a][2]).[2]

The changes to SSI were particularly dire to elderly and disabled immigrants, many of whom were Latino/as. Many already receiving benefits simply could not find work because of age or disability, lacked the ten-year work history, or were unable to naturalize due to lack of English proficiency. In 1997, however, a budget compromise reached by President Clinton and Congress restored SSI benefits to LPRs who had been in the country prior to August 26, 1996, the date of PRWORA's enactment, if they had already been receiving benefits or subsequently became disabled. Still, this means that immigrants who gained LPR status after August 26, 1996, are still barred from SSI and food stamps, at least until they become citizens or have worked the forty qualifying quarters in the United States. For most, the ten-year work exception is actually illusory because immigrants who have worked that long become fully insured under the Social Security Program, without the need to apply for SSI.[3]

In 2002, Congress also passed the Farm Security and Rural Investment Act, which restored food stamp eligibility to three groups of "qualified aliens": (1) persons who lived in the United States as "qualified" immigrants for at least five years; (2) children regardless of their date of entry; and (3) persons receiving disability-related assistance regardless of their date of entry (Farm Bill, 7 U.S.C. § 7911 *et seq.*).

Medicaid and TANF

PRWORA also restricted "qualified aliens'" access to other federal means-tested programs. Each year, through more than eighty such programs, the federal government provides benefits and services to individuals and families with low incomes. PRWORA explicitly exempted a number of programs from the term "federal means-tested public benefits" (PRWORA § 403[c][2]). In 1997, the U.S. Department of Health and Human Services (DHHS) issued an interpretation of the term "federal means-tested public benefits" and determined that only Medicaid and Temporary Assistance for Needy Families (TANF) are included in the exclusions. Medicaid is a medical assistance program jointly financed by state and federal governments for low-income individuals (Medicaid Act, 42 U.S.C. § 1396 *et seq.*). TANF, commonly known as welfare, is the monthly cash assistance program for poor families with children under age eighteen.

"Not-qualified aliens" for purposes of Medicaid and TANF include LPRs, at least for a period of five years after "entry" with LPR status into the United States or from the date of adjustment of status of LPR for those already in the country (PRWORA § 401[a]). LPRs who have worked for at least ten years are still eligible for these programs (PRWORA § 402 [a][1][B]). The 1997 federal budget compromise also restored Medicaid benefits to LPRs receiving benefits prior to August 26, 1996, as well as to those not yet receiving benefits but residing in the United States prior to August 26, 1996, who subsequently became disabled. Here again, certain classes of "qualified aliens" are exempted from Medicaid and TANF exclusions. Refugees, asylees, and those granted deportation withholding are thus eligible for these same means-tested benefits for their first seven years in the United States, as are Cuban and Haitian entrants (PRWORA § 403[d]). In addition, veterans, active-duty military personnel, and their spouses and dependents may qualify for exceptions (PRWORA § 403[a][1]).

Furthermore, for some LPRs meeting the five-year residency requirement, qualifying for Medicaid and TANF may still not be possible on the basis of income. About one-half of petitions for LPR status require that a sponsor file an "affidavit of support" on the petitioner's behalf to avoid being excluded on the basis that he or she "is likely at any time to become a public charge" (INA § 212[a][4]). Under the "deeming requirements" of the PRWORA, the income of the sponsor and/or the LPR's spouse must be considered in determining income eligibility for SSI and food stamps until the LPR becomes a citizen or for up to ten years (7 U.S.C. §2014[j][2] for food stamps; 42 U.S.C. § 1382j[b] for SSI). In fact, for all means-tested programs, the LPR is likely to become ineligible for benefits if the sponsor's income is reported, even if the LPR meets other qualifying criteria. If the LPR still receives benefits, the sponsor must reimburse government agencies for any benefits paid to or for the LPR whom they sponsor (PRWORA § 423[c]).

State Administration of Public Benefits

Since PRWORA, public benefits are no longer federally administered or uniformly applied. Congress transferred to the states much of the authority not only to design and implement benefit programs, but also to determine eligibility requirements affecting immigrants' qualification for most state and local means-tested programs (PRWORA §§ 402, 403). Prior to PRWORA, the federal government provided assistance through entitlement programs funded jointly with states and the DHHS, which monitored each state's performance to ensure compliance with federal standards. Now, these entitlements have been converted to block grants that states administer largely according to their own discretion. Although states must still submit their plans to DHHS, the agency's involvement is minimal.

State agencies responsible for administering public benefits programs must verify applicants' immigration and citizenship status to ensure that both "qualified" and "not-qualified aliens" do not receive inapplicable public benefits (PRWORA § 432). Verification should only occur when the benefit sought is contingent on citizenship or legal immigration status and applied only to persons receiving benefits. PRWORA, however, did not establish clear guidelines for verification purposes and, in fact, granted states discretion to adopt their own verification systems. Federal guidelines adopted post-PRWORA do exist, however. These guidelines recommend that state agencies remove questions from applications that are likely to chill participation of immigrant applicants. For example, social security numbers are sometimes required but should be limited to benefits where legal immigrant status is required. Further, PRWORA included some narrow provisions on reporting applicants to immigration authorities that apply solely to three programs (SSI, public housing, and TANF) and requires reporting only persons whom the agency knows are not lawfully present in the United States (PRWORA § 404).

Some states, like Arizona, have passed resolutions (e.g., Arizona Proposition 200) that would impose civil and criminal penalties against state employees who fail to verify immigration status and report to law enforcement applicants who do not qualify. At least seven other states—Arkansas, Alabama, Colorado, Georgia, Tennessee, Virginia, and Ohio—have introduced bills or ballot measures similar to Proposition 200. Although these state provisions go beyond federal regulations, PRWORA appears to authorize states to coordinate enforcement with immigration officials.[4] In fact, states must allow their public benefits administrators to disclose an applicant's un-lawful immigration status to immigration officials.

What You Should Do as an Undocumented Immigrant Before Seeking Government Benefits. The risk to undocumented persons of being reported to immigration agencies is thus likely to vary from state to state and from agency to agency. Undocumented persons, therefore, should take steps to learn about local practices before deciding to seek benefits. However, state employees who impose undue restrictions on eligible foreign nationals seeking benefits could run afoul of other federal verification and reporting guidelines and of civil rights protections. Title VI of the Civil Rights Act of 1964 prohibits these state agencies from discriminating on the basis of national origin, an obligation that includes providing reasonable language assistance to foreign nationals (42 U.S.C. § 2000[d]–[d][1], § 601).

State Responses Post-PRWORA
States have the option of denying or restoring federal means-tested benefits beyond what the PRWORA approved (PRWORA § 402[a][2][G] and [b][2][E]). Congress further permitted states to bar foreign nationals from participating in any of the benefit programs financed by Title XX block grants, such as child care, in-home assistance for disabled persons, and support services for abused and neglected children (PRWORA § 402[a][2][G] and [b][2][E]). Additionally, states may also include or exclude most current and future legal immigrants from state-funded benefit programs, although they cannot deny services to "qualifying aliens" who remain eligible for SSI and food stamps, or who have earned forty qualifying work quarters during their residence in the country (PRWORA § 412).

With some exceptions, state responses since PRWORA was enacted have been to attempt to restore certain benefits to legal immigrants. Over half of the states are spending their own money to cover at least some of the immigrants who are ineligible for federally funded programs, although these programs offer fewer benefits. Several state constitutions or laws require states to provide basic forms of aid removed by PRWORA. In addition, strong public policy reasons, particularly related to the adverse consequences of denying basic health care to immigrants (e.g., an increase in communicable diseases, decreased prenatal and preventive health care, complications from untreated chronic diseases) have pushed states to utilize state funds to provide essential health services removed by PRWORA.

Thus, for example, many states have also exercised the option to provide state-funded medical assistance to LPRs. Eligibility for these state-funded medical programs varies considerably and may depend on the LPR's age or length of residence in the state. Also, several states have chosen to provide state-funded food stamps to some or all legal immigrants while a few others provide emergency food assistance.[5] In addition, although immigrants may not receive federal TANF money for five years, some states provide state-funded TANF benefits. Several states have also established residency requirements in their TANF programs.

Citizenship

Nations define full membership in a society through the conferral of citizenship and, with membership, come rights, benefits, and duties. In the United States, for example, citizenship confers the right and duty to vote. It also grants greater access to social services and to family unification benefits under the immigration laws. Moreover, citizenship is increasingly essential for permanent residents (LPRs) to remain in the country, particularly given the expansion of grounds for removal and the reduction of any relief.

The United States generally recognizes three types of citizenship: (1) by birth in the country, or *jus solis;* (2) through naturalization; or (3) by descent or being the child of at least one U.S. citizen parent, also known as *jus sanguinis.*

Citizenship by birthright and through naturalization are constitutionally conferred through the Fourteenth Amendment of the U.S. Constitution, which reads in relevant part: "All persons born or naturalized in the United States, and subject to the jurisdiction thereof, are citizens of the United States and of the state wherein they reside." While the Constitution has never mandated citizenship by descent, Congress conferred such a right through statute as early as 1790. In addition, Congress is expressly authorized by the U.S. Constitution to establish a "uniform Rule of Naturalization" (U.S. Const. art. 1, § 8, cl. 4). The U.S. Supreme Court has interpreted the naturalization clause to include conferral of citizenship by descent (*Rogers v. Bellei*, 401 U.S. 815 [1971]).

Thus Congress cannot simply legislate away citizenship conferral. Congress does possess the authority to define the nature and scope of citizenship under the naturalization clause, at least with regard to citizenship through naturalization or descent. The limits on Congress's lawmaking authority in this area, in fact, are minimal. Still, Congress could not establish laws that restrict who can qualify for naturalization or citizenship by descent to the degree that the right would cease to exist. Congress may impose any condition on citizenship through naturalization or descent as long as it is not "unreasonable, arbitrary or unlawful" (*Rogers v. Bellei*, 401 U.S. 815 [1971]).

Furthermore, Congress cannot impose on birthright citizenship any conditions that violate the U.S. Constitution. Any such conditions must come from the U.S. Constitution itself. The judiciary is the final arbiter of interpreting the nature and scope of any constitutional limit on birthright citizenship. Understanding this basic principle is crucial, as groups opposed to immigration have sought to deny birthright citizenship to children born in the United States to undocumented parents.

Birthright Citizenship of Children Born in the United States to Undocumented Parents

Congress codified birthright citizenship under the Immigration and Nationality Act (INA) § 301(a), which, like the text in the Fourteenth Amendment, defines such a citizen as "a person born in the United States, and subject to the jurisdiction thereof." The attack on the birthright citizenship rights of children born in the United States to undocumented parents has turned on the qualifying phrase of the Fourteenth Amendment "subject to the jurisdiction thereof." The racial animus that motivates exclusion of certain foreign nationals born in the United States from citizenship is not new, despite the Fourteenth Amendment's origin from the civil rights struggle to end slavery and its granting of full membership rights to blacks.

Originally, the U.S. Constitution was silent as to birthright citizenship, and even the 1790 citizenship act did not recognize it as a right.[6] It was not until the aftermath of the U.S. Civil War, a struggle in part over slavery, that three constitutional amendments were adopted to foster racial equality: the Thirteenth Amendment, which abolished slavery; the Fifteenth, which prohibited race-based voting restrictions, and the Fourteenth, which, in addition to conferring citizenship rights, included a due process and equal protection clause. The Fourteenth Amendment overturned the Supreme Court precedent that declared that black slaves and free blacks were not "citizens," even if born in U.S. territory (*Scott v. Sandford*, 60 U.S. 393 [1856]).

But what did the phrase "subject to the jurisdiction thereof" mean? The question arose in another attempt to deny citizenship rights to nonwhites—this time, to U.S.-born Native Americans. In *Elk v. Wilkins*, 112 U.S. 94 (1884), the Supreme Court held that an "Indian" born in the United States but within tribal authority was not born "subject to the jurisdiction" of the United States and thus did not acquire U.S. citizenship at birth. That holding remains law today. It was only by subsequent statute that Congress conferred U.S. citizenship rights on Native Americans born on the reservation (INA § 301[b]).

In 1898, when Chinese immigrants with permanent lawful status but no eligibility for naturalization bore children in the United States, the Supreme Court resolved that "subject to the jurisdiction thereof" meant to exclude only Native Americans, children of diplomatic representatives in a foreign state, and children born of "alien enemies in hostile occupation" in the United States (*United States v. Wong Kim Ark*, 169 U.S. 649 [1898]). Thus, U.S. born children of Chinese parents residing lawfully in the country were declared citizens by birth.

The idea that birthright citizenship extended to children born in the United States to foreign nationals appears settled. However, in the 1980s, the argument surfaced that undocumented parents could be considered "alien enemies in hostile occupation," and thus, their children born in the United States would be excluded from Fourteenth Amendment rights. Moreover, since the early 1990s, a serious political movement to eliminate birthright citizenship has been afoot. To date, however, these efforts have failed.

Citizenship Through Naturalization

In 1990, Congress transferred the authority to grant naturalization to the attorney general (now the secretary of Homeland Security through the Department of Homeland Security). While Congress still establishes the requirements for naturalization through statute, DHS retains broad discretion in the interpretation of laws and their implementation. Thus, the naturalization process is primarily administrative—that is, courts do not play a significant role in its conferral. The judicial role, however, has not been entirely eliminated. The applicant may still elect or be required in many cases to take the final oath in a court of law, for instance. More importantly, courts retain jurisdiction to review denials of naturalization *de novo*, or anew (INA §§ 310 [b, c]).

Currently, there are eight basic statutory requirements to naturalization. The naturalization form itself (N-400), available at www.uscis.gov, contains questions to establish whether a person meets the following requirements. Lying on the application constitutes fraud, which could carry criminal consequences and possibly removal. (See Chapter 8 on immigration crimes.) In addition, naturalization requires a criminal background check. Thus, applicants with criminal histories must be careful because rather than serving as a process for obtaining naturalization, the application may result in removal.

1. *Lawful Permanent Residents.* Only persons lawfully admitted as LPRs are eligible for naturalization (INA § 318). INA § 318 also specifies that naturalization may not be conferred while removal proceedings are pending or while a final finding of removability is outstanding. If a person has honorably served in time of war or declared hostility, LPR status as a precondition is unnecessary (INA § 329).

2. *Residence and Physical Presence.* The applicant must have "resided continuously" after being admitted as an LPR in the United States for either (1) a five-year period immediately preceding the filing of the application (INA § 316[a]); or (2) a three-year period immediately preceding the filing of the application when the applicant became an LPR through marriage to a U.S. citizen and has been living in that marital union during that three-year period (INA § 319[a]). The INA defines residence as a "person's principal, actual dwelling place in fact, without regard to intent" (INA § 101[a][33]). However, because residence must also be continuous, long absences, even if the person meets the principal residence requirements, can disqualify the

person from citizenship. Generally, "continuous residence" means the applicant cannot have traveled outside the United States for more than six months, unless the applicant can establish that he did not intend to abandon his residence in the United States for such period (INA § 316[b]). The regulations at 8 C.F.R. § 316.5(c)(1)(i) provide examples that would support a claim that residence had not been interrupted even with an absence of between six and twelve months: (a) the applicant did not terminate her employment in the United States; (b) the applicant's immediate family remained in the United States; (c) the applicant retained full access to her U.S. abode; or (d) the applicant did not obtain employment while abroad. Absences for longer than a year break the continuity automatically, and the clock must begin anew (INA § 316).[7] In addition, the applicant must be physically present in the United States for at least half of the five- or three-year residency requirement (INA § 316[c]). There are more flexible requirements for children of U.S. citizens or for applicants who have served in the U.S. military (INA §§ 322 and 328). Part 7 on Form N-400, concerning all dates of entry and exit from the United States, must be carefully and accurately completed. At the interview, the USCIS may require copies of previously filed tax returns, verification of trips on the applicant's passport, and other proof if there is any doubt that the applicant has not met the requirement of "physical presence in the United States."

3. *Good Moral Character.* The applicant must demonstrate that he or she is of good moral character, at minimum for the periods for which residence and physical presence are required (INA § 316[a][3]). INA § 101(f) defines what acts would preclude a finding of good moral character, although the list is not exhaustive. These categories include alcoholism, the commission of specified crimes, being a professional gambler, the commission of fraud to obtain immigration benefits, and having been incarcerated for an aggregate period of 180 days or more. Some categorized activities, such as the commission of an aggravated felony as the term is defined in INA § 101[a][43], preclude a permanent finding of "good moral character."

4. *Age.* The applicant must be at least eighteen years old to apply for naturalization (INA § 334[b]). However, under the Child Citizenship Act of 2000, any child who (a) has a U.S. citizen parent; (b) is under age eighteen; and (c) resides in the United States as an LPR, in the legal and physical custody of the citizen parent, automatically becomes a citizen when the naturalization petition is approved for the parent (INA § 320). This provision applies to both biological and adopted children, although to qualify as a child under immigration laws, the child must have been adopted prior to reaching the age of sixteen (INA § 101[b][E][i]). Although such citizenship is automatic and does not require any application, such individuals are wise to obtain a passport or some other government-issued documentation confirming such citizenship. For children who do not qualify for automatic citizenship, INA § 322 allows parents to file on their behalf for naturalization,

as long as (1) the children have a U.S. citizen parent who files the application; (2) either the citizen parent or the children's citizen grandparent (parent of the citizen parent) has been physically present in the United States for five years, at least two of which were before either the parent or grandparent reached the age of fourteen; (3) the children are under the age of eighteen; and (4) the children reside outside the United States in the legal and physical custody of the citizen parent but are temporarily present in the United States after a lawful admission.

5. *English Language.* The petitioner must demonstrate during an interview with an immigration officer "an understanding of the English language, including an ability to read, write, and speak words in ordinary usage" (INA § 312[a][1]). Generally, this involves conversing and responding in English to questions on the civics test, described below. There are a few exceptions to the English-language requirement based on physical or mental disability, which must be substantiated through a medical examination (INA § 312[b][1]). The exception also applies to a person who is over fifty years of age and has been living in the United States for at least twenty years as an LPR, or a person who is over fifty-five years of age and has been living in the United States for at least fifteen years as an LPR (INA § 312[b][2]).

6. *Knowledge of Civics.* Applicants must demonstrate "knowledge and understanding of the fundamentals of the history, and of the principles and form of government, of the United States." CIS has designed a test of 100 questions, which an immigration officer randomly asks during an interview. Currently, CIS is seeking to redesign the test to include new questions that test concepts on democracy and the rights and responsibilities of citizenship, not just facts. The test, which is apparently harder, has pleased anti-immigrant groups and worried immigration advocates. That new test was administered in 2007 to 6,000 volunteers in 10 different cities, and consisted of 144 questions. Based on the results, CIS will create a new 100-question test and administer it to all applicants beginning in 2008. Whether the person passes the test is at the discretion of the interviewer, and persons generally have two opportunities to pass the test with each application. Persons with a medically demonstrated physical or developmental condition can be exempted from this requirement (INA § 312[b][1]), as can, at the discretion of the interviewing immigration officer, persons over sixty-five years old who have lived in the United States for more than twenty years (INA § 312[b][3]). Because there are fewer exceptions for the civics test than the English-language portion of the interview, the civics test may be taken in Spanish by persons who qualify for the English-language exception.

7. *Political Requirements.* INA § 313 disqualifies applicants who, either during the ten-year period immediately preceding the filing of the application or during the interval between the filing and the taking of the final oath of citizenship, have been affiliated with communist, totalitarian, or terrorist groups or have advocated their ideals, including through speeches and pub-

lications. The N-400 form attempts to discover grounds for disqualification by requiring applicants to list any membership association or to answer questions on political beliefs.

8. *Attachment to the Principles of the U.S. Constitution.* An applicant must demonstrate an attachment to the principles of the U.S. Constitution and allegiance to the U.S. government by taking an oath both in writing on the application and during the induction ceremony. The oath is a promise that the applicant supports the Constitution, renounces all foreign allegiances, is willing to defend all federal laws against all enemies, will bear true allegiance to those laws, and will bear arms for the United States if required by law (INA § 337[a]).

Beyond these eight statutory requirements for naturalization, DHS considers nonstatutory criteria that may include nonsupport of dependents; adultery; and failure to register with the Selective Service between eighteen and twenty-six years of age, but only if the applicant knowingly and willfully failed to register during the period for which the applicant must establish a history of good moral character. A person who fails to file taxes or to pay back-taxes prior to filing an application for naturalization could also be denied, especially since the failure to do so could be considered a crime.

Congress requires the applicant to reside for three months in the state or CIS district in which the naturalization petition is filed (INA § 316[a]). The application may be filed within three months prior to the applicant's meeting the residency requirement of either five or three years as an LPR. Depending on backlogs where the application is filed, the process could take between six months to a year or longer. If the immigration officer conducting the interview denies the petition, the applicant may request an evidentiary hearing before an immigration officer (INA § 336[a, c]). If that review is denied, the applicant may seek review in the U.S. district court for the district in which he or she resides (INA § 310[c]). Finally, applicants for naturalization should note that as of July 2007, application fees increased from $400 to $675.

Citizenship by Descent for Children Born Abroad

Under U.S. law, citizenship by descent is provided for primarily in sections 301(c), 301(g), 309(a), and 309(c) of INA. Sections 301(c) and 301(g) of the INA list universally applicable conditions for acquisition of citizenship by descent, and sections 309(a) and 309(c) provide overriding rules for persons born out of wedlock.

Citizenship by descent for children born to a married couple requires that at least one parent be a U.S. citizen at the time of the child's birth abroad. Citizenship by descent may also be conferred on a child who is adopted internationally and subsequently admitted as a child of a U.S. citizen (INA § 320).[8] The Child Citizenship Act of 2000 grants automatic citizenship to a child born abroad who (1) was fully and finally adopted; (2) is under eighteen years of age; (3) was admitted to the United States as an LPR; and (4) is in the legal and physical custody of at least one parent who is a U.S. citizen. In such cases, CIS will forward a certificate of citizenship to the adoptive parent within forty-five days of the child's entry into the United States. The U.S. citizen parent may also obtain a certificate by filing Form N-600.

In addition, laws require residency or physical presence in the United States by the citizen parent(s). The laws differ depending on whether the child was born to two U.S. citizen parents or to one U.S. citizen parent and a foreign national. If the child is born abroad to two U.S. citizen parents, then at least one of them must have resided in the United States or its outlying possessions prior to the birth of the child at any time and for however long (INA § 301[c]).[9] If the child is born to only one U.S. citizen parent, the U.S. citizen parent must have been physically present in the United States or its outlying possessions for cumulative periods totaling not less than five years, at least two of which were before the U.S. citizen parent was fourteen years old (INA § 301[g]).[10] The logic behind the physical presence requirement is that a citizen parent who spends enough time in the United States will absorb U.S. customs and values, which will then be transmitted to the child.

The INS definition imposes additional requirements for U.S. citizen fathers when the child is born outside the context of a traditional marriage. If the child is born out of wedlock, the father (though not the mother) must demonstrate a bona-fide parent-child relationship (INA § 101[b][D]). Before a child born abroad can gain U.S. citizenship, INA § 309(a) requires the unwed U.S. citizen father to establish that (1) clear and convincing evidence proves a blood relationship between father and child; (2) the father had U.S. nationality at the time of the child's birth; (3) the father (unless deceased) agrees in writing to provide financial support until the child reaches the age of eighteen; and (4) the father legitimated, recognized, or had a court declare parentage with the child. For children born out of wedlock to a U.S. citizen mother, INA section 309(c) does not provide conditions for the application of sections 301(c) and 301(g), but rather, supersedes them. According to section 309(c), "notwithstanding the provision of subsection (309)(a)," an out-of-wedlock child will be a citizen if its mother was a U.S. citizen at the time of its birth and "the mother had previously been physically present in the United States or one of its outlying possessions for a continuous period of one year." Because these additional requirements imposed only on fathers discriminate on the basis of gender, U.S. citizen plaintiffs have raised equal protection challenges to invalidate the provision. In *Nguyen v. INS*, 533 U.S. 53 (2000), however, a divided Supreme Court (five to four) upheld the law as constitutional.

The INA gives the Department of State responsibility for administering the law of citizenship by descent because a person who claims such citizenship will begin his life outside the United States and should have his citizenship administratively determined before coming to the country on a passport or visa. The secretary of state is charged with the administration of the INA as it relates to "the determination of nationality of a person not in the United States" and must also determine nationality in the course of issuing passports, which may only be issued to U.S. nationals (INA § 104[a][3]). CIS handles claims of citizenship by descent in particular, limited circumstances. These instances occur when a person previously entered the United States with or without authorization and seeks to acquire a certificate of citizenship (rather than choosing to apply for a passport); raises a citizenship claim belatedly as a defense against removal; makes his way to a U.S. port of entry without travel documents and seeks admission; or the less-than-sixteen-year-old foreign-born child of a U.S. citizen parent has a good-faith nationality claim denied by the Department of State while outside the United States and obtains a "certificate of identity" under section 360 of the INA in order to travel to a U.S. port of entry to apply for admission. Whichever administrative body is responsible for a citizenship claim, some form of judicial review will be available, and reviewing courts will vary in their deference to administrative determinations (INA § 360).

Family Unification

Congress has advanced family unification as a principal goal of immigration policy, although the recent failed comprehensive immigration reform efforts could predict a shift to a "merit-based" system in the future.[11] Until and if that happens, however, the INA will continue to permit U.S. citizens and lawful permanent residents to sponsor certain family members for permanent legalization.

Family-Based Immigration Priorities

The INA sets priorities for which family members may immigrate to the United States and grants certain family members immediate immigration privileges. Other members fall within one of four preference categories that are subject to annual numerical caps and per country limits.

Those who receive immediate immigration privileges are known as "immediate relatives," and they are the unmarried children under twenty-one years of age, spouses, and parents of U.S. citizens. A citizen son or daughter must also be over twenty-one years old to sponsor his or her parent (INA § 201[b][2][A][i]). Because the INA does not place a limit on the number of immediate relatives who can immigrate in any given year, visas are available to them without a waiting period. The only wait is for the processing of the application, which varies depending on where it originates. What happens, however, if the child turns twenty-one while the immigrant petition is still pending? The Child Status Protection Act of 2002 (CSPA) allows the beneficiary's age to be "frozen" as of the date the petition is filed, so that he still qualifies for immediate relative status once the application is processed (INA § 201[f][1]).

By contrast, other family members of U.S. citizens and LPRs who immigrate must wait for long periods. Because these visa categories are subject to numerical restrictions, the petitions may take up to twenty years. Each of the four family preference categories listed below is subject to different annual and per country numerical limits. The total annual worldwide limit for family-sponsored immigration is 480,000, minus the number of immediate relatives who were admitted in the preceding fiscal year, minus any children born to LPRs temporarily abroad, plus any available but unused employment-based visas from the preceding fiscal year (INA § 201[c][1][A][ii]). Also, in each fiscal year, the combined numbers of family-sponsored and employment-based immigrants from a single country may not exceed 7 percent of the total worldwide limits for immigrant visas (INA § 202[a][2]).

The family member categories and their corresponding numerical subceilings consist of the following:

- *First Preference*: Adult (over twenty-one years old) or married offspring of U.S. citizens (23,400 annually plus any unused fourth preference visas)
- *Second Preference:* (2A) Spouse and unmarried children (under twenty-one years of age) of LPRs; (2B) unmarried sons and unmarried daughters (twenty-one years of age or older) of LPRs (114,200 plus any unused first preference visas and any amount, if any, by which the total worldwide ceiling exceeds 226,000).
- *Third Preference:* Married sons and married daughters of any age of U.S. citizens (23,400 plus any unused first and second preference visas).
- *Fourth Preference:* Brothers and sisters of U.S. citizens where the citizen is twenty-one years of age or older (65,000 plus any unused first, second, and third preference visas).

Additionally, under INA § 203(d), a spouse or unmarried child under twenty-one years of age who is "accompanying, or following to join" an immigrant who is within any of the family-based categories above (except for "immediate relative") is entitled to the same preference status and to the same place on the wait list as the principal immigrant.[12]

The above are the family-based immigration categories the INA recognizes, which excludes married sons and daughters of LPRs, grandchildren, grandparents, uncles and aunts, and cousins.[13] In addition, while the INA does not define the term spouse, Article 3 of the Defense of Marriage Act declares that "in determining the meaning of any Act of Congress . . . the word 'spouse' refers only to a person of the opposite sex who is a husband and wife." Accordingly, court decisions have excluded homosexual partners from immigration benefits, even though a few states, like Massachusetts, recognize gay marriage.

The INA defines who is a "child." The definition of "child" affects the classification of a person as a "son or daughter," a "parent," and "brother and sister." That is, a parent relationship exists only when there is a child relationship. A "son or daughter" exists even if the person is now over twenty-one years old and/or married. A sibling relationship exists if the sponsor and the beneficiary were "children" of a common "parent" and if they are step-siblings, their relationship continues to exist. Generally, a child must be born in wedlock, unmarried, and younger than twenty-one years of age (INA § 101[b][1]). Additional requirements apply for children born out of wedlock, stepchildren, and adopted children. For example, a child becomes the step-child of the LPR or U.S. citizen spouse only if the marriage establishing the relationship takes place before the child turns eighteen (INA § 101[b][1][B]). An adopted child must have been under the age of sixteen when adopted, in the legal custody of the sponsoring parent, and have resided with the parent for at least two years (INA § 101[b][1][E]). A child born out of wedlock must have been legitimated by the father before she reaches the age of eighteen and/or be able to establish a bona fide parent-child relationship with the father (INA § 101[b][C] & [D]).

Backlogs

Numerical restrictions on family-based immigration result in more applicants each year than visas available. Consequently, long waiting periods exist for each of the four visa categories. Thus, each new family petition is assigned what is known as a "priority date," which is the date the I-130 petition is processed, in accordance to the category assigned. Filing an I-130 petition is the first step in any family-based petition. This is a simple application that generally (except for battered spouses and children) must be filed by the U.S. citizen or LPR who is sponsoring the visa on behalf of a family member. This priority date allows the applicant to wait in line, behind applicants whose applications were filed earlier. Each month, the Department of State publishes what is known as the Immigrant Visa Bulletin, in which it specifies what "priority dates" are being processed for each category. Because there is also a per-country limit, some countries, namely China, Mexico, and the Philippines, tend to have longer waiting periods for each category. Take, for, example, the State Department Visa Bulletin for June 2006, available at www.state.gov.

If, for example, an LPR of Salvadoran nationality wishes to immigrate his twenty-five-year-old son, he would look at the priority date visa category 2A, under the heading "All Chargeability Areas Except Those Listed," which applies to all countries except those specifically listed. That date is 01JUN02. This date means that for that visa category, the State Department is processing the ones assigned the priority date of June 1, 2002, the date CIS established that there was an applicable family relationship. Assuming the date now is July 1, 2007, the visa backlog is five years and one month. This provides an inexact estimate of how long an I-130 with a priority date of June 22, 2006 would take. The actual waiting period will depend on several factors, including the number of family-based visa petitions filed in the years between 2002 and 2007.

Given the long waiting periods that attach to family-based petitions with numeric restrictions, it is not uncommon for a "child" to turn twenty-one and/or get married while waiting for a visa. Unfortunately, sometimes getting married will render sons and daughters of LPRs ineligible for a visa altogether, unless the sponsoring parent becomes a citizen. At other times, turning twenty-one simply means the person switches categories from that of a 2A to a 2B, for example, in the case of a child of an LPR. Immigration procedures allow automatic conversion of a "currently valid petition previously approved" due to a change in the beneficiary's marital status, the beneficiary's aging out, or the naturalization of the petitioner (8 C.F.R. § 204.2[i]). When the petition converts automatically, the priority date remains the same as the date of proper filing of the original petition, except that as to some categories, the waiting period may be longer.

When age-out occurs, two things happen that could allow the beneficiary to retain the original visa category. First, the U.S. Patriot Act of 2001 grants a forty-five day grace period, only after which the age-out process would occur. Second, for applications filed after August 6, 2002, CSPA protects the child beneficiary of pending petitions from aging out, and still treats him as a child when the visa becomes available and is processed (INA § 201[b][2][a][i]). Thus, for example, if a son of an LPR within a 2A category files for adjustment of status, but turns twenty-one before adjudication of the application, he still remains eligible for the 2A visa, provided the beneficiary "took efforts to legalize" (i.e., filed for adjustment, hired a lawyer) within the one-year period after the visa became available.

At times, Congress has passed legislation to improve the long periods of physical separation that families must endure due to immigration backlogs. For example, in the LIFE Act of 2000, when the spouses and unmarried children under twenty-one years of age of LPRs have been waiting for three years or longer, they are able to apply for temporary visas. To be eligible, however, a spouse or child must have been a beneficiary of a 2A family petition filed before December 21, 2000, the date the LIFE Act came into effect (INA § 101[a][15][V]). The beneficiary may be inside or outside the United States to qualify for a V visa and subsequently apply for adjustment when the visa becomes available. This option is possible because the LIFE Act also removes the adjustment of status restrictions, with a penalty payment, that usually prevent persons without legal status from legalizing while in the United States (see below) (INA § 214[o] and 8 C.F.R. § 214.15[f]). In addition, in response to the backlog of immediate relative petitions for spouses of U.S. citizens waiting outside the United States, the LIFE Act expanded the temporary K visa to include spouses and their unmarried minor children accompanying them to the United States (INA § 101[a][15][K]).

Procedural Hurdles to Legalization Based on Illegal Entry or Unlawful Status

Anyone applying for an immigrant visa must also prove that she is admissible and not subject to the exclusion grounds found in INA § 212(a). In this section, we discuss only a few of these grounds with particular relevance to family-based petitions, namely those resulting from illegal entry and unlawful stay and the public charge ground. We also discuss relief from exclusion for family unification purposes. Many other grounds for exclusion as well as relief from removal are also for purposes of family unification, but these are taken up in separate chapters.

Presumably, without a visa, the beneficiary is still living abroad, and the visa petition is filed with the corresponding U.S. consulate. In the majority of cases, however, the family member is already in the United States, often without valid legal status. This fact has resulted in a number of procedural hurdles that, when added to the long wait for most family-based petitions, have made family unification difficult.

Beneficiaries of family-based petitions who are already in the United States may qualify for "adjustment of status," provided they meet several additional requirements. These requirements, however, include having entered the United States with a current and immediately available visa or being paroled (INA § 245[a] and [c]). Thus the requirements disqualify the majority of family-based beneficiaries, either because they entered the country illegally or because their visa has expired or will expire by the time the permanent visa becomes available. The only exception is that an "immediate relative" with an expired visa (but not one who entered without inspection) may still seek adjustment (INA § 245[c]). As a result, most family members, except those who benefit from the LIFE Act (see above) must exit the United States and return to their country of origin and wait to process their visa when it becomes available at the corresponding U.S. consulate. Unfortunately for most, unlawful entry into the United States or unlawful presence will bar them from legalizing for up to ten years, unless they qualify for a family-based hardship waiver.

In 1996, Congress added several exclusion grounds that arise from unlawful presence in the United States. One new ground makes inadmissible anyone (except battered spouses and children) "present in the United States without being admitted or paroled" or who arrives in the United States at other than a designated time or place (INA § 212[a][6][A]). This means the person cannot legalize while she remains in the United States without authorization. A related second exclusion ground applies to those who seek admission to the United States after having been "unlawfully present here for certain periods of time and voluntarily departing." Anyone who was unlawfully present in the United States for more than 180 days, but less than a year, and departed voluntarily before commencement of "removal proceedings" cannot legalize for three years from the date of departure (INA § 212[a][9][B][i][I]). If the unlawful presence exceeds one year, then the person becomes inadmissible for ten years from the date of voluntary departure (INA § 212[a][9][B][i][II]). This rule is known as the "3/10 year bar." Unlawful presence began to count as of September 27, 1997. Unlawful presence does not count, however, until the person is eighteen years old (INA § 212[a][9][B][ii]). In addition, there is a grace period of 120 days for persons who have been paroled or who filed a nonfrivolous application to extend their visas (INA § 212[a][9][B][iv]). For persons without current valid visas who must exit the United States to seek legalization, the 3/10 year bars apply.

The INA authorizes the CIS and immigration courts to waive the 3/10 year bar for the spouse, son, or daughter of a U.S. citizen or LPR if the refusal of admission would result in "extreme hardship" to the citizen or LPR spouse or parent (INA § 212[a][9][B][v]). Establishing extreme hardship is difficult, and while INA does not define the term, some guidance exists through cases: (1) hardship must include conditions or circumstances subsequent to the granting of status alone; (2) it may be considered in the aggregate—that is, hardship may be extreme as it affects two persons, although it would not be extreme if applied only to one; (3) economic loss alone does not satisfy the standard but is an additional factor that may be considered with others; (4) other factors include medical problems, the children's ages, effects of removal on the children's education, separation from other relatives, and difficulties in adjusting to life in a foreign country (see, e.g., *INS v. Jong Ha Wang*, 450 U.S. 139 [1981]).

Affidavits of Support

Another important exclusion ground that affects family unification is the inadmissibility of a person who is "likely to become a public charge" (INA § 212[a][4]). "Public charge" means that the person is likely to become "primarily dependent on the U.S. government for subsistence" based on such factors as poverty, age, education level and training, or illness (see 76 IR 980 [June 28, 1999]).

The "public charge" exclusion ground may be overcome, however, with an Affidavit of Support (Form I-864), which is required of all citizens or LPRs who sponsor their family members as immigrants (except for certain widowed or abused family members). The sponsor must be the petitioning citizen or LPR, although it is possible that she may join with another person as cosponsors if she does not meet the required income amount (INA § 213A[f][5]). The sponsor's income must be at least 125 percent of the poverty level (INA §§ 213A[f][1][E], 213A[f][6]). To evaluate income, the State Department uses the U.S. Poverty Income Guidelines prepared and revised annually by the Department of Health and Human Services, available at http://aspe.hhs.gov/poverty/. All sponsors must be over eighteen years of age and be domiciled in the United States (INA § 213A[f][1][A,B,C]).

The Affidavit of Support is a binding contract that becomes "legally enforceable against the sponsor by the sponsored immigrant, the Federal Government, any state (or any political subdivision of the state), or by any other entity that provides means-tested public benefit" (INA § 213[a][1][B]). The contract is binding for forty qualifying quarter-years after the immigrant last receives benefits or until naturalization if sooner (INA § 213A[a][2]). This means that for up to ten years (unless the beneficiary naturalizes), the sponsor could be responsible for paying back the government for certain public benefits received by the beneficiary. Keep in mind, however, that the recipient of the visa will be ineligible for the first five years to receive these benefits (see above discussion on government benefits). Programs that fall within this definition of public charge are not generally available to LPRs, including Supplemental Security Income (SSI) and Temporary Assistance for Needy Families (TANF). The State Department also offers as examples programs that would not create a public charge problem for LPRs: the Food Stamp Program; Medicaid (other than long-term care); the Child Health Insurance Program; emergency medical services; the nutritional program for women, infants, and children; Head Start; job training programs; and provision of in-kind services such as soup kitchens or crisis counseling. In addition, the sponsor's assets and income are treated as if they belong to the beneficiary when calculating the foreign national's eligibility for public benefits. Thus, in most cases, even after the five years, the beneficiary is unlikely to qualify for benefits based on income.

Special Rules for Marriage-Based Petitions

Under U.S. immigration law, marriage to a U.S. citizen confers "immediate relative" status to the foreign national. Marriage to an LPR confers second preference status, allowing the spouse to accompany or file to join the principal visa holder. Because of the immigration benefits attached to marriage, Congress has been concerned that some may decide to marry solely to obtain the immigration benefit. As a result, Congress has required that only bona fide marriages receive the immigration benefit and has created a series of additional visa requirements or restrictions to detect sham marriages.

One way to curtail marriage fraud is to view marriage in very conventional terms for visa approval, which CIS or the State Department investigates during the adjustment or consular visa processing interview. Usually, there are ten red flags that may signal a sham marriage: large age disparity; language difficulties between the couple; vast differences in cultural or ethnic backgrounds; family or friends being unaware of the marriage; marriage arranged by a third party; marriage while in proceedings; discrepancies in statements where a husband or wife should have common knowledge; no cohabitation since marriage; beneficiary being a friend of the family; petitioner previously filing visa petitions for other foreign nationals, particularly if they were prior spouses. Should any of these factors be present, the interviewing immigration or state department officer could investigate the matter closely and require the petitioners to provide voluminous evidence to establish the bona fide nature of the marriage. If the petitioners fail to do so, the immigration petition could be denied based on suspicion of fraud.

In addition, since Congress passed the Immigration Marriage Fraud Amendments in 1986 (IMFA), individuals filing marriage-based family petitions, when the marriage is less than two years old at the time of visa approval, have received only conditional permanent resident status (INA §§ 216[a][1], [g][1]).[14] A child who immigrates derivatively through the marriage-based application also acquires the same conditional status residency (INA § 216[g]). As a practical matter, most marriages are already two years old by the time the immigrant petition is approved, either because of backlogs in processing or visa availability. When this happens, the following conditional status restrictions do not apply.

Conditional status imposes certain conditions subsequent to receipt of the visa:

- First, if, at any time during the individual's first two years of conditional LPR status, CIS finds that the marriage was entered into for purposes of procuring immigrant status, or that the marriage has been judicially annulled or terminated (other than by the spouse's death), or that a fee (other than an attorney fee) was given for the filing of the petition, then the permanent resident status is terminated (INA § 216[b][1]). The beneficiary may contest the finding at a removal hearing at which the government will bear the burden of proving that the marriage was a fraud or is no longer valid (INA § 216[b][2]).
- Second, the conditional resident and her spouse have an affirmative duty to petition jointly for the removal of the conditional status and to appear for an interview in connection with that petition to establish that the marriage is bona fide (INA § 216[c]). This petition must be filed during the ninety-day period immediately preceding the second anniversary of the person's admission for permanent residence (INA § 216[d][2][A]). Here, the visa holder must establish that the marriage was legally valid, that it has not been judicially annulled or terminated (other than through death of the spouse), that it was not entered into for immigration purposes, and that no fee (except attorney's fees) were paid (INA §§ 216[c][3][A] and [d][1]). If the resident status is terminated, the visa holder may contest the finding in a removal hearing, where, again, the government must prove that the marriage was a fraud or is no longer valid (INA § 216[c][3][D]). If the joint petition is not filed on time, or if without good cause either spouse fails to appear

at the interview, the permanent residence status is also terminated (INA § 216[d][2][A]). In such cases, the conditional resident could provide CIS with a written explanation of the good cause of the omission, together with a properly completed joint petition for removal of conditions, or attempt to reopen the case (8 C.F.R. §§ 103.5[a][1][i] and 216.4[a][6]).

If the visa holder cannot file jointly for removal due to refusal of the spouse to cooperate or because the marriage is no longer viable or has ended, there are certain waivers available (under INA § 216[c][4]) that may be filed with Form I-751. One basis for a waiver is a finding that the removal would entail "extreme hardship." The provision does not specify who must suffer the "extreme hardship" (see above), but it has been interpreted to include the visa holder, the spouse, and any dependent child (see 67 IR at 341 Question 57 [1990]). The second ground for a waiver is when the marriage has ended in divorce or annulment, notwithstanding that it was entered into in good faith. Here, the petitioner must wait until the divorce or annulment is final before filing. The standard for establishing the bona fide nature of the marriage is the same as applied during the initial approval of the marriage. Usually, the couple must document the history of the relationship, which includes proof of joint property ownership (real or personal) or joint tenancy; documents demonstrating commingling of financial resources, such as joint bank accounts, jointly issued credit cards, jointly filed tax returns, bills in the names of both parties; birth certificates of children born of the relationship; and affidavits from persons with personal knowledge of the parties' relationship. The third waiver is for a battered spouse or child and allows removal of the conditional resident status if the battered spouse or child can show that the marriage was in good faith but that the spouse either physically abused her child or subjected her to extreme cruelty. If the waiver is denied, the conditional resident may seek review before an immigration judge and subsequently appeal to the Board of Immigration Appeals (INA §§ 216[b][2], [c][2][B] and [c][3][D]). Further review, however, may not be available since the INA restricts judicial review of discretionary decisions by the immigration agencies (INA § 242[a][2][B]).

Several other INA provisions exist to curtail marriage fraud. INA § 204(g), for example, disallows a family-based petition when the marriage that would confer the benefit takes place during a removal hearing. Here, the foreign national spouse must reside outside the United States for two years before filing the petition. The presumption is that eleventh hour marriages are a sham or for the sole purpose of avoiding removal. Since 1990, however, Congress has recognized an exception that allows the foreign national spouse to overcome the presumption of a sham marriage. The applicant must present clear and convincing evidence that the marriage was entered into in good faith and in accordance with the laws of the place where the marriage took place; the marriage was not entered into for the purpose of procuring the visas; and no fee was paid for filing the petition (INA § 245(e)[3]). Additionally, CIS cannot approve a second preference visa petition for a spouse of the LPR petitioner who immigrated less than five years previously through a prior marriage to a U.S. citizen or LPR, unless the petitioner supplies "clear and convincing" evidence of the bona fides of the prior marriage (INA § 275[c]). Finally, INA §204(c) prohibits any person who committed marriage fraud from ever being able to file a future immigrant visa petition.

Removal: Reasons, Process, and Relief

A lawful permanent resident (LPR) of the United States is entitled to work and live in the country indefinitely, without becoming a citizen. LPR status, however, hardly guarantees permanence. Indeed, tens of thousands of LPRs every year lose their status and are removed. Some of them are long-term residents, perhaps since they were children, and must leave behind family, friends, jobs, property, and community ties.

Removal of LPRs has increased especially since 1996, when Congress passed the Illegal Immigration Reform and Immigrant Responsibility Act (IIRIRA) and the Antiterrorism and Effective Death Penalty Act of 1996 (AEDPA). AEDPA expanded the removal grounds that applied to LPRs and narrowed discretionary relief, particularly relating to crime and national security. IIRIRA similarly expanded the substantive grounds for removing LPRs, further restricted discretionary relief, introduced a number of "expedited" removal procedures, and restricted judicial review.

The Department of Homeland Security (DHS) may employ various laws to remove an LPR. First, DHS can remove an LPR if within the first five years after the LPR obtains that status, DHS obtains information that indicates the erroneous granting of LPR status (INA § 246). Second, at any time, DHS may place the recent immigrant in removal proceedings if the LPR was not actually eligible at the time DHS granted her admission (INA § 237[a][1][A]). One common use of INA § 237[a][1][A] occurs when the LPR committed fraud to obtain the immigration benefit. In cases of fraud, a limited waiver from removal is authorized to promote family unification or for victims of domestic violence who are eligible to self-petition (see Chapter 11 for special rule applying to victims of domestic violence) (INA § 212(a)(1)[H]).

An LPR can also lose her status for myriad reasons. She may be deemed to have abandoned her residency if she leaves the United States for more than a year or if she has a pattern of lengthy absences even if none equals a year. An LPR filing taxes as a nonresident may also indicate abandonment of LPR status. Also, the DHS can initiate removal proceedings against an LPR for events that occur after she attains LPR status.

The grounds for which LPRs (and other persons with temporary visas) may be removed are spelled out in Section 237 of the INA. Most of these grounds are aimed to remove persons Congress perceives as a threat to public health or safety, public morality, the economy, and national security.

Most of the criminal-related grounds for removal of LPRs were already covered in Chapter 8 in the section on immigration consequences of crime. In this chapter, we discuss the remaining removal grounds applicable to LPRs and any applicable exceptions or waivers. In addition, we discuss the different procedures available to the DHS to effectuate the removal. Finally, we address any relief from removal that may be available to LPRs.

Post-entry Deportability Grounds
Relevant to LPRs: Immigration Control

- *Smuggling.* An LPR who, prior to entry into the United States, or within five years of any entry, knowingly assists another foreign national to enter the country, becomes deportable (INA § 237[a][1][E]). Generally, an LPR effectuates an "entry" anytime she enters the United States from a foreign port, provided the presence in that foreign port was voluntary. Thus, even if an LPR has been in the United States with that status for twenty years, she could still be subject to deportation if she has left and reentered the country within five years of the date of the smuggling. Also, smuggling occurs regardless of whether there was any monetary gain from the activity and includes activities beyond physical transport of someone across the border. In fact, the Department of State considers "smuggling" to include making a false oral or written statement on behalf of a visa applicant. Smuggling can also include sending money home to assist family members to enter the United States. DHS may waive this deportation ground but only when the LPR helped smuggle solely the LPR's spouse, parent, son, or daughter (INA § 237[a][1][E][iii]).
- *Failure to Register.* INA §§ 261–266 authorize DHS to impose certain registration, address reporting, and other requirements on foreign nationals, including LPRs. Post-9/11, INA § 265 was employed to require certain foreign nationals mostly of Arab and Muslim descent to register. Failure to register can result in removal (INA § 237[a][3][A]).
- *Document Fraud.* An LPR who commits document fraud under INA § 274C is removable. INA § 274C addresses presenting a document for entry before boarding a common carrier and then failing to produce that document to an immigration officer upon arrival in the United States. A timely retraction, if made at the first opportunity, purges the fraud.
- *Falsely Claiming Citizenship.* An LPR who falsely claims U.S. citizenship to obtain any immigration or public government benefit is removable (INA § 237[a][3][D][i]). A limited exception is permitted for

a reasonable mistake by an LPR who has at least one U.S. citizen parent and who resided in the United States before the age of sixteen (INA § 237[a][3][D][ii]).

Security and Related Grounds

Other deportability provisions are related to security reasons and apply to foreign nationals said to be engaged in terrorist activities as these are broadly defined under INA § 212[a][3][B]) or who have been associated with terrorist organizations (INA § 237[a][4][B]) or have received military training by a terrorist organization (INA § 237[a][4][E]); those who will be adverse to U.S. foreign policy (INA § 237[a][4][C]); those who participated in Nazi persecution, genocide, or the commission of any act of torture or extrajudicial killing (INA § 212[a][4][D]); and those who participated in the commission of severe violations of religious freedom (INA § 237[a][4][E]).

Public Charge

An LPR who within five years after the date of entry becomes a public charge is also deportable (INA §237[a][5]). The 1996 welfare reforms made most LPRs ineligible for most public benefits, and therefore this provision is unlikely to apply. Nevertheless, an LPR who otherwise meets welfare eligibility should consider this provision before deciding to apply. It is important to note that the mere receipt of public funds does not make a person a public charge. Rather the U.S. State Department has defined "public charge" as "primarily dependent on the U.S. Government for subsistence," as demonstrated by "the receipt of public cash assistance for income maintenance" or "institutionalization for long-term care at U.S. Government expense" (9 F.A.M. § 40.41 n.2a).

Unlawful Voters

An LPR who votes unlawfully in any election, whether federal, state, or local, is removable (INA § 237[a][6][A]). A limited exception applies to an LPR who reasonably believed she was a U.S. citizen because either parent is a U.S. citizen and the LPR resided in the United States prior to age sixteen (INA § 237[a][6][B]).

Removal Process

If a lawful permanent resident falls within any of the removal grounds and is detected, the Immigration and Customs Enforcement may detain her (INA § 242[a]) or issue a Notice to Appear (NTA) to place her in removal proceedings.[15] When the LPR is arrested, within forty-eight hours of the arrest (or within seven days if she is certified as a terrorist under INA § 236A[a][5]), ICE must decide whether there is sufficient evidence that the LPR is in the United States in violation of immigration laws, unless she departs voluntarily (see below) (8 C.F.R. § 287.3[b]).[16] If so, ICE issues an NTA, gives a copy to the LPR, and files it with the immigration court, which officially commences the removal process (8 C.F.R. §§ 239.1, 1239.1). The NTA explains the nature of the proceedings; specifies the grounds for removal; recites the factual allegations behind the charges; states the time and place of the scheduled hearing before an immigration judge; instructs the LPR to keep ICE apprised of any address changes; and states the consequences for failure to do so, including removal in absentia (INA § 239[a][1]).

ICE also decides during this forty-eight hour period whether to continue detaining the LPR. The power to arrest an LPR not in custody remains. Detention is mandatory for LPRs who have been charged as aggravated felons or who meet most other crime-related or national security grounds (INA §§ 236[c][1] and 241[a]). In all other cases, DHS has the discretion to detain the LPR without bond, release on cash bond of at least $1,500, or release on "conditional parole" (INA § 236[a]). Release is permitted only if DHS decides the LPR "would not pose a danger to property or persons and . . . is likely to appear for any future proceedings" (8 C.F.R. § 236.1[c][8]). The LPR may appeal the decision to detain to an immigration judge in a bond hearing. If a judge posts bond, that decision is automatically stayed if DHS appeals it to the Board of Immigration Appeals, until the BIA makes a finding (8 C.F.R. § 1003.19). The detention decision is important because removal proceedings can take from several months to several years.

The LPR does not enjoy the same due process rights as would a person charged in a criminal proceeding. For example, with limited exceptions, neither the Fourth nor Fifth Amendment rights apply, nor does the LPR have a right to counsel, unless at her own expense (INA § 240[b][4][A]). The immigration court provides an interpreter. Usually, the hearing is open to the public (8 C.F.R. § 1003.27).[17] At the commencement of the hearing, the LPR must plead to acceptance or denial of the charges in the NTA. The LPR also may designate the country to which she wishes to be removed, in the event such an order is given.

At the hearing, ICE has the burden of proving by clear and convincing evidence that the LPR is a foreign national and not a U.S. citizen. Only then does the burden shift to the LPR to prove with clear and convincing evidence that she is lawfully present pursuant to a prior admission. If the LPR is successful, the burden of proof shifts back to ICE, which must demonstrate with clear and convincing evidence that the grounds charged and factual allegations are valid and true. This includes proving the elements of each charged deportability ground and the nonapplication of all asserted exceptions. The LPR, however, has the burden of establishing eligibility for any waiver of the deportability ground, or of any affirmative relief (see below) (INA § 240[c][4][A]). Proof is usually given through evidence, including witnesses. Formal rules of evidence do not apply in immigration proceedings.

After reviewing the evidence, the immigration judge issues a ruling, either orally or in writing, which contains the findings as to removability, and if so ordered, the country to which the LPR must be removed. The BIA decides most cases by single-member "affirmances without opinion." The remaining cases are decided by a three-member panel and reasoned opinions. This expedited BIA process is controversial since it severely curtails reviewability on the merits to improve efficiency.

Ordinarily, within thirty days of the BIA decision, ICE or the LPR may appeal to the U.S. Court of Appeals for the circuit in which the removal hearing was held. The reviewing court must decide the case on the basis of the reviewing record and cannot consider new evidence. Some important removal decisions, however, are not subject to judicial review, including most removal orders based on crime-related deportability grounds and almost all denials of discretionary relief (INA § 242[a][2][C]). Some LPRs have filed habeas corpus petitions in the district court when judicial review has been unavailable, and in 2001, the Supreme Court confirmed the availability of habeas corpus review in such cases (*INS v. St. Cyr*, 533 U.S. 289 [2001]). In 2005, however, Congress responded to *St. Cyr* by amending section 242(a)(2)(C) and all other court-stripping provisions of the INA to state explicitly that the bar on judicial review bars all other provisions of law, statutory or nonstatutory, including habeas corpus review (REAL ID Act, 119 Stat. 231). As a compromise, however, Congress added new INA § 242(a)(2)(D), which specifies that judicial review does not preclude "review of constitutional claims or questions of law raised upon a petition for review." Congress's goal was to channel all judicial review to the courts of appeals, rather than the district courts. Thus, in May 2005, district courts were required to transfer all pending habeas corpus claims to the courts of appeals. Courts of appeals therefore continue to review whether a crime for which an LPR was convicted fits within one of the crime-related deportability grounds (e.g., aggravated felony), or whether the applied INA provision raises a constitutional question. Courts of appeals will also continue to have some review of legal questions related to most discretionary relief.

In addition, the LPR or ICE may petition the immigration court or the BIA for a motion to reopen or reconsider, although doing so does not stop the clock on the thirty-day period within which to file a judicial appeal. The motions are filed with the BIA if it has already rendered a decision or, otherwise, with the immigration judge. In general, a motion to reopen is appropriate when one of the parties discovers previously unavailable evidence that might alter the decision, while a motion to reconsider typically challenges the correctness of the decision.

While on appeal or while a motion to reconsider is pending, the LPR's removal is not automatically stayed unless the court or the decisionmaker grants it formally. ICE has ninety days within which to effectuate the removal (unless there are stays), during which time the LPR must be detained, certainly if the person was removed for criminal reasons (INA § 241 [a][1] and [2]). Beyond the ninety days, ICE may detain for up to six months; then, if the LPR provides a good reason why removability is not reasonably foreseeable in the future, DHS must release the individual, unless DHS can show that removal is foreseeable (*Zadvydas v. Davis*, 533 U.S. 678 [2001]). However, if the secretary of homeland security has "reasonable grounds to believe" that the LPR is removable on national security or terrorism grounds or "is engaged in any other activity that endangers the national security of the United States," the LPR may be detained indefinitely in renewable six-month increments (INA § 236A [a][6]).

Relief from Removal

Most LPRs in removal proceedings may petition for removal relief. One possibility is to apply for asylum (see Chapter 11). In addition, LPRs may qualify for other types of relief, including cancellation of removal, withholding of removal, or through the Convention Against Torture or private bills. Also, though not a remedy to removal, voluntary departure allows LPRs to avoid the exclusion grounds related to removal in case they decide to reapply for admission.

Relief carries certain requirements and limitations. First, foreign nationals who are properly notified of their removal hearings and fail to appear, or who received voluntary departure (explained below) and fail to leave on time, become ineligible to apply for any of the several specified types of relief from removal for ten years (INA § 240[b][7], 240B[d]). Second, aggravated felons and in some cases other criminal offenders are expressly disqualified from most of the major relief provisions and may also be precluded from a showing of good moral character, which is a required element of some of the relief provisions detailed below. Third, foreign nationals removed for national security grounds, especially for terrorism, are barred from several forms of discretionary relief. Fourth, foreign nationals applying for discretionary relief must provide certain biographical and biometric data, which permits immigration agencies to conduct extensive background checks (8 C.F.R. § 1003.47). Fifth, persons seeking relief may have to do so while in detention (INA § 236[a]). Sixth, these forms of relief are discretionary, and their denial is not subject to judicial review, save on questions of law or constitutionality (INA § 242[a][2][B]).

Cancellation of Removal

An immigrant who has had LPR status for not less than five years and has resided continuously in the United States for seven years since being admitted under any status—that is, as an LPR or on a temporary visa—and who has not been convicted of an aggravated felony may petition to have his removal cancelled (INA § 240A[a]). LPR status terminates only after a final BIA removal order but will not count if procured through fraud. Continuous residence, however, ends when the LPR receives an NTA or commits a crime, whichever is earlier (INA § 240A[d][1]). An LPR who does not meet these basic requirements can also apply for cancellation of removal also available to other foreign nationals, including the documented. (See Chapter 11 under Relief for Removal for those requirements.)

Withholding of Removal

Subject to some exceptions, the INA provides relief against removal to a country where the foreign national's life or freedom would be threatened because of the foreign national's race, religion, nationality, membership in a particular social group, or political opinion (INA § 241[b][3]). Only a future threat to one's life or freedom qualifies, and past persecution is not a basis for relief. Withholding also differs from asylum (see Chapter 11) because the latter grants a right to stay as opposed to just the right "not to be returned." An immigration judge will deny withholding of removal when she finds "reasonable grounds" that the person is a danger to U.S. security (INA § 241(b][3][B][iv]). Under this provision, terrorists are specifically ineligible. Committing a particular serious crime also disqualifies. The INA does not define "particular (nonpolitical) serious" crime, and courts decide the issue on a case-by-case basis. The term usually refers to violent crimes against a person or property. An aggravated felony is automatically "particularly serious" if the sentence is at least five years in prison (INA § 241[b][3][B]).

Convention Against Torture Relief

Article 3.1 of the United Nations Convention Against Torture and Other Cruel, Inhuman or Degrading Treatment or Punishment (U.N.G.A. Res. 39/46), ratified by the United States, provides that "no state Party shall expel, return (refouler) or extradite a person to another state where there are substantial grounds for believing that he would be in danger of being subjected to torture." Torture occurs when a state actor or person with state acquiescence inflicts severe pain and suffering in order to obtain a confession, punish (unless it is a lawful sanction), intimidate, coerce, or discriminate (Art. 1.1 of the Torture Convention). Thus, acts of third parties, including guerrilla groups, may not meet the definition unless there is a showing that the government knew of the activity and failed to act to prevent it.[18] Also, as with withholding of removal, what matters is a "more likely than not" probability that the person will be subjected to future acts of torture, not whether torture was committed in the past.

Private Bills

The other remedy of last resort is for a Congressperson to sponsor a "private bill" to confer LPR status on a foreign national who is ineligible or has lost the status. These acts, however, will occur only in extraordinary circumstances.

Voluntary Departure

A person who accepts voluntary departure under INA § 240B leaves the United States "voluntarily," and, in exchange, no formal removal order is issued. This option allows foreign nationals to avoid the ten-year bar that attaches to a formal removal order when the foreign national reapplies for admission (INA §212[a][9][ii]). As well, voluntary departure can waive the three-year bar that applies for unlawful presence in the United States between six months and up to a year so long as voluntary departure occurs after commencement of removal hearings and is made by an immigration judge (INA §212[a][9][B][i][I]). If the foreign national does not voluntarily depart as agreed, however, voluntary departure automatically becomes a removal order.

There are two types of voluntary departure. Under subsection (a), foreign nationals may depart voluntarily, at their own expense, before the commencement or completion of removal proceedings. "Before proceedings" means that the decision is made by the DHS officer. "After proceedings have commenced" means that the decision is made by an immigration judge. The remedy, however, is not available to persons apprehended at the border (INA § 240B[a][4]). Also ineligible are aggravated felons, individuals who are inadmissible as terrorists, and those who were previously removed and returned (INA § 240B[a][1]). The foreign national may be required to post bond, and the voluntary departure period may be as long as 120 days (INA § 240B[a][2]).

Subsection (b) imposes additional requirements but authorizes voluntary departure at the conclusion of removal proceedings. In addition to the same disqualifications that apply under subsection (a), the foreign national is disqualified unless (1) she has one year of physical presence in the United States immediately preceding the NTA; and (2) she is a person of good moral character for the five years immediately preceding the application (INA 240B[b][1]). Posting bond for subsection (b) relief is also mandatory (INA § 240B[a][3]), and the maximum period allowed to leave the country is sixty days (INA § 240B[b][2]).

Appendix

Government Immigration Resources

- For the most current visa bulletin, which tells you how long you must wait for your visa petition, visit http://travel.state.gov/visa/frvi/bulletin/bulletin_1360.html.
- Immigration forms are available for free at http://www.uscis.gov.
- To find out the status of your immigration case in the immigration court, you can call toll free at 1-800-898-7180; make sure to have your "alien registration number" (A#).

- You may call U.S. Citizenship and Immigration Services (USCIS) toll-free for automated information and live assistance concerning immigration services and benefits at 800-375-5283. The TTY number is 800-767-1833. You may also visit its website at http://uscis.gov/graphics/index.htm where you can find out the status of your case, find out how to post a bond for an alien in detention, download forms, learn about detainee rights, learn how to file forms, and for more information on finding the status of your case.
- For information about a matter before the Board of Immigration Appeals (BIA) you may call 703-605-1007.

For Help About Immigration Detainees

- For help, visit http://www.detentionwatchnetwork.org/.
- For information on filing immigration detainee complaints, visit http://www.abanet.org/publicserv/immigration/Complaint_Processes_Immig_Detainees.pdf.

Resources on Public Benefits for Documented and Undocumented Migrants

- *U.S. Department of Agriculture (USDA)*. Local food stamp offices can provide information on eligibility of legal immigrants to receive food stamps. All such local offices are listed on the USDA's website at http://www.fns.usda.gov/fsp/faqs.htm. The USDA also operates a toll-free number (800-221-5689) for information about the Food Stamp Program. Most states also have a toll-free information number.
- *U.S. Department of Health and Human Services, Center for Medicare and Medicaid Services.* Visit http://www.cms.hhs.gov.
- *U.S. Department of Social Security.* http://www.ssa.gov.
- *Urban Institute*. A nonpartisan social and economic policy research institution, http://www.urban.org.
- *National Conference of State Legislatures (NCSL)*. A bipartisan organization that serves legislators and staffs of the nation's fifty states, its commonwealths, and territories. NCSL's Immigrant Policy Project provides legislative research and analysis on immigration policy issues, such as the provision of benefits, health care, education, housing, and integration assistance; see http://www.ncsl.org/programs/immig/index.htm.
- *Center on Budget and Policy Priorities*. A policy organization working at the federal and state levels on fiscal policy and public programs that affect low- and moderate-income families and individuals, including on issues of welfare reform; http://www.cbpp.org.

- *The National Health Law Program (NHELP).* A national public interest law firm, www.healthlaw.org, that seeks to improve health care for America's working and unemployed poor, minorities, elderly, and people with disabilities. NHELP serves legal services programs, community-based organizations, the private bar, providers and individuals who work to preserve a healthcare safety net for the millions of uninsured or underinsured low-income people. NHELP has published a resource manual, *Immigrant Access to Health Benefits*, by Claudia Schlosberg.
- *The National Center for Children in Poverty (NCCP).* NCCP is the nation's leading public policy center dedicated to promoting the economic security, health, and well-being of America's low-income families and children. Using research to inform policy and practice, NCCP seeks to advance family-oriented solutions and the strategic use of public resources at the state and national levels to ensure positive outcomes for the next generation; http://www.nccp.org.
- *The National Immigration Law Center (NILC).* A national public policy organization that seeks to promote rights and opportunities for low-income immigrants and their family members. NILC conducts policy analysis and impact litigation and provides publications, technical advice, and training to a broad constituency of legal aid agencies, community groups, and pro bono attorneys; http://www.nilc.org. NILC publishes the *Guide to Immigrant Eligibility for Federal Programs*, which includes a list of states that provide state-funded programs to expand immigrants' access to public benefits.

Notes

1. In addition, in 2000 Congress passed legislation conferring eligibility for most federal public benefits to victims of human trafficking. The Victims of Trafficking and Violence Protection Act of 2000, 114 Stat. 1464 § 107 (2000).

2. Ten years equals forty qualifying quarters, and the LPR can include the quarters worked by her spouse and minor children. PRWORA § 435.

3. For social security eligibility, visit http://www.socialsecurity.gov/ssnvisa/.

4. *Friendly House et al. v. Napolitano*, Order, CV-04-649, Dec. 22, 2004 (D. Ariz.), available at http://www.ilw.com/immigdaily/cases/2005,0104-house.pdf (finding that the PRWORA authorizes the reporting of immigrants for attempted or the commission of public benefits fraud by state agencies).

5. These states are California, Colorado, Florida, Illinois, Maryland, Massachusetts, Minnesota, Nebraska, New Jersey, New York, Rhode Island, Texas, and Washington.

6. The Constitution did attach several privileges to birthright citizenship, such as being able to become U.S. president.

7. LPRs should also keep in mind that absences from the United States in excess of 180 days could mean that he could be considered to be seeking admission, which

would render him subject to exclusion, both in terms of substantive grounds for removal and procedural safeguards (INA § 101[a][13][C]).

8. The INA establishes certain requirements on international adoptions for immigration benefits found in §§ 101(b)(F) and (G).

9. The term *the United States* as used here also includes the U.S. territories of Puerto Rico, Guam, and the U.S. Virgin Islands, as well as the Commonwealth of the Northern Mariana Islands (INA § 101[a][38]). The term *outlying possessions* means Samoa and Swains Islands (INA § 101[a][29]).

10. Physical presence includes time in the military or employment in the U.S. foreign service (INA § 301[g]).

11. The June 2007 failed comprehensive immigration reform proposal in the Senate virtually would have eliminated family unification provisions, save those for immediate family, and replaced them with a competitive "merit-based" point system that gave preference to education and skills, including English proficiency.

12. A spouse or child will be regarded as "accompanying" the principal immigrant until six months after the issuance of the principal immigrant's visa (22. C.F.R. § 40.1[a]). There is no analogous time limit for a spouse or child who is "following to join."

13. Other special categories of family members who may acquire immigration status include spouses and children of asylees and refugees, Amerasian children, fiancées, and certain widows of U.S. citizens.

14. The conditional status does not apply to accompanying or following to join spouses or children under INA § 203(d) (family members who were already married when the beneficiary sought his or her visa). INA § 216(g)(1).

15. The removal process for LPRs differs in some significant ways from the removal process that may apply to foreign nationals who are apprehended at a border checkpoint. Those removal proceedings are found in INA § 235. The removal process described in this chapter is also similar to that available to undocumented foreign nationals who entered without inspection. There are, however, some important differences, including that when removing LPRs, the government must prove that the LPR is removable. When the foreign national entered without inspection, in contrast, the foreign national must prove he or she has a right to stay. The subtleties of these differences are beyond the scope of this chapter.

16. The regulations also allow "an additional reasonable period of time" beyond the forty-eight hours when there is an "emergency or other extraordinary circumstance" (8 C.F.R. § 287.3[d]). Based on this regulation, post-9/11, DHS also delayed this process to allow the government to investigate the foreign national for potential terrorist leads.

17. Post-9/11, however, an increasing number of removal hearings were closed.

18. See *Ali v. Reno*, 237 F.3d 591 (6th Cir. 2001).

11

Undocumented Migrants

Government Benefits

Since 1996, when Congress enacted the Personal Responsibility Act and Work Opportunity Reconciliation Act (PRWORA), "not-qualified aliens" became ineligible for almost all federally means-tested public benefits. "Not-qualified aliens" include the undocumented as well as persons with temporary visas or nonimmigrant status, those granted temporary protected status, and other persons who have applied for but not yet received legal immigration status (PRWORA § 431[b]).

In 1998, the U.S. Department of Health and Human Services decided which of thirty-one federal programs were subject to PRWORA's "federal public benefit" definition (63 Fed. Reg. 41657). These included Temporary Assistance for Needy Families (TANF), food stamps, Medicaid, supplemental security income (SSI), unemployment compensation, schools loans and grants, and subsidized housing.

Under law prior to PRWORA, foreign nationals were eligible to receive Medicaid, SSI, and Aid to Families with Dependent Children (now TANF) if they were "permanently residing in the United States under color of law." PRWORA disallowed such aid, including when persons had employment authorizations and a valid social security number. Now, all these programs are foreclosed to all persons considered "not-qualified," and federal agencies and states are required to verify immigration and citizenship status of applicants to ensure their eligibility.

"Not-qualified aliens" are still eligible for some public benefits. These same programs are also available to the "qualified alien," including lawful permanent residents (LPRs). None of the major public health, mental health, or family planning block grants, for example, are defined as programs that exclude the undocumented.[1] PRWORA also includes a range of

205

"protected" benefits that must be available to all persons in need. These exempt, or protected, benefits are

- emergency Medicaid
- immunizations
- diagnosis and treatment of communicable diseases
- short-term, in-kind, noncash emergency or disaster relief services
- school lunch, breakfast, and other child nutrition programs
- Head Start
- means-tested programs under the Elementary and Secondary Education Act of 1965
- access of undocumented children to a public elementary and secondary education (see Chapter 6)
- any program necessary to protect life and safety that is not income-conditional. These programs include child and adult protective services; programs addressing weather emergencies and homelessness; shelters, soup kitchens, and meals-on-wheels; police, fire fighters, and ambulances; disability or substance abuse assistance necessary to protect life or safety.

In addition, some states have enacted legislation restoring or conferring a few state or locally funded benefits since PRWORA's enactment, mostly to pregnant women and undocumented children.

In this chapter, we discuss a few specific public benefits still available to "not-qualified aliens" either because PRWORA retained them or states have restored them for public policy or rights-based reasons. In addition, Congress adopted post-PRWORA federal legislation conferring broader immigration and public benefits to certain foreign nationals who have been victims of violence, including victims of domestic violence. Such legislation is discussed later in this chapter. Undocumented persons should also read the section in Chapter 10 on Government Benefits, particularly the section discussing state administration of public benefits, verification of immigration status, and reporting requirements.

Emergency Medicaid

PRWORA denied all "not-qualified aliens" eligibility for federally funded health care, including Medicaid, except under conditions of medical emergency (PRWORA § 401). The federal Medicaid program requires that all state Medicaid programs reimburse health providers for the cost of emergency services to foreign nationals who would otherwise be income-eligible for Medicaid. In addition, the Emergency Medical Treatment and Active Labor Act (EMTALA) (42 C.F.R. § 489.24 [a][1][i]) requires every hospital with an emergency room to screen every person who requests care and to treat and stabilize any detected emergency need. Hospital district indigent care or uninsured programs also must ensure that the "protected benefits" are provided without respect to citizenship. States are reimbursed for part of the costs of the emergency Medicaid program by the federal government.

In practice, uninsured foreign nationals who do not qualify for Medicaid must either pay out-of-pocket for a private doctor or visit the emergency room for care. However, emergency room doctors must only treat emergencies, as narrowly defined under federal law. For purposes of emergency Medicaid, an emergency medical condition is defined as one manifesting itself in acute symptoms of sufficient severity (including severe pain), such that the absence of immediate medical attention could reasonably be expected to result in (1) placing the patient's health in serious jeopardy; (2) serious impairment to bodily functions; or (3) serious dysfunction of any bodily organ or part (42 U.S.C. § 1396b[v][3]). This definition includes emergency labor and delivery of babies. The Medicaid regulations also require a "sudden onset" of an illness or injury (42 C.F.R. § 440.255[b][1]), which courts have interpreted to mean as occurring unexpectedly over a short period of time, as in the case of a stroke, heart attack, or auto accident. Emergency condition, however, does not include chronic illnesses, even if these are extremely serious absent immediate life-threatening factors.

Hospitals and doctors concerned with unpaid medical services will sometimes be hostile to uninsured patients and refuse to treat them. To receive Medicaid funds, however, hospitals must screen and stabilize emergency room patients. Refusing to do so for purely economic reasons, called "patient dumping," is forbidden under EMTALA, which extends responsibility beyond hospitals to emergency room physicians and doctors on call. The law provides for administrative penalties and for civil damages in separate lawsuits filed by, or on behalf of, improperly treated ER patients. Doctors and hospitals that violate EMTALA also risk exclusion from Medicaid and other government health insurance programs and fines of up to $50,000 per violation.

What You Should Do as an Undocumented Migrant If You Are Denied Emergency Medical Care. There have been very few settlements against doctors in administrative hearings, in part due to underreporting and in part due to the discretion accorded doctors in deciding what conditions constitute an emergency. Therefore, patients seeking emergency assistance for chronic conditions and who suffer immediate harm as a result of being denied treatment might pursue other alternatives. That patient might visit a different hospital or the same emergency room when a more flexible doctor is on duty. The patient might also file an internal complaint with the hospital against the doctor that refused care to alert the hospital of the doctor's conduct.

State Initiatives for Public Assistance to Undocumented Migrants

PRWORA expressly prohibited states from providing undocumented persons with state-funded public benefits, unless states subsequently passed affirmative legislation conferring such benefits (PRWORA § 1621[c] and [d]). Some states have done so but with wide variation. States with the most extensive coverage include California, Washington, Hawaii, Connecticut, Massachusetts, Rhode Island, Minnesota, New Jersey, New York, Pennsylvania, and Wisconsin.

For example, PRWORA barred undocumented women's access to federally funded prenatal health care, despite the serious health consequences to the unborn likely U.S. citizen. LPRs are also ineligible for free prenatal health care for the first five years after obtaining LPR status. Since PRWORA, however, approximately twenty states have restored eligibility for prenatal care to LPRs with less than the five-year residency requirement and sometimes to all other foreign nationals, including the undocumented. Similarly a few states like New Jersey and Washington provide state-funded health insurance to the elderly and disabled.

Eligibility for the Supplemental Nutrition Program for Women, Infants, and Children (WIC), a federal nutrition program providing access to food, counseling, and other health and nutrition services to low-income mothers and their babies and children under five years old, is at the states' discretion. To date, all states provide the program to pregnant women, regardless of immigration status.[2] States have the option of restricting access by certain groups of legal immigrant women and children and all undocumented women and children. However, states that deny any category of migrants' entrance into the WIC program would risk losing federal WIC funding and would also risk overspending on administrative time determining eligibility, possibly resulting in increased state Medicaid spending on low birth-weight babies.

Through the State Children's Health Insurance Program (SCHIP), some states have provided medical insurance to documented and undocumented children who became ineligible for Medicaid under PRWORA. SCHIP is jointly financed by the federal and state governments and helps participating states expand health care coverage to more than five million of the nation's uninsured children. The SCHIP statute does not require that children be "qualified aliens" to be eligible. However, under SCHIP, states can receive federal matching funds to pay for specialized types of expenditures, as long as those costs do not exceed 10 percent of the state's total expenditures on SCHIP benefits (unless the state receives a variance). These expenditures include providing child health benefits that are in addition to the basic benefit package the state already provides and promoting health service initiatives to protect public health. More specifically, all immigrant children, regardless of status, can benefit from health education activities, school health programs, and direct services such as newborn screening and lead testing.

Federally qualified health centers (FQHCs) also receive grants from the federal government to provide health services to underserved populations without regard to income or immigration status (42 U.S.C. § 254b *et seq.*) These populations include migratory and seasonal agricultural workers, the homeless, public housing residents, and people who face barriers accessing health services because they cannot pay or due to language and cultural differences.

Access to Higher Education

Every year, approximately 65,000 students graduating from U.S. high schools face limited prospects for completing their education or working legally in the United States because their parents brought them to the country as undocumented children. One significant impediment for undocumented students is denial of college admission. Another significant hurdle is ineligibility for student loans or tuition aid, particularly when colleges or universities may charge them out-of-state residency fees. Despite this impediment, thousands of undocumented students enroll in community colleges or universities.

Constitutional protection against state discrimination targeting aliens in higher education has extended only to lawful permanent residents and certain temporary residents (nonimmigrants) who can establish "residency" in the United States. In *Nyquist v. Mauclet*, 432 U.S. 1 (1977), the Supreme Court struck down New York's bar to state-funded scholarships to those aliens who would not affirm their intent to become citizens as soon as they were eligible. Then in 1982, in *Toll v. Moreno*, 458 U.S. 1 (1982), the Court struck down the University of Maryland's policy of charging out-of-state tuition rates to G-4 visa holders because under federal immigration policy, G-4 visa holders could establish residency. The holding, however, left open the door to distinctions targeting nonimmigrants who could not establish residency in the United States. The ruling did not address whether states can discriminate against undocumented students who, by virtue of their unauthorized stay in the United States, would be ineligible for residency.

Since *Nyquist* and *Toll*, some states have charged out-of-state tuition fees for higher education to nonimmigrant and undocumented students, based on the premise that such state residency requirements are consistent with federal immigration policy.

But why might the Court refuse to extend the Constitution's Equal Protection clause to protect nonimmigrant and undocumented students from discrimination in higher education in the same way that it chose to protect the children in *Plyler* (see Chapter 6)? There are at least two legal explanations. First, higher education is not considered a fundamental or quasi-fundamental right, so that discrimination against foreign nationals is permitted so long as states have a rational basis for the disparate treatment. Second, students in higher education are more clearly not a "protected class" for equal protection purposes, given that most are young adults with autonomy and no longer the young and "innocent" children in *Plyler*. In *Plyler*, the Court did not consider undocumented migrants to constitute a suspect class entitled to special constitutional protection. Still, the Court recognized undocumented children as deserving some protection, in part, because it would be unfair to penalize children for their parents' choice to bring them to the United States unlawfully. The imposition of blame for remaining unlawfully in the country after a child reaches adulthood, however, is also consistent with the minor exception for unlawful presence granted by the Immigration and Nationality Act (INA), which does not count children's unlawful presence in the United States until they reach the age of eighteen (INA § 212[a][9][B][iii]). Under an Equal Protection analysis, when states discriminate against a class that is not protected and deny a privilege, the practice is likely to be upheld as long as the state can offer one legitimate or rational basis for the distinction (e.g., saving money).

In the absence of constitutional protection for discrimination against most nonimmigrant and undocumented students in higher education, Congress and state legislatures have introduced legislation either to create a statutory right or to deny the privilege. A few states have sought to deny the undocumented admission into public universities. In Virginia, for example, the attorney general issued a 2002 memorandum stating, "The attorney general is strongly of the view that illegal and undocumented aliens should not be admitted into our public colleges and universities at all."[3] This memorandum caused Virginia's colleges and universities to implement, or to continue to enforce, policies that deny admission to the undocumented. When challenged, the U.S. District Court of Virginia upheld the admission bar, as long as the state resorted to federal standards for establishing who is and is not undocumented (*Equal Access Educ. v. Merten*, 305 F.Supp.2d 585, 591 [E.D. Va. 2004]).

Other state legislatures have passed or introduced legislation to either grant or deny in-state tuition benefits to the undocumented. Courts have consistently upheld the power of states to charge higher tuition rates to nonstate residents. This policy is based, in part, on the notion that state taxpayers should have access to the universities at a lower cost than individuals who do not pay taxes in that state. In addition, the state has a legitimate interest in seeing that its residents, who are more invested in the state, have a greater opportunity to attend the universities and remain in the state after graduation. Undocumented migrants may pay their fair share of taxes, and many are longtime residents in their respective states; yet, these same policies are not always applied to them because their illegal residence violates federal immigration law. As of early 2008, at least nine states have passed laws to grant in-state tuition to the undocumented or temporary residents,[4] while a few have passed laws denying benefits.[5] In 2001, Texas was first to allow undocumented students in-state tuition benefits. Under Texas law, eligible undocumented students included those graduating from Texas high schools who resided in the state for at least three years prior to high school graduation, and who signed an affidavit stating their intent to seek legalization as soon as it was available (Tex. Educ. Code Ann. § 54.052[j]).

States also cannot divorce their policies on access to higher education to undocumented and nonimmigrant students from federal legislation. Higher education institutions were already affected by the 1996 welfare reforms that restricted student aid eligibility to foreign nationals. Section 505 of the Illegal Immigration Reform and Immigrant Responsibility Act of 1996 (IIRAIRA) proscribed states from conferring upon undocumented immigrants any postsecondary education benefits based on residency status within the state unless the state was willing to offer the same to any other U.S. citizen or national regardless of residency status. At the same time, PRWORA denied the undocumented any postsecondary monetary assistance in the form of grants, loans, and work-study. Any state wishing to make an undocumented person eligible for any state or local public benefit would have to enact a state law providing for such eligibility. Subsequently, Congress created Section 1623, which appears to withdraw state discretion to grant in-state tuition to undocumented students but actually requires states to take an affirmative step to change residency requirements to permit undocumented students to be eligible for in-state tuition. That provision reads, "notwithstanding any other provision of law, an alien who is not lawfully present in the United States shall not be eligible on the basis of residence within a state . . . for any postsecondary education benefit." The effect of these measures has been to require states to change residency requirements for all students so as to effectuate meaningful access to higher education.[6]

Since 2001, however, members of Congress have introduced bipartisan legislation to repeal IIRAIRA provisions on higher education and to offer a means for certain undocumented children to earn legalization. If passed, the legislation would effectively trump any state measure that denies admission to the undocumented and would remove any disincentive for charging in-state tuition rates to undocumented or nonimmigrant students. The proposed legislation, introduced as either the Development Relief and Education for Alien Minors (DREAM) Act (S. 1545) or the Student Adjustment Act (H.R. 1684), would repeal Section 505 of the IIRAIRA and allow states to offer in-state tuition rates to undocumented students. The DREAM Act also provides qualifying youth access to certain government financial aid. In addition, the legislation would legalize young people who possess good moral character, can establish five years' residency in the United States, are under twenty-one years of age, have earned a high school diploma, and who complete at least two years of college or military service.

Despite support by several members of Congress, neither the DREAM Act nor the Student Adjustment Act has become law. In 2006 and again in

2007, the DREAM Act was incorporated into the Comprehensive Immigration Reform Acts, which failed to pass as law. Senate efforts in 2007 to include the DREAM Act by amendment in the defense authorization bill, or to pass it independently, failed.

Ordinary Living

An estimated twelve million unauthorized migrants reside in the United States. Nearly half entered the country legally and overstayed their visas. Others crossed the border without inspection. Despite their lack of immigration documentation, these foreign nationals work and live in the United States for lengthy time periods and engage in "ordinary living": they have jobs, open bank accounts, take out loans, rent apartments, purchase homes, drive cars, and travel. Increasingly, however, since the terror attacks of September 11, 2001, these "ordinary living" tasks are becoming more difficult for unauthorized migrants.

The primary obstacle to "ordinary living" has been the denial of U.S. issued identification forms, such as driver's licenses and social security numbers (SSNs), not only to undocumented persons but also those with temporary visas. Under federal law, SSNs have never been available to most foreign nationals, except lawful permanent residents (LPRs) and certain temporary immigrants (nonimmigrants) eligible to work in the United States. Driver's license restrictions for foreign nationals, based on immigration status, increased significantly after the September 11 attacks. By January 2005, twenty-four states had legislation requiring a lawful presence requirement for the issuance of a driver's license, while only eleven states expressly did not.

Then, the federal government, considering the issuance of driver's licenses a national security issue, imposed national standards on their issuance. The U.S. Congress signed into law the Intelligence Reform and Terrorism Prevention Act (IRTPA) of 2004 and the REAL ID Act of 2005. IRTPA and the REAL ID Act require that all state-issued driver's licenses comply with proof of identity standards and machine-readable identity (biometric) information, such as a picture or other unique identifier. In addition, the REAL ID Act imposes SSN and legal residency requirements on state-issued driver's licenses, at least if these are to be used as a form of identification before federal agencies for official purposes (REAL ID Act § 202[c]). Further, the REAL ID Act authorizes the issuance solely of temporary licenses and identification cards for persons holding temporary visas or whose petitions are pending. The temporary licenses expire when the person's authorized stay in the United States expires or after one year if there is no definite end period (REAL ID Act § 202 [c][2][C]). Eligibility for federal funding to implement the REAL ID Act requires states to share information about its drivers with other states through an interstate database (REAL ID Act § 203).

States are not mandated by law to comply with IRTPA and the REAL ID Act; however, there are important incentives to do so. A resident from a noncomplying state would be turned away when trying to conduct business with a federal agency, unless that person had a federally issued ID, such as a passport. Recognizing that compliance is likely necessary, many states have complained that laws were passed unfunded and that the cost to states will be high. Nevertheless, within four months of the passage of IRTPA and the REAL ID Act, twenty-four states had already introduced legislation to conform state law to the federal requirements. By January 2007, at least twenty-seven states had a lawful presence requirement for the issuance of a driver's license, while only eight did not.[7]

The consequences of driver's license denials to foreign nationals are dire. It is not simply a denial of a "privilege" to drive. In many cities, the denial of a driver's license exacerbates the underclass status of immigrants because the ability to drive is usually necessary to earn a living. Furthermore, denial of a driver's license amounts to a denial of identity. Driver's licenses have become the primary form of identification U.S. residents must use to conduct most essential activities of ordinary living, whether with private or public entities. Driver's licenses are widely accepted and sometimes required to obtain services from federal and state agencies, open a bank account, request credit, rent an apartment, or buy a home. Moreover, the lack of a driver's license deeply affects the nature of immigrants' interaction with law enforcement by increasing the racial profiling of Latino/as, especially during traffic stops (i.e., for immigration enforcement). In turn, this decreases the trust that local police departments have worked to build for more effective community policing.

A few states, including Tennessee, have issued driving certificates in lieu of driver's licenses (Tenn. Code Ann. § 55-50-331). These driving certificates are not to be used as a form of personal identification but solely authorize the holder to drive. In fact, "for driving purposes only" is usually inscribed in the certificate. Driving certificates solve only part of the problem by licensing foreign motorists to drive and obtain car insurance. They do nothing to resolve the lack of personal identification that would allow foreign nationals to engage in "ordinary living."

Some foreign governments responded to driver's license restrictions by issuing their own consular identification or Matricula Consular card (MC) to their nationals residing in the United States. The first country to do so was Mexico, followed by Guatemala and Argentina, with at least seven other countries following suit or considering doing the same: Poland, Brazil, Honduras, Peru, El Salvador, Bolivia, and Nicaragua. To obtain an MC, foreign nationals must usually provide at least a birth certificate, another official document, such as a national identification card, passport, or voter registration card, and evidence of the individual's permanent residence in the United States, such as a utility bill. Most MCs include a hologram or other embedded design to make it tamper proof. They also contain the name, signature, date and place of birth, and U.S. address of the bearer, as well as a serial number, date of issue, expiration date, and the name of the issuing consulate. Consulate offices, however, do not conduct criminal background checks of applicants, nor do the consulates maintain a database of issued cards. Guatemala's MC issuance process is based on the country's passport database, which includes fingerprint verification capability.

The issuance of MC cards is consistent with the general scope of permissible consular functions and has been codified in the Vienna Convention on Consular Relations. Historically, foreign governments have issued consular identification cards solely to enable their nationals abroad to seek consular assistance, such as applying for a passport. Since 2002, however, these consular cards began to replace the driver's license as personal identification for transactions in the United States, including contact with police, opening bank accounts, gaining a driver's license (at least in those ten states that allow it),[8] and receiving local services or public benefits. Additionally, the card is accepted by numerous telephone and utility companies, hospitals, insurance companies, and video stores, among other establishments.

As the issuance and acceptance of MCs have increased, however, so have the criticisms and restrictions. Criticisms range from national security to concerns over infringement by foreign governments on U.S. sovereignty. MC restrictions also began at the local level and subsequently have been "federalized," although the effect has been on public, not private, institutions. In May 2003, for example, Colorado became the first state to restrict public acceptance of MCs. The New York Police and Motor Vehicle Departments have also refused to add the MC to their lists of acceptable identity documents. Subsequently, in IRTPA, Congress required the Secretary of Homeland Security to propose minimum standards for identification documents to be used by airline passengers (IRTPA § 4012). Furthermore, in the REAL ID Act, Congress included a provision specifying that an official passport was the only acceptable foreign identity document (REAL ID, § 202). The REAL ID Act also established that driver's licenses are the only identification accepted at federal sites. This requirement seems to preclude the use of MCs at airports or other federal institutions.

In contrast, financial institutions can find federal legislative or regulatory support for accepting MCs for banking services. Section 326 of Title III of the U.S. Patriot Act added a new subsection authorizing the Secretary of Treasury to issue minimum standards relating to identification and verification of any person who applies for a bank account. The final regulation as issued by the secretary permits financial institutions to accept MCs as long as these are safe and fraud-proof (68 Fed. Reg. 25090, 25109). This is important to foreign nationals, who, without a bank account, subject themselves to inordinate costs of cashing checks or sending money abroad and even to increased property crime. MCs are also important to banks, which profit by increasing their business and savings rates. In addition, some banks have begun to provide undocumented persons with loans to purchase homes. Foreign nationals who have borrowed loans to purchase their homes have presented the MC or the individual taxpayer identification numbers (ITINs) issued by the Internal Revenue Service. Some banks also rely on ITINs for other banking transactions.

Opponents of MCs have argued that their acceptance by institutions could give rise to criminal or civil liability. For example, a group called Friends of Immigration Law Enforcement (FILE) threatened to sue banks under a federal law that prohibits the harboring of undocumented migrants. FILE argues that acceptance of MCs is a criminal violation of 8 U.S.C. § 1324 because it "encourages" and "induces" undocumented foreign nationals to reside in the United States by conferring them benefits. This broad interpretation of the statute, however, is likely incorrect, given that the government would have to show that the accepting entity intended or had the mental state to commit the crime of encouraging illegal immigration. Indeed, institutions cannot know the immigration status of MC holders because consular officers issue these cards to their nationals residing abroad whether the residents are legal or undocumented. In addition, allowing foreign nationals to possess a bank account does not "encourage" illegal immigration, as many foreign nationals reside in the United States with or without a bank account.

Legalization, Removal, and Relief from Removal

As of 2008, the estimated twelve million undocumented migrants residing in the United States have little hope of finding a clear path to legalization. Therefore, millions of undocumented migrants will continue to live and work in the United States vulnerable to exploitation, subject to the increasing anti-immigrant local measures that restrict their access to ordinary living, and in fear of deportation, particularly as immigration raids increase.

In this chapter we address a few exceptions that may allow some undocumented migrants to legalize. This section explains the substantive and procedural requirements for permanent legalization. It also explains a few additional temporary grants of stay, including temporary protection status (TPS). It also addresses issues of removal and relief for removal for undocumented migrants. More flexible legalization requirements and relief from removal may apply to persons receiving special protection under the Immigration and Nationality Act (INA), including, for example, spouses and children of U.S. citizens and LPRs who have been victims of domestic violence. A discussion of those special legalization provisions appears later in this chapter.

How You Can Obtain Legalization. Legalization is minimally a two-step process. First, the person must qualify for an immigrant visa. Second, the person must establish that she is admissible.

To qualify for a visa, a foreign national must be eligible for at least one of the four categories of available visas based on (1) family relationships (see the discussion in Chapter 10 on family unification); (2) employment; (3) diversity; and (4) refugee or asylum status. Most family- or employment-based visas require a sponsor. For example, a U.S. citizen or LPR relative would file Form I-130 for family-based petitions, or an employer would file Form I-140 for employment-based visas. By contrast, the foreign national self-petitions for a diversity visa or for asylum and refugee status. Each visa also requires certain characteristics of the foreign national, such as a family relationship or education level, or seeks to address special circumstances important to U.S. policy, such as attracting the best and brightest to U.S. jobs, increasing diversity among immigrants, and providing refugee status to those facing persecution in their own countries. In the following section we address the basic requirements for employment-based and refugee and asylum petitions.

Admissibility means the foreign national is not excluded from legalization based on such factors enumerated in INA § 212(a). The INA groups exclusion grounds into ten broad categories, including health, criminal background (see Chapter 8), public charge (see Chapter 10 on family unification), immigration control, and national security. These exclusion grounds apply whenever a foreign national applies for a visa, whether permanent or temporary, whether from abroad or in the United States. This section discusses the health, immigration control, and national security exclusion grounds, their exceptions, and any available waivers or discretionary relief.

Employment-Based Immigrant Visas

Employment-based visas are reserved for highly skilled, educated, or extremely talented foreign workers. Undocumented workers in the United States who lack an education or are working in jobs considered "unskilled," such as in restaurants, landscaping, or general construction, do not qualify. Undocumented workers with great hopes of obtaining legal status sometimes allow ignorant or, worse, ill-intentioned lawyers or legal assistants to process employment-based visas on their behalf. Often, instead of achieving legalization, after several years of waiting, the worker is deported. Understanding which employment-based visas are available is therefore important to safeguard against falling prey to false promises of legalization.

There are five different employment categories, ordered in terms of preference. First preference is for persons with "extraordinary ability in the sciences, arts, education, business, or athletics"; "outstanding professors and researchers"; and certain "multinational executives and managers" (INA §

203[b][1]). The second preference is for "members of the professions, holding advanced degrees" (usually meaning graduate degrees) and foreign nationals "of exceptional ability" (INA § 203[b][2]). The third preference is for "skilled workers, professional" (without advanced degrees), and other workers who can show that the United States needs their labor (INA § 203[b][3]). The fourth preference is for certain "special immigrants," who include, among others, religious workers and certain long-term foreign employees of the U.S. government (INA § 203[b][4]). The fifth preference is for entrepreneurs or investors who plan on operating a business in the United States and creating jobs (INA § 203[b][5]). These visas are also numerically restricted but few backlogs occur unless the number of petitions exceeds the number of available visas. As of July 2007, for example, all employment-based visas were current.[9]

In most cases, a foreign national seeking an employment visa must have a job offer from an employer who petitions on her behalf (8 C.F.R. § 204.5[h]).[10] Furthermore, with few exceptions, second and third preference employment-based visas require labor certification; that is, a showing that able, willing, and qualified U.S. workers who are citizens or LPRs are not available and that the applicant's employment will not adversely affect the wages and working conditions of similarly employed U.S. workers (INA § 212[a][5]). Labor certification is always the first step in applying for an employment-based visa and must be completed by the employer before filing the petition.

Current labor certification procedures usually require the employer to determine whether the job appears in Schedule A or B as published by the U.S. Department of Labor [20 C.F.R. § 656.10). Schedule A lists occupations precertified for labor certification that do not require a separate process; currently, however, this list contains only physical therapists, nurses, and immigrants of "exceptional ability in the sciences and arts" (20 C.F.R. § 656.5). Schedule B, by contrast, lists hundreds of unskilled jobs for which labor certification would not be granted, unless the employer applies for a waiver and makes a special showing (20 C.F.R. §§ 656.11 and 23).

If the job is not listed in Schedule A or B, the employer may file an application with the U.S. Department of Labor's Employment and Training Administration (ETA). First, however, the employer must request from the state workforce agencies (SWA) the prevailing wage for the particular job and take specified recruiting steps to determine if qualified U.S. workers are available for the job. An ETA official, known as a "certifying officer," determines whether to grant certification. If the employer is denied, he may seek review by the Board of Alien Labor Certification Appeals. To do so, the employer must act within thirty days of receiving written notification of the denial.

The labor certification process is complex, expensive, slow, and subject to long delays. The process involves both SWAs and the ETA. Most of the delays occur at the SWAs, where waiting times vary considerably from state to state. Up-to-date estimates of waiting times at both the state and federal levels are available at http//:www.ows.doleta.gov/foreign/times.asp#reg. Delays in the labor certification process affect not only the employer's and employee's ability to fill the job promptly, but they also create procedural difficulties, particularly for foreign nationals seeking to adjust status while still in the United States. Without delays in labor certification, adjustment of status would allow a foreign national with a current temporary visa, such as a student or worker H1B visa, to process her legalization without leaving the United States (INA § 245[a] and [c]). With delays, however, even if the employment-based visa is available, the person's temporary visa would no longer be current by the time the process is complete. In this case, except for a 180-day grace period (INA § 245[k]), the foreign national may no longer adjust status and must leave the United States for consular processing of the visa.

Another result of delays is that a foreign national seeking to adjust to permanent status while holding a temporary visa must keep it current by remaining with the same employer, despite any difficulties, until the labor certification is complete. Since 2000, however, a foreign national who has been waiting for labor certification for longer than 180 days may switch to a new job without the need for preapproval (INA §§ 2004[j] and 212[a][5][A][iv]).

Asylum or Refugee Status

A few persons who wish to escape or who have escaped from persecution in their own country for political, religious, or other reasons recognized by law are also eligible for legalization by applying for asylum or refugee status. Refugees and asylees must meet similar requirements under the INA. Asylum seekers are those who meet the refugee definition and are already in the United States. These individuals may either file an affirmative application for asylum (8 C.F.R. § 208.4[b][3]) or seek asylum while in removal proceedings (8 C.F.R. § 208.4[b][3]). Overseas refugees apply from abroad. For this latter group, the U.S. president determines how many overseas refugees will be admitted every year, after "appropriate consultation" with Congress (INA § 207[a]). That number has been steadily declining, ending at 70,000 in 2005.

Legalization through asylum is not an easy path. Strict legal requirements render most persons ineligible. Political bias has also favored persons coming from certain communist countries, to the detriment of other nations such as Colombia (which is still in the midst of a civil war). Furthermore, statutory requirements blatantly intend to discourage potential asylees from filing claims. For example, the asylum application must be filed within one year of the applicant's arrival in the United States, with some exceptions (INA § 208[a][2][B]).[11] As a result, many asylum seekers become ineligible when they delay filing. In addition, if the application is filed while the person is in removal proceedings (as opposed to an affirmative application), the

applicant will likely be detained while the petition is adjudicated (INA §
236[a]). Moreover, an applicant who knowingly files a "frivolous" claim for
asylum — one lacking merit — runs the risk of becoming permanently ineligible for any immigration benefit, including legalization though family or employment (INA § 208[d][6]).

Unfortunately, many undocumented migrants unwittingly hire others to
file weak asylum petitions on their behalf, only to be denied and placed in
removal proceedings. Additionally, there have been times, especially in the
1990s, when the backlog of asylum petitions filed, principally by Central
Americans in countries at war, resulted in the delayed adjudication of those
applications. In the meantime, those who filed the asylum petitions received
work authorizations, as permitted by law. Now, however, more than a
decade later, those applications are finally being adjudicated, and persons,
especially from Guatemala, are being ordered removed by the thousands.
With few exceptions to those who qualify for legalization under special legislation, such as the Nicaraguan Adjustment and Central American Relief
Act (NACARA, see below), the changed conditions in those nations means
that they will be deported even if their application for asylum had merit
when originally filed.

The procedural and substantive requirements for refugee or asylum status are complex. The following section provides only the basics, so that a
person may make a preliminary determination of whether to consider pursuing an asylum claim.

In 1980, the United States adopted the Refugee Act. The Refugee Act
provides the first definition of "refugee," which appears in INA §
101(a)(42), and requires a showing of "persecution or a well-founded fear of
persecution on account of race, religion, nationality, membership in a particular social group, or political opinion." Fear of persecution must be the
primary motivation for seeking refuge. Economic reasons, for example, are
not valid. This definition also applies to persons in the United States seeking
asylum under INA § 208.

A person cannot seek asylum unless she has been persecuted or has a
well-founded fear of persecution if she were to return. The applicant need
not show a real possibility of being singled out for persecution. Rather, she
can meet the burden by establishing a pattern or practice in her country
against a group of persons similarly situated to her on account of the enumerated statutory reasons (8 C.F.R. § 208.13[b][2][iii]).

Harm that constitutes persecution must meet a threshold level of seriousness, measured by an "objective" observer. The meaning of persecution generally requires either a "threat to life or freedom, or the infliction of suffering or harm upon an individual in order to punish him for possessing a belief
or characteristics the persecutor seeks to overcome"[12] or the "infliction of
objectively serious harm or suffering that is subjectively experienced as serious harm by the applicant, regardless of whether the persecutor intend[ed] to

cause the harm" (67 Fed. Reg. 76588, 76597). The statute provides examples of persecution, including forced sterilization or coerced abortion on account of political or religious opinion (INA § 101[a][42]). There is disagreement among the BIA and other appellate courts as to whether punishment must be the motivation of persecution. Courts generally agree, however, that economic or employment discrimination does not constitute persecution. Persecution must be individualized so that "generally harsh conditions shared by many others [do] not amount to persecution" (see, e.g., *Ahmed v. Ashcroft,* 341 F.3d 214, 215–216 [3d Cir. 2003]). Furthermore, persecution must generally be conducted by a state actor, although private actors also persecute when the state will not or cannot take reasonable efforts to halt them.

Furthermore, the persecution must be "on account of" one of the statutorily recognized grounds. What the term means and how it applies are complex questions. "On account of" is referred to as the "nexus requirement" because it connects the persecution to one of the protected grounds. What the degree of nexus should be has created some confusion, but it has generally meant *because of* or *based on.* Furthermore, the "on account of" reason need not be the sole reason for the persecution but one of the central ones (REAL ID Act, § 101[a][3]). What "central" means is determined on a case-by-case basis.

Some of the protected categories also give rise to complexities. Establishing that the persecution is based on political opinion, for example, generally requires the applicant to act or refuse to act because he or she is motivated by an expressed political choice. In *INS v. Elias-Zacarias,* 502 U.S. 478 (1992), the Supreme Court did not consider that the applicant could meet the "on account of political opinion" prong when he refused to join the guerrilla army in the absence of an express political opinion supporting the refusal. The applicant, however, may be successful in his claim if he demonstrates that his acts did or would lead his persecutors to impute a political opinion through his acts. This is true even when the persecutor imputes on the victim a political opinion he knows she does not possess. This was the result in *Lazo-Majano v. INS,* 813 F.2d 1432 (9th Cir. 1987), where a Salvadoran woman was granted asylum because an army sergeant, who repeatedly raped her and kept her in bondage, falsely accused her of subversion if she were to leave or file a complaint against him. Furthermore, some but not all courts view a person's position of "neutrality" in a civil war as a political opinion.

Another category that raises questions about the scope and purpose of refugee protection is persecution that occurs on "account of membership in a particular social group." Generally, the term "particular social group" has required that the shared characteristic of the group be "immutable" or innate, such as sex, color, or kinship ties. In some circumstances, courts have also considered a shared past experience among members of a group. These have included former military leadership or land ownership, but not necessarily holding a job that may require a person to perform a political activity. Engaging voluntarily in socially undesirable activity such as gang membership is not included. The term must also be narrow enough to allow limitations. For example, in *Sanchez-Trujillo v. INS*, 801 F.2d 1571 (1986), the Ninth Circuit declined to consider a class of young, urban, Salvadoran working-class males as constituting a particular social group because there were too many differences among the members of the group. In addition, proposed Department of Justice rules on the meaning of "particular social group" list several factors for its definition, none of which are determinative: (1) the members of the group are closely affiliated with each other; (2) the members are driven by a common motive or interest; (3) a voluntarily associational relationship exists among the members; (4) the group is recognized as a societal faction or is otherwise a recognized segment of the population in the country in question; (5) members view themselves as members of the group; and (6) the society in which the group exists distinguishes members of the group for different treatment or status than is accorded to other members of the society (Proposed Rule, modifying 8 C.F.R. § 208.15). Among those included as members of a "particular social group" have been homosexuals[13] and women, when the persecution was "on account of" their gender.[14]

Special Legalization Avenues

Congress enacted special provisions (the Cuban Refugee Adjustment Act) that allow Cuban refugees to become eligible to adjust to LPR status after one year of admission or being paroled into the United States. This law also benefits Cubans who entered without inspection as long as they turn themselves in. The benefit extends to spouses and children of Cubans whether or not they are Cuban citizens as long as they reside with the Cuban applicant in the United States.

Periodically, Congress has passed legislation granting certain undocumented persons residing in the United States the right to permanent legalization. One example is the Immigration Reform and Control Act of 1986, which granted legalization to foreign nationals residing in the United States since 1982. Similarly, Cuban and Nicaraguan nationals became eligible for legalization if they were physically present in the United States for a continuous period beginning on or before December 1, 1995, and filed the application before April 1, 2000 (Nicaraguan Adjustment and Central American Relief Act).

NACARA also benefited Guatemalans and Salvadorans (as well as nationals of former Soviet bloc and Eastern European nations). The legislation gave them the opportunity to apply for suspension of deportation under rules that preceded the Illegal Immigration Reform and Immigrant Responsibility Act of 1996 (IIRIRA). These requirements are taken up in Chapter 10 in the section on relief from removal.

Admissibility

Once an I-130 (family-based) or an I-140 (employment-based) petition has been approved, the applicant must establish that she is admissible. Most exclusion or inadmissibility grounds are subject to exceptions, which must be applied, or waivers, which are discretionarily granted. Refugees and asylum seekers (and many others under the special legalization venues) are automatically exempted from certain exclusion grounds, including labor certification and public charge, and USCIS has the authority to waive most others (INA § 207[c][3]). In addition, by statute most exclusion grounds are waived for victims of domestic violence who are self-petitioning and for those applying under NACARA. However, asylum cannot be granted when the applicant is a national security risk to the United States or when the applicant has committed particular, serious crimes (INA § 208[b][2][A][5]). The INA does not define "particular (nonpolitical) serious" crimes, and courts decide the issue on a case-by-case basis. Usually, a particular, serious crime involves violent crimes against a person but can also include crimes against property. For example, an aggravated felony, as the term is defined in the INA, is automatically "particularly serious."

A foreign national who entered the United States on a still valid visa may usually apply for adjustment of status by filing Form I-485 (INA § 245). All other persons must apply from abroad and go though consular processing, usually by filing Form DS 156 (22 CFR § 22.2). With few exceptions, those who entered or have resided unlawfully in the United States and who then apply from abroad are subject to a three- to ten-year bar to legalization unless a family-based waiver applies. The following are in addition to those exclusion grounds discussed in Chapter 10 on Family Unification and Chapter 8 on Immigration Consequences of Crime.

Inadmissibility on Health-Related Grounds

• *Communicable Diseases.* In general, a foreign national who has a communicable disease of public health significance is inadmissible (INA § 212[a][1][A][i]). Such diseases include "infection with the etiologic agent for acquired immune deficiency syndrome" or HIV. INA § 212(g)(1) authorizes a waiver of this ground for a person with certain family relationships to a U.S. citizen or LPR.

• *Failure to Vaccinate.* Anyone who fails to present documentation of being vaccinated against vaccine-preventable diseases is inadmissible (INA § 212[a][1][A][ii]). A limited exception applies to children adopted abroad by U.S. citizens. The children must be ten years old or younger and be vaccinated in the United States within thirty days of entry (INA §212[a][1][C]). A limited waiver is also available for medical or religious reasons (INA § 212[g][2]).

• *Physical or Mental Disorder.* INA § 212(a)(1)(A)(iii) renders inadmissible a foreign national with a mental or physical disorder who poses or has posed a threat to self, property, safety, or the welfare of others, unless the foreign national receives a waiver subject to the necessary terms, conditions, and controls imposed by immigration officials (INA § 212[g][3]).

• *Drug Abuser or Addict.* INA § 212(a)(1)(A)(iv) renders inadmissible persons who are drug abusers or addicts, and no waiver is authorized. Additionally, the Center for Immigration Services (CIS) issued a policy memorandum explaining that an applicant with a significant record of alcohol-related driving accidents may be inadmissible.

Immigration Control

• *Failure to Attend Immigration Court Proceedings.* A person is inadmissible for five years after the date of departure from the United States if he or she, without reasonable cause, fails to attend or remain in attendance at a hearing to determine removal (INA § 212[a][6][B], 8 U.S.C.A. § 1182).

• *Immigration Fraud.* Foreign nationals who have committed specified forms of document fraud are subject to administrative fines under INA § 274(C)[15] and are also inadmissible under INA § 216(a)(6)(F), subject to a few discretionary waivers for humanitarian reasons and in certain family-based circumstances (i.e., the only such offense was committed solely to assist or aid a spouse or child) (INA § 212[d][12]). Foreign nationals who procure visas, admission, or certain other documents or benefits by fraud or misrepresentation become inadmissible for life (INA § 212[a][6][C][i]). Misrepresentation or fraud contains three elements: (1) a misrepresentation, either orally or in writing to an immigration officer, that is (2) willful or with knowledge of its falsity and (3) material (i.e., affects the outcome). An INA § 212(i)(1) waiver excuses this ground of inadmissibility. To qualify, the foreign national must be a resident seeking permanent legalization, must be the spouse, son, or daughter of a U.S. citizen or LPR and must show that extreme hardship would result to his spouse or parent if he were inadmissible. False claims of citizenship, both oral and written to anyone, are independent grounds for inadmissibility, unless the foreign national reasonably believed he was a citizen based on the citizenship of at least one of his parents and residence in the United States (INA § 212[a][6][C][ii][I]–[III]).

• *Smugglers.* Under INA § 212(a)(6)(E), any foreign national who has knowingly encouraged or aided in any way another foreign national to enter or attempt to enter the United States without authorization is inadmissible. This ground applies regardless of whether there was any monetary gain from the activity and includes activities beyond physical transport of someone across the border. The State Department considers "smuggling" to include a knowingly false oral or written statement by a foreign national on behalf of a visa applicant. Smuggling can also include sending money home to assist family members to enter the United States. There is a limited exception to the smuggling ground for persons with certain family members legalizing under IRCA, and a discretionary waiver to LPRs who proceed abroad temporarily or persons seeking admission under one of the family-based immigrant categories (except brothers and sisters), if the smuggling was only of their spouse, parent, son, or daughter (INA § 212[d][11]).

• *Not being in possession of valid immigration entry documents.* INA § 212(a) 7(A)(i) and 7(B)(i) excludes foreign nationals who lack a valid passport and visa or other valid entry documents, unless a person holding a permanent visa but who lacks other required documentation is still allowed in at the discretion of the attorney general. Parallel provisions applying in special cases are INA § 212A(a)(5)(A) for the person lacking a labor certification, and INA § 212(a)(6)(D) for stowaways. A foreign national denied admission is generally removed under INA § 235(b)(1) and faces other exclusion for five years because of her removal if she attempts to reapply for admission, as discussed below.

• *After Removal.* A person removed administratively (i.e., without a hearing) at a port of entry is inadmissible for five years after the date of removal; twenty years if there is a second removal order; or permanently if he has been convicted of an aggravated felony. If the foreign national is ordered removed after an immigration hearing under INA § 240, the exclusion is for ten years after the removal or departure; twenty years if there is a second removal order; or permanently if he has been convicted of an aggravated felony (INA § 212[a][9][A][i] or [ii]). Certain foreign nationals can overcome these bars only with permission from CIS, by filing Form I-212 with the district director having jurisdiction over the place where removal proceedings were held (8 C.F.R. § 212.2[d]). Favorable factors to receive permission include the applicant's moral character, his respect for law and order, evidence of reformation and rehabilitation, family ties and responsibilities, hardship to himself or others resulting from the removal, and the need for his services in the United States.

• *Ineligible for Citizenship and Draft Evaders.* INA § 212(a)(8) renders inadmissible a foreign national who is permanently ineligible for citizenship and any person who left the United States to evade the draft.

• *Unlawful Entrant After Removal.* INA § 212(a)(9)(C)(i) makes inadmissible a person who has been ordered removed and who subsequently enters or attempts to reenter without being admitted. Such a person faces a permanent bar to admission but may seek consent to reapply for admission after being outside the United States for ten years.

National Security Provisions

Other inadmissibility provisions are related to security reasons, including foreign nationals engaged in terrorists activities (INA § 212[a][3][B][ii][V]) or who have been associated with terrorist organizations (INA § 212[a][3][B]); those who will be adverse to U.S. foreign policy (INA § 212[a][3][C]); those who have been members of a totalitarian party, with some exceptions for involuntary and past membership (INA § 212[a][3][D][i]); and those who participated in Nazi persecution, genocide, or the commission of any act of torture or extrajudicial killing (INA § 212[a][3][E][i]).

Miscellaneous Provisions
Additionally, the INA excludes foreign nationals who practice polygamy (INA § 212[a][10][A]); have engaged in international child abduction (INA § 212[a][10][C]); have voted unlawfully (INA § 212[a][10][D]); or who renounced their U.S. citizenship for purposes of avoiding tax liability on or after September 30, 1996 (INA § 212[a][10][E]).

Relief from Removal
Most undocumented migrants in removal proceedings have little hope of relief, but some exceptions occur. In addition to asylum, certain undocumented migrants qualify for other specific forms of relief, including cancellation of removal, NACARA relief, withholding of removal, Convention Against Torture (CAT) relief, adjustment of status, and possibly private bills. Moreover, though not a remedy to removal, voluntary departure allows some foreign nationals to avoid the exclusion grounds related to removal orders under INA § 212(a)(9) discussed above. The requirements for withholding of removal, CAT relief, private bills, and voluntary departure are the same as for documented immigrants, and are explained in Chapter 10. Restrictions to relief from removal also apply equally to documented and undocumented immigrants. For a discussion of these restrictions, see Chapter 10.

Cancellation of Removal
Cancellation of removal is available to undocumented migrants who otherwise meet four stringent eligibility requirements: (1) ten years of continuous physical presence in the United States; (2) good moral character; (3) no criminal convictions of certain crimes; and (4) proof that removal would result in exceptional and extremely unusual hardship to the petitioner's spouse, parent, or child who is a U.S. citizen or LPR (INA § 240[A][b]). Only 4,000 foreign nationals per year may be granted cancellation of removal every year (INA § 240 [e][1]).

The requirement for "continuous presence" is demanding, not only because it is for ten years but because certain acts will make the clock stop. For example, the time stops the moment a foreign national receives a Notice to Appear about the commencement of removal proceedings (INA § 240A[d][1]). Also, the clock will stop the moment the foreign national commits any crime that would render him inadmissible (INA § 240A[d][1]). Temporary absences from the United States, however, that are innocent, casual, and brief will not interrupt continuous presence. However, a single departure of more than ninety days or cumulative absences of more than 180 days will (INA § 240A[d][2]). In some cases, it may be that the commission of any crime or other violation while abroad may destroy continuous presence, even if the visit abroad is brief.

The good moral character requirement (defined in INA §101[f]) is the same as it is for naturalization (see Chapter 10), except the required residency period is ten years rather than five. The no criminal conviction requirement applies to all criminal and national security grounds that would render the foreign national excludable or removable.

Additionally, perhaps one of the most difficult requirements to meet is the "exceptional and extremely unusual" hardship prong. In Chapter 10 on Family Unification, we explained the "extreme hardship" requirement that must be established to qualify for certain waivers to the exclusion grounds. The difference between that standard and this is one of degree. Usually, it is not enough that the foreign national's spouse or children (who must be U.S. citizens or LPRs) are so acclimated to the United States that removal to another country would be difficult. For example, in *Matter of Monreal-Aguinaga*, 23 I. & N. Dec. 56 (2001), the Board of Immigration Appeals did not grant cancellation or removal relief to an undocumented Mexican national who had resided in the United States since age fourteen and had two U.S. citizen children, ages eight and twelve, and whose LPR parents and seven LPR siblings also lived in the United States. Although the circumstances must not be "unconscionable," they do have to be unique; examples might include a very sick child who cannot receive proper medical attention in the country of removal.

NACARA Relief

NACARA provides a special form of cancellation of removal (formerly known as suspension of deportation) under more flexible standards for Salvadorans, Guatemalans, and nationals of the former Soviet Union and Eastern European countries. The NACARA requirements are seven years of continuous physical presence, good moral character during that period, and extreme hardship to the LPR or U.S. citizen spouse, parent, or child but also to the applicant. Further, under NACARA, the clock does not stop when removal proceedings commence.

NACARA applies to the following groups:

- Salvadoran nationals who were not apprehended after December 19, 1990, at the time of entry, and who first entered the United States on or before September 19, 1990, and registered under the *ABC* settlement (*American Baptist Churches v. Thornburgh*, 760 F. Supp. 796 [N.D. Cal. 1991]) on or before October 31, 1991, or applied for Temporary Protected Status (TPS) (see below) on or before October 31, 1991. The ABC settlement, based on a lawsuit alleging disparate treatment in the adjudication of refugee and asylum petitions by Salvadorans and Guatemalans, allowed eligible class members from Guatemala and El

Salvador to register for certain benefits, including applying again for asylum or having their asylum applications reconsidered.

- Guatemalan nationals who were not apprehended after December 19, 1990, at the time of entry, and who first entered the United States on or before October 1, 1990, and registered for *ABC* benefits on or before December 31, 1991.
- Nationals of Guatemala and El Salvador who applied for asylum on or before April 1, 1990.
- Spouses and children (under twenty-one years old, unmarried) of a person granted suspension or cancellation under NACARA if they were spouses and children at the time relief was granted.
- Unmarried sons or daughters of a parent granted suspension or cancellation under NACARA, if the son or daughter was twenty-one years of age or older at the time of relief and entered the United States on or before October 1, 1990.

Adjustment of Status

Since 1986, adjustment of status has been available to very few people in removal proceedings because the applicant must have been admitted or paroled, have a current visa, and be applying for a visa that is immediately available (INA § 245[a]). The only foreign nationals exempted from the current adjustment of status requirement are "immediate relatives" (spouses and unmarried children under twenty-one years old) of U.S. citizens who entered the country with a visa that has since expired and special immigrants whose visas expired due to technical reasons through no fault of their own (INA § 245[c][2]). For this limited category, those applying must still be eligible for a visa that is immediately available, and they must also be admissible.

Other Temporary Options

In addition to a few permanent legalization options, there are a few temporary status options, some of which could ultimately lead to permanent legalization to the undocumented. Other temporary visa options available to undocumented persons who are victims of domestic violence are covered later in this chapter.

Temporary Protected Status

The INA permits DHS to designate nationals from a country or area of a country for temporary protective status (TPS) upon a finding of ongoing armed conflict, earthquake, flood, or other environmental disaster, or due to temporary inability of a country to accept the return of its nationals (INA § 244A[b][1][A]–[C]). Persons with TPS status are authorized to work in the United States and may apply for a work permit (INA § 244[a][1][B]). Once the status expires, individuals return to being in undocumented status and subject to removal. All TPS applicants must apply for the status by the date specified in the regulations. Other application requirements are that the applicant (1) must be admissible as an immigrant with certain exceptions; and (2) must not be convicted of one felony or two or more misdemeanors (INA §§ 244[f], 244[c][2][B]).

Of Latin Americans, only Salvadorans, Hondurans, and Nicaraguans have received such benefits. Migrants from El Salvador were given TPS designation on February 13, 2001, for all those present in the country as of that date, extending for eighteen months until September 6, 2002, then again extended until September 9, 2006, and most recently extended again until March 9, 2009 (70 Fed. Reg. 1450). TPS benefits a total of 248,282 Salvadoran nationals. Hondurans received TPS if they had been physically present since January 5, 1999, and had continuously resided in the United States since December 30, 1998. Their status expired July 5, 2006, but was extended again until January 5, 2009 (69 Fed. Reg. 64084). TPS benefits 78,000 Hondurans. Nicaraguans originally received TPS on January 5, 1999 (64 Fed. Reg. 526 [1999]) and have received several extensions, with the most recent until January 5, 2009. TPS benefits 4,000 Nicaraguans.

Victims of Human Trafficking

The ugliest face of immigration policies is human trafficking. Every year, tens of thousands of persons are trafficked to work as slaves, including in the sex industry. The Trafficking Victims Protection Act of 2000 (TVPA) (codified at INA § 101[a][15][T]) created a T visa to protect women, children, and men who are the victims of human trafficking. T visas allow qualifying victims to live and work legally in the United States for three years. After three years, T visa holders may apply for permanent legalization. Victims may apply for their spouses and children, and those under twenty-one may also apply for their parents and unmarried siblings under eighteen. There is an annual cap of 5,000 T visas available. Unfortunately, despite high numbers and extreme facts of victimization, immigration agencies have approved only about 600 visas for victims of sexual human trafficking since 2002.

To qualify, the foreign national must (1) have been the victim of a "severe form of human trafficking"; (2) be physically present in the United States; (3) reasonably provide assistance in investigating or prosecuting acts of trafficking persons (or be under age eighteen); and (4) be someone who would suffer extreme hardship involving unusual and severe harm if removed from the United States (INA § 101[a][15][T]). To show evidence of being a victim of a severe form of human trafficking, a person may submit a law enforcement agency endorsement or submit credible secondary evidence describing the nature and scope of force, fraud, or coercion used against the victim (8 C.F.R. § 214.11[f] [2002]). The applicant must also be physically present in the United States on account of the trafficking (8 C.F.R. § 214.11[g]). To show compliance with reasonable requests from a law enforcement agency, an applicant may submit law enforcement certification or other secondary evidence. To meet the hardship requirement, lack of social or economic opportunities upon removal is not enough (8 C.F.R. § 214.11[i][1]). Rather, the applicant must include the traditional extreme hardship factors associated with trafficking, which are listed in the regulations: (1) age and circumstances of the applicant; (2) serious physical or mental illness requiring treatment not available in the foreign country; (3) the nature of the physical and psychological harm suffered by the victim; (4) the loss of access to the criminal justice system in the United States; (5) severe penalties in the foreign country for being a victim of trafficking; (6) likelihood of revictimization; (7) likelihood that the trafficker or others acting on his or her behalf would harm the applicant in the foreign country; and (8) the likelihood of danger due to civil unrest or armed conflict in the country of origin (8 C.F.R. § 214.11[i]). Finally, T visa applicants may receive a waiver for certain inadmissibility grounds, including the public charge or certain other immigration violations if these were the result of the applicant's victimization (67 Fed. Reg. 4784, 4789).

Domestic Violence: Legalization of Victims and Removal

Just as domestic violence affects marriages between citizens, so does it affect marriages between foreign nationals or between foreign nationals and citizens. In the latter two cases, immigration status itself has aggravated the abuse, especially for women. For example, an abuser with an exclusive right to petition to immigrate the spouse or child could threaten not to file on behalf of the victim if she reported the violence. Similarly, he could threaten to report the victim to immigration authorities and separate her from her children. If the victim left the abuser of her own accord, she lost the right to legalization. When she left, her undocumented status substantially limited her employability and access to public services. In addition, the victim's acts of self-defense against the abuser might be treated as a crime of moral turpitude and render her excludable or removable, or disqualify her from naturalization or other relief from removal.

Congress has passed various pieces of legislation to improve the plight of abused undocumented women and children. In 1986, Congress allowed a battered spouse and child to file independently of their abusive spouses to remove the conditions that attach to a marriage-based visa. This was an exception to the requirement that a married couple file jointly. Still, this law only benefited victims who already possessed LPR status, even if conditionally. In 1994, Congress passed the Violent Crime Control and Law Enforcement Act, or the Violence Against Women Act (1994 VAWA). The 1994 VAWA allowed abused spouses and children of LPRs and U.S. citizens to self-petition for immigration status without the participation of their abuser and expanded the types of evidence that victims could present to substantiate the abuse. The act also allowed battered spouses and children of LPRs and U.S. citizens to apply for cancellation of removal in removal proceedings under standards significantly more flexible than those that traditionally applied. While 1994 VAWA was a good start, the act still required victims to stay in the relationship to self-petition and to have good moral character for cancellation of removal. The latter requirement sometimes disqualified a victim who acted in self-defense against the abuser.

Thanks to the lobbying efforts of victim advocates, Congress passed the Violence Against Women Act of 2000 (2000 VAWA), which included amendments to fix many of the remaining impediments to immigration remedies. Critical changes created by 2000 VAWA included the ability of victims to self-petition even after severing the relationship with the abuser, as long as the self-petition was filed within two years of the divorce. The act also included changes improving access to cancellation of removal. In addition, 2000 VAWA amended several of the waivers from certain criminal grounds of exclusion or deportability to make them available to persons who were eligible to self-petition or to apply for cancellation of removal based on the abuse.

More recently, Congress reauthorized VAWA with the passage of the Violence Against Women and Department of Justice Reauthorization Act of 2005. This act eliminated lingering obstacles victims faced in seeking legalization and expanded protection to a larger group of victims. Since 2005, for example, elder victims of abuse who have been battered or subjected to extreme cruelty by their adult U.S. citizen sons or daughters may self-petition (VAWA 2005, § 816).

Not all foreign nationals who are victims of domestic abuse and who reside in the United States benefit from these laws. A victim will only benefit if she has a spousal or child relationship with the abuser, and the abuser is a U.S. citizen or LPR as explained below. Thus, abused women and children who are married to or are children of an undocumented foreign national do not qualify for these benefits (8 C.F.R. §§ 204.2[c][1][i][A] and [e][1][i][A]). A U nonimmigrant or temporary visa that could provide a path to legalization to certain domestic violence and sexual assault victims who do not have the qualifying relationship to a U.S. citizen or LPR was created by the 2000 VAWA. Requirements for a U visa are also explained in this section, as is the option of pursuing asylum for certain cases involving domestic abuse. Additionally, this section addresses the potential removal consequences to the LPR abuser when the battered spouse or child reports the abuse and pursues legalization on her own.

The Right to Self-Petition

Since 1995, a qualifying victim of domestic abuse has been able to self-petition as an "immediate relative" (a spouse or child of a U.S. citizen) or as a second family preference immigrant (a spouse or child of an LPR) by filing form I-360 (INA §§ 204[a][1][A] and [B]). Either the abused spouse self-petitions and includes the children as derivative beneficiaries (whether or not the children were abused), or the children can themselves self-petition when they have been abused, when the abused parent does not petition (INA §§ 204[a][1][A][iv] and [B][iii]). A parent can also self-petition on behalf of her biological child when the child does not also qualify as a child of the abuser but has been abused, even if the spouse herself has not been abused (8 C.F.R. § 204.2[c][1][i][E]).

Qualification for self-petition on the basis of an abusive relationship requires several steps. First, the self-petitioner or the parent of the self-petitioner child must be, or have been, or intended to be married to her abuser (INA §§ 204[a][1][A][iii]). Cohabitation is not sufficient, but a good faith marriage with a bigamist qualifies as a marriage. In addition, the marriage to the U.S. citizen or LPR abuser must have been entered into in good faith and not solely to obtain an immigration benefit (INA §§ 204[a][1][A][iii][I][aa]). However, a self-petitioning child who is abused by the U.S. citizen or LPR parent or stepparent need not prove the good faith of the marriage between the parent and the abuser (INA § 204[a][1][A][iv] and [B][iii]).

Since 2000, the abused self-petitioner has been able to file up to two years after the relationship has ended, including through divorce, or because the abuser has died. In addition, if the abuser loses his LPR status (see below) for a reason related to domestic violence, the abused spouse or intended spouse or the child may still self-petition if she otherwise meets all the other eligibility criteria and files within two years of the LPR's loss of status. VAWA 2005 also allows an abused child to self-petition up to age twenty-five, if the abuse was one of the central reasons for the filing delay (VAWA 2005, § 805[c]).

Second, the self-petitioner must prove that during the marriage or intended marriage, she "has been battered by, or has been the subject of extreme cruelty" by her spouse or intended spouse (INA §§ 204[a][1][A][iii][I][bb]). The abuse may be physical, sexual, psychological, or emotional (8 C.F.R. § 204.2[c][1][vi]). Psychological abuse may consist of social isolation, stalking, interrogating friends, not allowing the victim to work, controlling all money, or denigrating the victim.

Third, the self-petitioner must have resided with the abuser at some point during the marriage, even if the abuse did not occur in the United States (INA §§ 204[a][1][A][iii][II][dd] and [iv]). For a self-petitioning child, visitation periods with the abusive parent will satisfy this requirement (INA §§ 204[a][1][A][iv] and [B][iii]).

Fourth, the self-petitioner must be a person of good moral character, as the term is defined in INA § 101(f). The commission or conviction of most crimes will disqualify the victim from the good moral character definition. However, 2000 VAWA added a provision specifying that a disqualifying act or conviction encompassed in INA § 101(f) that would be waivable if classified as a ground of exclusion or deportability (see below) will not preclude a finding of

good moral character if the act or conviction was related to the abuse (INA §
204[a][1][C]). A willful failure to support dependents and the commission or
conviction of crimes not related to the abuse, however, will not result in a
finding of good moral character, unless the self-petitioner can show extenuat-
ing circumstances (8 C.F.R. § 204.2[c][1][vii]). In addition, a self-petitioning
spouse or child forced into prostitution by the abuser will still be deemed to
be of good moral character if there was no conviction (8 C.F.R. §
204.2[c][1][vii]). INA § 101(f) grants the decisionmaker discretion, however,
to find that good moral character is lacking under circumstances more expansive than those listed. This has led some immigration judges or officers of the
US Center for Immigration Services to deny the self-petition when, for example, the self-petitioner has not filed taxes, has had an affair or a child out of
wedlock, or has received public benefits, the latter despite 2000 VAWA provisions permitting victims to receive benefits for a limited period. Advocates
should also note that CIS or immigration judges must take into account positive factors of the self-petitioner's character to ameliorate any negative ones.[16]

The self-petition will not create a right to work authorization; however,
once approved, the self-petition allows the immigrant to apply for work authorization. Additionally, although marriage or remarriage will not result in
the revocation of an approved self-petition, victims should not marry or re-
marry while the petition is pending as doing so could bar the self-petitioner
from VAWA relief. There are important confidentiality provisions related to
self-petitions, with civil penalties attached in case of violation (INA §§
210[b][6] and 245[c][5]). If CIS intends to deny the self-petition, it must notify the applicant and provide her an opportunity to rebut the denial. If denial stands, the self-petitioner may appeal to the Associate Commissioner
for Examinations.

Special Adjustment of Status Rules

The approval of the I-360 petition is only the first step to legalization for
battered spouses and children. The self-petitioner must next apply for admissibility. Foreign nationals who entered the United States without inspection or have an expired visa usually are not able to legalize (adjust their status) while remaining in the United States (INA § 245[a] and [c]).
Furthermore, to be eligible for adjustment of status, the petitioned visa must
be immediately available (INA § 245[a]). Special provisions and procedures,
however, permit domestic violence victims to adjust their status, even when
they entered without inspection, have an expired visa, or their visa is not immediately available.

Immediate relatives—those self-petitioners who are married or are children of U.S. citizens—may adjust their status right away as there is no wait
period for those visas, and the INA exempts their unlawful entry or expired
visa status (INA § 245[a] and [c]). Some CIS adjudicators have taken the position that despite the exemptions in INA §§ 245(a) and (c), victims who en-

tered without inspection still cannot legalize because INA § 212(a)(6)(A)(i) makes any foreign national who entered without inspection inadmissible. This interpretation should be judicially challenged, as it is inconsistent with Congress's intent in 2000 VAWA. Support for permitting adjustment for undocumented VAWA petitioners is also in the 2005 legislation, which authorizes immigration agencies to use discretion to allow even reapplication for admission after a previous removal order (VAWA 2005, § 813[b]).

For spouses and children of LPRs, status adjustment is even more difficult. Under current law, the self-petitioner who does not have a current visa at the time of filing the petition is potentially removable until the visa becomes available. Yet, the wait period for a second preference family-based visa is approximately six years. In most cases, however, when CIS grants the self-petition, it also grants "deferred action" status, which allows the self-petitioner to remain in the United States until a visa becomes available.

If the self-petitioner must leave the United States, she may process the immigrant visa from the corresponding consulate abroad. However, that victim is likely to have lived in the United States without status for an extended period of time, and her departure may make her ineligible to legalize for up to ten years unless she qualifies for a family-based waiver. In 2000 VAWA, an exception to the so-called 3/10 year bar for battered spouses and children was ostensibly created. However, to qualify, the self-petitioner must demonstrate a "substantial connection" between the battery and extreme cruelty and her unlawful status, which is a difficult standard (INA § 212[a][6][A][ii][II]). Even if she is eligible for the exception or a waiver, the petitioner may have to remain outside the United States for an extended period.

Exemptions and Waivers to Exclusion Grounds

Further provisions accommodate the victim of domestic violence but only when she is admissible. One provision exempts VAWA self-petitioners from the public charge exclusion ground and the need to supply an I-864 affidavit of support. The same provision also allows receipt of public benefits without adverse affect upon approval of the self-petition (INA §§ 212[a][4][C] and [p]).

In addition, VAWA self-petitioners are eligible for additional or more flexible waivers for certain exclusion grounds, in addition to those already available to all other applicants for admission. For example, they may receive a waiver against health-related exclusion grounds due to infectious diseases, including HIV or AIDS (INA § 212[g]). VAWA self-petitioners are also eligible for the INA § 212(h) waiver that applies to certain criminal-related grounds, without having to establish a family unity objective or waiting fifteen years to reapply for admission. In addition, the extreme hardship requirement of the INA § 212(i) waiver that applies to immigration fraud is more flexible for VAWA self-petitioners because the extreme hardship can be to themselves, their children, or parents.

Cancellation of Removal

A victim of domestic violence can file a VAWA petition while in removal proceedings, if a self-petition has not been adjudicated and denied. If a VAWA self-petitioner's application is denied and she is placed in removal proceedings, she is still eligible for all removal relief otherwise available to other undocumented migrants similarly situated. However, VAWA created special rules pertaining to cancellation of removal that are significantly more flexible than are otherwise available to undocumented immigrants who are not abuse victims. Each of the applicants seeking cancellation must file her own petition and establish abuse. For children, however, the witness of the abuse against the parent alone can be sufficient proof. A VAWA cancellation of removal applicant may be the U.S. citizen or LPR's spouse (even if the abuser has been ordered removed), child, or the child's parent, even if the parent has not been abused.

VAWA self-petitioners significantly benefit from three aspects of cancellation of removal proceedings: (1) a reduction in the physical presence requirement from ten to three years; (2) a good moral character prong that exempts otherwise disqualifying acts related to the abuse; and (3) a more flexible hardship standard. Issuance of the Notice to Appear will not stop the clock for accrual of physical presence for VAWA petitioners, in contrast to regular cancellation relief (INA § 240A[b][2][A][ii]). The commission of a crime that would render the victim excludable or deportable (i.e., not justified by the abuse) will stop the clock on the date of the offense. In addition, a single absence from the United States of ninety days, or a total of 180 days in the aggregate, will make a victim ineligible for cancellation, except when the absence was related to the abuse (INA §§ 240A[b][2][B] and [d][1]). Any such absence, however, must be deducted from the years totaling the required three years of physical presence.

As to the good moral character requirement, VAWA exempts those acts related to a domestic violence crime under INA § 237(a)(2)(E) when the victim demonstrates a connection between the acts and the abuse and shows that a waiver is "otherwise warranted" (INA § 240A[b][2][A][iv]). This waiver is available if the abuse victim can show that she acted in self-defense, or that the offense did not result in serious bodily injury, and there was a connection between her crime and the abuse. The waiver is also available if she can show that the protection order she violated was actually issued for her own protection. Only those actions or convictions that specifically render a person ineligible to apply for cancellation may not be waived when the immigration judge is considering the victim's good moral character. These include unexcused (not related to the abuse) crime-related grounds, national security grounds, marriage fraud, document fraud, and false claims to citizenship. These bars are actually more onerous than those applied to persons seeking regular cancellation of removal. Therefore, victims who have committed the unexcused crimes and who have resided in the United States for ten years or more should consider whether qualifying for regular cancellation of removal is more feasible.

As to the hardship requirement, the standard for abuse victims is "extreme" hardship, not "exceptional and extremely unusual," which applies to other undocumented migrants (8 C.F.R. §§ 240.58[c] and 240.20). Such hardship can be to the victim herself, the victim's child, or the victim's parent. The hardship must address both what the victim would lose if she could not stay in the United States and what she would suffer if she returned. The court would consider abuse-related hardship factors, including the nature and extent of the abuse and its physical and psychological consequences; the need for access to U.S. courts, to the U.S. criminal justice system, and to family law proceedings; the need for social, medical, mental health, or other services for the victim and her children that are not "reasonably accessible" in the removal country; laws, social mores, and customs in the home country that would ostracize or penalize the victim for being a victim of abuse, for leaving the relationship, or for taking actions to stop the abuse, including a divorce; the abuser's ability or inclination to follow the victim after removal; the home country's inability to protect the victim from the abuse; and the likelihood that the abuser's family, friends, or others would physically or psychologically harm the victim and her child (8 C.F.R. § 240.58[c]).

VAWA victims applying for cancellation are eligible for a few additional procedural benefits. For example, applicants seeking cancellation of removal or suspension of deportation are exempt under VAWA 2005 from the motion to reopen filing deadlines and numerical limits, provided the applicants are physically present in the United States at the time of filing (VAWA 2005, §825). VAWA also allows a foreign national granted VAWA suspension to request that her children—or if she is a child, her parent—receive parole and be allowed to stay in the country or to join the victim in the country, even if the children or parents are ineligible for cancellation or immediate legalization. According to 2000 VAWA, parole must be granted, with work authorization, until the family members paroled become eligible for legalization (INA § 240A[b][4]).

Asylum for Victims of Domestic Violence

An asylum seeker must prove that she has a well-founded fear of persecution based on race, religion, nationality, membership in a particular social group, or political opinion. Victims of domestic violence have attempted to seek asylum in the United States based on the extreme abuse they have experienced and the absence of protection from the state. These cases, however, have not neatly fit all of the doctrine's requirements, even with the often grave nature of the claims. Despite these challenges, there remains hope that the doctrine will sufficiently evolve to embrace asylum claims in particularly egregious domestic violence cases.

One obstacle has been that the asylum seeker must establish that her persecution or well-founded fear of persecution is based on one of the enumerated grounds of protection. Generally, domestic violence claims fall within the social group membership, in this case, gender. However, the applicant must also prove that the persecution was on account of the membership in the social group (e.g., women), which has been more difficult to prove. Furthermore, the fact that the abuse has often come from a private actor has been an impediment insofar as U.S. asylum doctrine requires state action for an act to qualify as persecution.

A story that highlights the plight of domestic violence asylum seekers is the case of Rodi Alvarado (*Matter of R.A.* [Rodi Alvarado] [In Re R-A-, 22 I. & N. Dec. 906 (BIA 1999), vacated by Attorney General Reno on Jan. 19, 2001]). Alvarado fled Guatemala, a country where murder rates against women are among the highest in the world and where a third of the killings result from domestic violence. At age sixteen, Alvarado married Francisco Osorio, a former soldier, who immediately began to threaten and violently assault her for the next ten years. Osorio raped and sodomized Alvarado, infecting her with sexually transmitted diseases, broke windows and mirrors with her head, dislocated her jaw, and tried to abort her child by kicking her violently in the spine. Despite several attempts to flee and seek help from the authorities, neither the police nor the courts in Guatemala intervened.

Initially, an immigration judge granted Alvarado's request for asylum; however, the BIA reversed the decision. The BIA admitted that the abuse against Alvarado was "heinous" and that her severe injuries rose to the level of harm sufficient to constitute persecution. The BIA also found that Alvarado established the government's unwillingness or inability to protect her and its tolerance of spouse abuse. Nevertheless, the BIA denied asylum, reasoning that Alvarado failed to demonstrate the necessary nexus between her social group membership as a woman and her plight.

In December 2000, the U.S. Department of Justice issued proposed regulations to address gender claims, and subsequently, Attorney General Janet Reno vacated the BIA's decision in Alvarado's case, directing the BIA to redecide the case once the regulations were issued in final form. In 2004, after opposing Alvarado's asylum for eight years, the Department of Homeland Security, which replaced the Department of Justice in the enforcement of immigration laws, reversed its position and endorsed the issuance of regulations that would allow granting Alvarado asylee status. The proposed rules on the meaning of "particular social group" lists several additional factors that should be considered in the definition, none of which are determinative: (1) the members of the group are closely affiliated with each other; (2) the members are driven by a common motive or interest; (3) a voluntarily associational relationship exists among the members; (4) the group is recognized as a societal faction or is otherwise a recognized segment of the population in the country in question; (5) members view themselves as members of the group; and (6) the society in which the group exists distinguishes members of the group for different treatment or status than is accorded to other members of the society (Proposed Rule, modifying 8 C.F.R. § 208.15). Among those included as members of a "particular social group" have been homosexuals and women, when the persecution was "on account of" of their gender.

The U Visa

The 2000 VAWA created a new U visa, intended to benefit foreign nationals who suffered "substantial physical or mental abuse" as a result of being a victim of a broad range of criminal activities, and who had been or were willing to help in the investigation or prosecution of the crime (INA § 101[a][15][U]). This new visa may provide a remedy for undocumented victims of domestic violence who do not qualify under VAWA because they are not married to their abusers or because their abusers lack LPR or U.S. citizen status. Unfortunately, to date, not a single survivor of violence who, despite having cooperated with law enforcement to prosecute their victimizers, has received a U visa. On March 7, 2007, in fact, Catholic Charities and Sanctuary for Families filed a lawsuit against USCIS to force the agency to comply with the six-year-old statute and grant immigration relief to these victims.

The range of crimes that may qualify a victim for a U visa include rape, torture, abusive sexual conduct, prostitution, sexual exploitation, female gender mutilation, hostage taking, peonage, involuntary servitude, slave trading, kidnapping, abduction, unlawful criminal restraint, false imprisonment, blackmail, extortion, manslaughter, murder, felonious assault, witness tampering, obstruction of justice, perjury or attempt, conspiracy, or solicitation to commit any of these crimes (INA § 101[a][15][U][iii]). The visa application must include law enforcement certification that the foreign national has been helpful or is likely to be helpful to the investigation or prosecution.

One significant advantage of this visa is that USCIS may grant it to a qualifying foreign national who entered without inspection or has an expired visa. Furthermore, CIS may waive nearly all grounds of exclusion that would apply if doing so is in the public or national interest (INA § 212[d][13]). In addition to the victim, the spouse, children, and, if the applicant is a child, the parent may also obtain status if CIS finds that they will suffer extreme hardship if removed, and if, additionally, a law enforcement official certifies that the investigation or prosecution would be harmed without the relative's assistance (INA § 101[a][15][U][iv]). Only 10,000 U visas are issued annually, although relatives who qualify for them are not counted against the cap (INA § 214[o][2]). In addition, a U visa holder is entitled to employment authorization (INA § 214[o][2]) and may apply for permanent legalization after being continuously present in the United States for three years since the visa issuance, and if she establishes that her "continued presence is justified on humanitarian grounds, to ensure family unity, or otherwise in the public interest" (INA § 245[l][1]). A single ninety-day absence, or absences of 180 days in the aggregate from the United States will break the continuity of physical presence unless the absence was related to the criminal investigation or prosecution (INA § 245[l][2]). Permanent legalization may also be denied if CIS finds that the U visa holder "unreasonably" refused to help in the criminal investigation or prosecution (INA § 245[l][1]).

Public Benefits Eligibility for VAWA Petitioners

Despite the 1996 restrictions on public benefits eligibility to foreign nationals, VAWA petitioners who have filed Form I-360 or filed for cancellation of removal are eligible for certain federal public benefits if they can show they are no longer living with the abuser and a substantial connection exists between the battery and the need to receive public benefits (Illegal Immigration Reform and Immigrant Responsibility Act [IIRIRA] § 501). Furthermore, because a VAWA petitioner is not required to file an affidavit of support to overcome the public charge exclusion ground, any sponsor's income should not be counted ("deemed") for assessing means-tested benefit eligibility. Still, after the IIRIRA amendments, VAWA petitioners' eligibility still depends on their date of entry into the United States (prior to August 22, 1996) or is subject to the five-year residency bar (see Chapter 10 for the discussion of government benefits for documented immigrants). To receive benefits, the self-petitioner must have separated from the abuser and either have an I-360 approved or produce a statement from USCIS that the application is likely to be approved.

In addition, federal funds provided to local social service programs or to states for state-based programs are not "federal public benefits," and immigrant access to these programs is not restricted. For example, battered women's shelters receive funding from a variety of federal sources without immigration restrictions. The source of these programs include, but are not limited to the Family Violence Prevention Services Act; community and migrant health centers; Community Services Block Grants; and substance abuse, mental health, and maternal and child health centers. Other state-funded sources may be available to certain undocumented migrants, especially health services to women and children (see discussion above on government benefits to undocumented migrants).

Domestic Violence as a Deportable Offense

Since 1996, certain domestic violence offenses may become the basis for removal of LPRs or others holding a temporary visa. INA § 237(a)(2)(E) provides that a foreign national who "at any time after entry is convicted of a crime of domestic violence, a crime of stalking, or a crime of child abuse, child neglect, or child abandonment is deportable." This removal ground includes acts of violence against a nonspouse or former spouse; who is cohabiting or has cohabited with the abuser; or who has had a child with the abuser. The abuser may also be removed if he has any other relationship with the victim not mentioned above but encompassed under domestic violence protections under federal law or the laws of any state or Native American tribal government. This removal ground also applies to a foreign national who is determined at any time after entry to have violated a protective or restraining order granted on the basis of domestic violence. In addition, a domestic violence offense may fall within the definition of a crime involving moral turpitude for persons who are subject to exclusion, not deportation grounds.

While the removal of the abuser from the United States may offer protection to victims of domestic violence, to some victims, it is a double-edged sword. Removal of the LPR parent will separate the abuser from his children and may sever economic support from the parent, an outcome that many victims may not want, even if they wish to end the abuse by separating.

Appendix

Undocumented Students' Access to Higher Education

- For information about Dream Act Initiatives, visit the National Council of La Raza at http://www.nclr.org/content/policy/detail/1331.
- For information on in-state tuition initiatives for undocumented students, read "In-State Tuition for Undocumented Immigrants: States' Rights and Educational Opportunity" by Arlene Russell, a state policy scholar of the American Association of State Colleges and Universities, available at http://www.aascu.org/policy_matters/pdf/in-state_tuition07.pdf. See also "Update: State Policies Regarding In-State Tuition for Undocumented Students, Jobs for the Future," available at http://www.achievingthedream.org/_pdfs/_publicpolicy/Undoc ImmigUpdate_0307.pdf.

On Driver's Licenses for the Undocumented

- For detailed information about the REAL ID Act and state legislation on driver's license requirements, visit the National Immigration Law Center at http://www.nilc.org/immspbs/DLs/index.htm.
- For policy and advocacy help with driver's license legislation, visit the National Council of La Raza at http://www.nclr.org/content/policy/detail/1060.

Anti-Immigrant Local Ordinances

For general information about local ordinances, visit

- The American Civil Liberties Union on local anti-immigrant cases at www.aclu.org/immigrants/discrim/27848res20070105.html.

- The Society of American Law Teachers' Statement on Post-9/11 Anti-Immigrant Ordinances, at http://www.saltlaw.org/~salt2007/files/uploads/2007_SALT_immigrationordinances_0.pdf.
- The National Council of La Raza on Talking Points on Anti-immigrant Ordinances, at http://www.nclr.org/content/publications/detail/48107.

Notes

1. Programs that are not "federal public benefits" and thus may not screen out undocumented persons include Title V (the Maternal and Child Health Block Grant); Title X (Family Planning); the Primary Care Block Grant; and funds for federally qualified health centers.

2. See http://www.fns.usda.gov/cnd/SCHIP/factsheet.htm for the United States Department of Agriculture's SCHIP program overview and details.

3. Memorandum from the Commonwealth of Virginia Attorney General, *Immigration Law Compliance Update* 5 (September 5, 2002).

4. These are Texas, California, New York, Utah, Washington, Illinois, Kansas (*Day v. Bond,* 500 F.3d 1127 [10th Cir. 2007] [upholding dismissal of equal protection challenge to Kansas law for want of standing because the plaintiff failed to show injury]), New Mexico, and Nebraska. See National Immigration Law Center, *Basic Facts About In-State Tuition for Undocumented Immigrant Students,* available at www.nilc.org.

5. These include Arizona, Georgia and, in some college appropriations bills of late, Mississippi. Oklahoma once granted in-state tuition to undocumented immigrants, but reversed this treatment in the Oklahoma Taxpayer and Citizen Protection Act of 2007.

6. Importantly, § 1623 provides in full:

> An alien who is not lawfully present in the United States shall not be eligible on the basis of residence within a state (or political subdivision) for any postsecondary education benefit unless a citizen or national of the United States is eligible for such a benefit (in no less an amount, duration, and scope) without regard to whether the citizen or national is such a resident.

Thus, states, notwithstanding the desire of Congress, have the power to determine what constitutes state residency. Such a determination of residency is a "status benefit," not a "monetary benefit." Therefore, states can decide whether "to confer (or, more importantly, not to confer) residency status upon the undocumented in their public postsecondary institutions." Michael A. Olivas, "Lawmakers Gone Wild? College Residency and the Response to Professor Kobach," *SMU L. Rev.* 61 (forthcoming 2008), 101.

7. See http://www.nilc.org/immspbs/DLs/state_dl_rqrmts_ovrvw_2007-01-31.pdf.

8. As of January 2007, the ten states were Idaho, Indiana, Michigan, Nebraska, New Mexico, Oregon, Texas, Utah, Washington, and Wisconsin.

9. See http://www.google.com/search?hl=en&q=2007+july+visa+bulletin.

10. Only persons with "extraordinary ability in the sciences and the arts, education, business, or athletics" and entrepreneurs or investors may self-petition for an employment-based visa. Second preference applicants may waive the job offer and labor certification requirements if they can show that their immigration to the United States is in the national interest of the United States (8 C.F.R. § 204.5[k][4][ii][2004]).

11. The two exceptions are "changed circumstances which materially affect the applicant's eligibility for asylum or extraordinary circumstances relating to the delay in filing" (INA § 208[a][2][D]). The regulations define "extraordinary circumstances" as "events or factors directly related to the failure to meet an exhaustive list of possible 'extraordinary circumstances'" including physical, mental, or legal disabilities, and ineffective assistance of counsel.

12. *Matter of Acosta,* 19 I. & N. Dec. 211 (BIA 1985).

13. See *Matter of Toboso-Alfonso,* 20 I & N. Dec. 819 (BIA 1990).

14. See *Fatin v. INS,* 12 F.3d 1233 (3d Cir. 1993).

15. INA § 274(C) makes it unlawful for "any person or entity knowingly" to make a false document; to use or possess a false document; to use a lawful document issued to another; to accept or give a lawful document to another; to prepare or assist another in preparing an application or document required under the INA; knowing or recklessly disregarding that the application or document is false or relates to another; or to present an entry document before boarding a common carrier and fail to present such document to immigration officials upon arrival in the United States.

16. See *Torres-Guzman v. INS,* 804 F.2d 531 (9th Cir. 1986); *Matter of Sanchez-Linn,* 20 I. & N. Dec. 362 (BIA 1991).

12
Conclusion

We set out to write a handbook that addressed the primary flashpoints that result in unique and often marginalized treatment of Latino/as under U.S. law—immigration status, language barriers, and racial and ethnic discrimination.

In Chapter 2 we provided an overview of the many different contexts of employment law as it applies to Latino/as. The complex law of employment discrimination involves many federal laws that overlap and interact in ways that are very complicated, with each of the statutes protecting different classes of workers and each covering different types of employment-related activity. Thus, the sections of the chapter relating to employment discrimination addressed questions of hiring, terms and conditions of employment (including promotions and harassment), dismissal, and retaliation. We also explained legal distinctions based on national origin, ancestry, language, alienage, and citizenship status, which are subject to different analyses depending on the legal argument the worker makes. Latinas suffer multiple forms of discrimination, so we outlined the rights they have to be free from sexual harassment, which often also has racist overtones.

We recognize the reality that there are many undocumented workers who also need to know their rights. Therefore, we included an entirely lawful strategy whereby both the employer and the workers can maximize their mutual protection in the workplace. Because many undocumented and other Latino/as work in agriculture, we also explained rights that apply specifically to farm workers.

In Chapter 3 we addressed the problem of discrimination against Latino/as when they rent an apartment or buy a home. We also explained the rights tenants have once they move into a rental unit. Another problem that is increasingly being experienced by Latino/as is discrimination in the process of borrowing money for housing (getting mortgages). We illustrated common pitfalls and practices of which consumers should be aware and explained the federal laws that protect Latino/as in the lending context.

In Chapter 4 we confronted several situations where the language barriers faced by some Latino/as were exploited or otherwise triggered adverse legal consequences. In the prevailing U.S. climate that increasingly demands fluency in English, there is no comprehensive legal protection for those unable to understand English. Several states and local governments have embraced so-called official English and English-only laws. In other jurisdictions, in the absence of an enabling statute, generally there is no right to insist on translations from the government. Exceptions with sources in the Constitution that apply in the context of the criminal justice system were discussed in Chapter 8. Attacks on the Spanish language and on those who do not speak English have gone beyond government communications to reach the language used by parents with their children, the language spoken in a business establishment such as a restaurant or tavern, and even the language an employer allows an employee to speak on the job (see Chapter 2). Other language issues discussed in this book include language barriers between landlords and tenants (Chapter 3) and the current campaign to eradicate bilingual education (Chapter 6).

In Chapter 5 we discussed an unfortunate by-product of the anti-Latino/a sentiment in the United States—hate speech. We learned that hate speech on the job that is repetitive and severe may invoke legal remedies for the targeted employee, but that hate speech enjoys much greater protection outside the context of employment, such as on the street. Still, if that racial hate is expressed through a crime such as assault, the perpetrator of that hate crime might be punished in many states under penalty enhancement laws. Derogatory media stereotypes are a species of hate speech, but we saw that constitutional guarantees of free speech and other legal constraints leave Latino/as with only strategies such as protest to combat these images. Because Latino/as traditionally have countered discriminatory practices by employing self-help such as walkouts, protests, and boycotts, Chapter 5 concluded with an overview of the constraints on these nonlegal remedies.

Chapter 6 explored many dimensions of the challenges Latino/as face today in the context of education. It discussed the No Child Left Behind Act, a law that establishes standards for school districts with the intention of improving education; however the act lacks the funding necessary to reverse the growing incidence of Latino/as failing to graduate from high school.

We also discussed aspects of affirmative action, in higher education (colleges and universities) as well as in secondary education (high schools). There remain opportunities for Latino/as to access financial aid and admission to higher education that are based on the obstacles they have overcome that relate to their heritage. Difficulties that arise from lack of English-language proficiency, economic factors, and lack of educated role models continue to be considered in the admissions process. Racial and ethnic isolation in education before college is another subject that school districts have addressed, and what they can do about it is also explained.

No doubt the acquisition and application of political power would help combat many of the adverse consequences in U.S. law and life for Latino/as that we have discussed. In Chapter 7 we addressed the legal and structural barriers that thwart effective political participation in national, state, and local elections. To confront these barriers, we suggested political reforms, but recognized that these reforms themselves are at the mercy of a political system weighted against Latino/as. Therefore, we discussed a litigation strategy to combat discriminatory election systems, as well as the potential protections available under the federal Voting Rights Act for certain covered jurisdictions.

In Chapter 8 we discussed the criminal justice system, an arena in which our three flashpoint areas of focus—immigration, language barriers, and racial/ethnic discrimination—collide. We acknowledged how discriminatory attitudes lead some law enforcement and immigration officials to target Latino/as through racial profiling. Language barriers disadvantage Latino/as at all stages of the criminal justice system—from initial encounters with police, to interrogation, trial, and even in prisons. But we saw that a combination of constitutional and statutory measures sometimes ensures accommodation of Spanish and other non-English-language speakers in the criminal justice arena. Immigration came into play in our discussion of crimes associated with immigration, and of the consequences to immigrants, documented or not, of criminal behavior. Finally, we covered issues of more general application to Latino/as (and other groups) regardless of their language or citizenship status, particularly such constitutional guarantees as the Miranda warning before interrogation, voluntariness of confessions, and the privilege against self-incrimination.

In Chapter 9, we provided specific advice to immigrants on how to choose legal representation in immigration matters affecting themselves or their family members. Unfortunately, stories abound of lawyers and non-lawyers who provide bad legal representation to immigrants who as a result may end up in removal proceedings. Immigrants' dire need for legalization makes them particularly vulnerable to false hopes offered by service providers who may lack training in immigration law or intentionally misguide clients. Immigration law is complex and inflexible, and immigrants, particularly those who entered the country without authorization or who have a criminal history, must learn to be cautious. This chapter also addressed the duty of immigrants who live and work in the United States to pay taxes and the liability for failure to do so, including adverse immigration consequences.

Lawful permanent residents in the United States soon realize that their legal status does not guarantee them equal treatment under the law compared to citizens. Thus, for example, in Chapter 10 we explained when and how LPRs may lose their immigration status and can be removed. We also addressed immigration family unification benefits available to LPRs under the immigration laws, which are limited to spouses, minor children, and unmarried sons and daughters and are subject to long wait periods. LPRs are also ineligible for most government benefits available to the indigent unless they can establish additional residency or work history requirements, a topic we also explore in Chapter 10. We therefore included a section on citizenship, including naturalization. LPRs who naturalize would not increase their access to immigration and government benefits but would gain the right to vote and to full political participation in this country.

The most vulnerable residents in the United States, of course, are still those who lack immigration status, either because they entered without authorization or overstayed their visas. This growing population of about twelve million is increasingly the target of federal and local anti-immigrant measures that deny access to basic services available to citizens and most legal residents. In Chapter 11, we took up some of the most pertinent areas, including government benefits, access to higher education, and driver's licenses. We explained the legal limitations imposed on undocumented immigrants but also provided some examples of alternative treatment by some states that recognize immigrants' economic contributions and their basic human rights. With the defeat in 2007 of comprehensive immigration reform, we included a section in Chapter 11 detailing the few legalization provisions available to undocumented immigrants under the law today, including relief from removal and special provisions that provide greater immigration benefits to victims of domestic violence.

That defeat of immigration reform may prove to have set the pace for the continuing decline in fair treatment of Latino/as under U.S. law. Yet the activism among Latino/as and community groups responding to that decline may spark a legal and social renaissance for this vulnerable population. Some of the suggestions in this book, we hope, help chart that course.

Index

Accent discrimination, 25–26
Acosta, Oscar "Zeta," 138
Admitted foreign nationals, 145, 147; distinguished from nonadmitted foreign nationals, 146–147
Affirmative Action, 80–87; public opposition to, 84
Aggravated felonies: as grounds for removal, 150; as defined by immigration law, 150
Alcohol education programs, language of, 135
Asylum, 218–222
At-will employees, 8

Bilingual education, 92–95. *See also* No Child Left Behind Act
Bilingual Education Act, 93–94
Bilingual workers, 21–22. *See also* English-only rules in the workplace; English fluency requirements of employees
Board of Immigration Appeals (BIA), 148–149
Border, Mexican, 141–142
Boycotts, 73–74
Breathalyzer tests, 132–133
Bus sweeps by government officials, 116

California, Fair Employment and Housing Act of, 9
California, Four-Percent Plan, 85–86
California, Proposition 209, 84, 85
California, Proposition 227, 94
"Captive audience," 69
Citizenship, 178; birthright, 179–180; by descent, 183–184; discrimination based on, 12; through naturalization, 180–182; types of 178–179
Civil Rights Act of 1866, 8, 38; application to at-will employees, 8; cause of action under, 8; damages under, 8
Civil Rights Act of 1964, 4, 7, 10, 27, 37, 49, 93
Civil Rights Act of 1968, 37
Civil Rights Act of 1991, 10
Consent to searches, monolingual Spanish-speakers' ability to, 130–131
Court Interpreters Act, 134, 136, 137
Crime, as defined by immigration law, 148
Criminal conviction, as defined by immigration law, 146
Cuban Refugee Adjustment Act, 221

Deportation, statute of limitations for, 150

Derogatory media stereotypes, 71-73

Development Relief and Education for Alien Minors Act (DREAM), 211–212

Discrimination, defined, 9

Discrimination in lending, 46–49

Discriminatory effect, under the Fair Housing Act, 41

Disparate impact, 8, 9; as related to terms and conditions of employment, 15; Bona fide Occupational Qualification (BFOQ) exception, 11–12; business necessity defense, 11, 15; employer's motive, 10; as related to tenant language ability, 45; use of height requirements, 11; use of statistical hiring data; 10

Disparate treatment, 8, 9; as related to housing, 38–39, 41; as related to terms and conditions of employment, 15; circumstantial evidence of, 9; direct evidence of, 9; liability under, 9; pretext, 9

Document fraud. See Immigration document fraud

Dog sniffs, use and validity of, 117, 120

Domestic violence, as a deportable offense, 238–239; asylum for victims of, 235–237; legalization of victims of, 229–230; right to self-petition on account of, 230–232

Driver's license, 133; denial of, 212–213

"Driving while brown," 117–118

Due Process clause, 126–128; involuntary statements under, 126

"East LA Blowouts," 73

Emergency Medicaid, 206–207

Emergency Medical Treatment and Active Labor Act (EMTALA), 206

Employer immigration crimes, 144–145

Employer retaliation, 18; establishing a claim of, 18; employer's defense to, 18; filing a claim for, 33

Employment-based immigrant visas, 216–218

English fluency requirements of employees, 24– 25

English-only court orders in custody disputes, 55

English-only rules in places of entertainment, 57–59; proving racial discrimination due to the use of, 58

English-only rules in the workplace: business justifications for, 22–24; customer preference for, 23–24; legality of, 21–22

English-only state laws, 52–53; history of, 52

Equal Credit Opportunity Act (ECOA), 46, 47, 48

Equal Educational Opportunity Act, 93, 95

Equal Employment Opportunity Commission (EEOC), 7–8, 11–12, 15–22, 24–25, 34–36, 67

Equal Protection, 4, 5, 82

Exclusionary remedy, 120, 129–130

Fair Employment Practices (FEP), 8. See also State antidiscrimination laws

Fair Housing Act (FHA), 4, 38, 41, 44–46, 49. See also Title VIII

Fair Labor Standards Act (FLSA), 28, 31–32, 33

Family-based immigration priorities, 185–187; priority dates, 187–189

Farm Labor Contractor Registration Act (FLCRA), 31

Farm Security and Rural Investment Act, 174–175

Farm worker wages, 31; laws applicable to, 31

Fifth Amendment, 122–123, 127, 131, 138. See also Miranda rights

"Fighting words," as defined by the Supreme Court, 68

Financial aid for Latinos in higher education, 86–87
First Amendment, 5, 65, 71, 74, 142
Florida, Talented 20 Program, 86
Food stamps, 174
Fourteenth Amendment, 14
Fourth Amendment, 114–116, 117, 118–120, 130; public v. private actors under, 115
"Frito Bandito" advertising campaign, 71, 72
"Fruit of the poisonous tree" doctrine, 120, 129. See also Exclusionary remedy

Government accommodation of Spanish speakers, 53–54; in relation to standardized K–12 tests, 79; translation of government occupational testing/licensing, 55. See also Translation of government forms
Government benefits, documented immigrants, 173–178, 176–177; undocumented migrants, 205–207
Greaser Act, 3

Habitability of housing, 43
Harassment by third parties, 17
Harboring undocumented persons, 142–143
Hate crimes, 70–71; committed by government officials, 70
Home loans, 45–46. See also Discrimination in lending
Home Ownership and Equity Protection Act, 47
"Hostile audience," 70
Hostile work environment, 16; establishing a cause of action for, 16; hate speech as constituting a, 65–67
Human trafficking, victims of, 228–229

Illegal Immigration Reform and Immigrant Responsibility Act (IIRIRA), 211, 238

Immigration, 1–2; bracero program, 1, 2; brief history of, 1; federal law regulating, 1, 2, 5; legislative history surrounding, 2; Operation Wetback, 1; rights of undocumented immigrant children, 2; role of courts, 5; state law regulating, 5
Immigration document fraud, 143–144
Immigration enforcement, 118–119
Immigration hearing, 121
Immigration raids, 29–30, 118, 119; strategies in response to, 31, 121
Immigration Reform and Control Act of 1986 (IRCA), 12, 26, 28, 221; covered employees under, 13; unfair immigration–related practices under, 12–13
Incitement of an immediate crime, 67–68
Individual Taxpayer Identification Number (ITIN), 166-168; how acquired, 167
Intelligence Reform and Terrorism Prevention Act (IRTPA), 212, 214
Interrogation techniques, 127. See also Police interrogations
Involuntary confessions, 126–128

Jurors, English fluency requirements, 138–140

Language fraud in the marketplace, 59–61; door- to-door salesmen, 60
Landlord discrimination, 37; English-ability requirements of tenants, 44–45; failure to renew lease, 42; failure to respond to complaints of racial harassment, 42; legal defenses to, 39; proving, 39
Lawyer, acquiring a, 159–160
League of United Latin American Citizens (LULAC), 110
Lease agreements, fairness in, 42; translation of lease requirements, 44
Legalization, 215–216; denial of, health-related grounds, 222–223; denial of, legal grounds, 223–224

Legal representation, sources of free, 157; responding to inadequate, 162–164

Magnuson-Moss Warranty Act, 60
Marches, as a form of protest, 74–75
Marriage-based petitions, 191–194
Medicaid, for documented immigrants, 175–176
Mexican American Legal Defense and Educational Fund (MALDEF), 110
Migrant and Seasonal Agricultural Worker Protection Act (MSAWPA), 31–32, 34
Migrant worker, defined, 31
Miranda rights, 122–126; custodial interrogation, defined, 123–124; distinction from Due Process clause, 126; language in which administered, 131–132; reasonable person test under, 123; waiver of *Miranda* rights, 124–125
Moral turpitude, crimes involving, 149–150

National Association of Latino/a Elected and Appointed Officials (NALEO), 110
National Labor Relations Act (NLRA), 26–27, 73
National origin, 8; EEOC definition of, 8; distinguished from citizenship, 12
Naturalization, disqualification from, 151
Nicaraguan Adjustment and Central American Relief Act (NACARA), 219, 221, 226–227
No Child Left Behind Act, 77–78, 91, 93–94
Nonadmitted foreign nationals, 145–146; distinguished from admitted foreign nationals, 145–147
Nonlawyers, use of, 157–159, 161
Notaries, 158
Notices, government, language of, 133

Operation Tarmac, 145

Oregon, requirement for interpreter during interrogation, 132

Personal Responsibility and Work Opportunity Reconciliation Act of 1996 (PRWORA), 91, 173, 174, 175, 176, 177, 205–206, 208, 211
Police interrogations, 122; required language of, 131–132
Police lies, 128
Pregnancy Discrimination Act, 19
Prisoners, language rights of, 140–141
Privilege against self-incrimination, 122, 123, 128–129

Quid pro quo sexual harassment, 19–20

Race-conscious measures in grades K–12, 87–89
Racial balancing in housing, 41
Racial profiling, generally, 114–122; defined, 115. *See also* "Driving while brown"
Racial slurs and jokes, use of, 16. *See also* Hostile work environment
Raid. *See* Immigration raid
Rallies, as a form of protest, 74–75
Real Estate Settlement Procedures Act (RESPA), 48, 60
REAL ID Act, 147–148, 212–213, 214, 220
Reasonable suspicion, 115, 116, 119
Removal, 145–151, 194–195; cancellation of, 199–200 234–235; criminal–related grounds for, 148–149, 195–198; duration of, 147; judges discretion in, 145; relief from, 147, 199, 225–226
Residency, for tax purposes, 166
Right to remain silent. *See* Fifth Amendment or *Miranda* rights

Searches by public actors, 115; consensual searches, 116. *See also* Fourth Amendment
Segregation, 4; school segregation, 4; private segregation, 4

Seizures by public actors, 115–116
Sexual Harassment, 18–21; filing a complaint for, 20
Sit-ins, as a form of protest, 75
Sixth Amendment, 137, 138
Smuggling undocumented persons, 142–143
Spanish-language evidence presented at trial, 139
Standardized tests, use of, 77–79. See also No Child Left Behind Act
State antidiscrimination laws, 8–9, 28
State Children's Health Insurance Program (SCHIP), 208
State initiatives for public assistance to undocumented migrants, 208
Students, undocumented, 209–212
Subprime lending, 48–49
Supplemental Nutrition Program for Women, Infants and Children (WIC) 208
Supplemental security income (SSI), 174, 205

Tax violations, consequences for, 168–170; effect on immigration proceedings, 17–171
Taxes, 164–170; filing without a social security number, 166–168
Temporary Assistance for Needy Families (TANF), 175, 176, 191, 205
Temporary Protected Status, 227–228
Tendency to confess, 123
Terms and Conditions of Employment, 14–15; use of statistics to prove disparity, 15
Texas Ten-Percent Plan, 85
Title VI, 93, 97
Title VII, 27, 65–67; application to undocumented workers, 27; coverage of, 7,13; damages under, 8; initiating a claim under, 7. See also Disparate impact; Disparate treatment
Title VIII, 37–38, 40–41, 46, 48

Torture, use of, 127
Translation at trial, 134–137; translation of court documents, 137; translation of criminal charges, 137. See also Court Interpreters Act
Translation of government forms, 54–55. See also Notices, government, language of
True threats, 69
Truth in Lending Act, 60
Truth in Savings Act, 60

U Visa, 237–238
Undocumented children, rights of, 89–92
Undocumented workers, 26–28; state laws affecting, 28
Uniform Residential Landlord and Tenant Act (URLTA), 43
Unions, right to organize into, 26–27. See also National Labor Relations Act
United Farm Worker boycotts, 74
Unlawful entry (into the United States), 142
Unlawful reentry (into the United States), 142

Vagrancy Act, 3. See also Greaser Act
Violence Against Women Act (VAWA), 229, 232, 233, 234, 235, 238
Visas, qualifying for, 216. See also Employment-based immigrant visas
Voting, requirement of citizenship for, 98–99; disenfranchisement of convicted felons, 100; disenfranchisement of Puerto Ricans, 100; Latino/a voting strength, 100–101; methods of election, 101–103; special election districts, 108–109
Voting Rights Act, 53–54, 98–99; bilingual election process, 99; Section 5 Preclearance, 105–107

Walkouts, as a form of protest, 74

About the Authors

Steven W. Bender, the James and Ilene Hershner Professor of Law at the University of Oregon School of Law, is author of *Greasers and Gringos: Latinos, Law, and the American Imagination* (2003). **Raquel Aldana** is professor of law at William S. Boyd School of Law at the University of Nevada, Las Vegas. **Gilbert Paul Carrasco**, Professor of Law at Willamette University College of Law, is a noted expert in civil rights law, immigration law, and constitutional law. **Joaquin G. Avila** is a MacArthur Foundation Fellow and assistant professor at Seattle University School of Law.